PIMLICO

209

WHAT DID YOU DO IN THE WAR, MUMMY?

Mavis Nicholson is one of Britain's best-loved TV interviewers. She was born in 1930 in South Wales, and told the story of her childhood in *Martha, Jane & Me*. After university she became a copywriter and then for ten years a full-time mother. She was a forty-year-old mother of three when she presented her first TV series, *Good Afternoon*, which was followed by many other programmes, including *Mavis on 4*. Now a grandmother, she lives with her journalist husband in Powys.

WHAT DID YOU DO IN THE WAR, MUMMY?

Women in World War II

MAVIS NICHOLSON

PIMLICO

PIMLICO
An imprint of Random House
20 Vauxhall Bridge Road, London SW1V 2SA

Random House Australia (Pty) Ltd
20 Alfred Street, Milsons Point, Sydney
New South Wales 2061, Australia

Random House New Zealand Ltd
18 Poland Road, Glenfield
Auckland 10, New Zealand

Random House South Africa (Pty) Ltd
PO Box 337, Bergvlei, South Africa

Random House UK Ltd Reg. No. 954009

First published by Chatto & Windus 1995
Pimlico Edition 1996

3 5 7 9 10 8 6 4 2

Papers used by Random House UK Ltd are natural,
recyclable products made from wood grown in
sustainable forests. The manufacturing processes
conform to the environmental regulations of the
country of origin

Printed and bound in Great Britain by
Butler and Tanner Ltd, Frome, Somerset

ISBN 0–7126–7464–0

To those who shared their memories of the last war:
Denise Aylmer-Aylmore, Helen Bamber, Doris Barry, Helen Brook,
Joyce Carr, Pauline Crabbe, Mary Fedden, Ann Fox, Clemency Greatorex,
Kathleen Hale, Odette Hallowes, Nicola Harrison, Denise Hatchard,
Peggy Hill, Sister Hussey, Diana Hutchison, Evelyn Jones, Christina Kirby,
May Lawton, Edna Morris, Renate Olins, Pat Parker, Phyllis Pearsall,
Patricia Pitman, Myra Roberts, Anne Shelton, Doreen Tagholm, Peggy Terry,
Molly Weir, Mary Wesley, Phyllis Willmott, Jean Wynne. And to
Jane Nicholson, who faithfully transcribed them.

CONTENTS

PREFACE

Date: Sunday, 3rd September 1939
Time: 11 o'clock
Place: Near a wireless set.

A YOUNG WIFE IN LEEDS: *We could eat no breakfast hardly and just waited with sweating palms and despair for 11 o'clock. When the announcement was made, 'The country is at war with Germany,' I leant against my husband and went quite dead for a moment or two.*

A GENTLEWOMAN IN ESSEX: *I had been told by my gardener that an important announcement would be given out on the wireless. It would either be peace or war and anxiety increased as the time drew near. Then it was the latter. I stood up for 'God Save the King' and my little dog got out of her basket and stood beside me. I took her on my lap for comfort.*

A 48-YEAR-OLD SCHOOLMISTRESS, IN A SMALL COUNTRY TOWN: *At 11.15 we sat round listening to Chamberlain speaking. I held my chin high and kept back the tears at the thought of the slaughter ahead. When 'God Save the King' was played we stood.*

A GIRL OFFICE WORKER OF 21, IN SHEFFIELD: *Glorious morning, Mum and Dad and self listening to every bulletin. War declared. Funny feeling inside me, and yet we all stood at attention for 'The King' and I know we were all in the same mind, that we shall and must win.*

From *War Begins at Home* by Mass Observation
(Chatto and Windus, 1940)

MAVIS NICHOLSON, A GIRL OF 8 IN SOUTH WALES: *I heard the news down the back kitchen, on my grandmother's wireless – a big wooden set run on accumulators with the label:* DANGER ACID – Do Not Touch. *I was sitting up on her table watching my father shaving in a mirror on the door of a metal cabinet. He was in his vest, with his braces dangling over his trousers. As he heard Chamberlain's words he nicked his face with the razor and said, 'Bloody hell.'*

I slid off the table and ripped a piece off the corner of a newspaper without any print on it so that he could wet it and stick it on the cut to stop it bleeding.

'What's war like, Dad?' I asked. He flicked the last streak of lather off his face. And pointing his razor he said, 'Don't ask me about war.'

I knew he'd say that. For I'd tried many times before to get him to tell me about the Great War, when he had lied about his age so he could join up. I knew he had fought in rat-infested trenches, and that he thought animals had been better treated than soldiers. Now he said he was bloody glad he was too old to be called up. He pitied the poor buggers who would go off believing, as he had done, that this war was the war to end all wars.

I thought no more about it for the rest of my busy day – Sunday School all afternoon, playing cards with my grandma in the evening.

It was not until I was coming home from school the next day with the older girls that the message about the war got through to me. Perhaps my mother and father had deliberately played it down. But the big girls were very dramatic about it. They convinced me we were going to be invaded any minute. I burst into tears and ran the rest of the way home in order to be with my family in case the Germans were on their way.

The blackout was a real reminder of the perils of war. We knew that a chink of light seen at the window could mean a direct hit. *'Put that light out'* was said with relish by the people who volunteered to join the ARP as air-raid wardens.

It was comforting, however, seeing sandbags stacked outside the police station. Big rolls of barbed wire barricading our beaches. Criss-cross sticky brown paper on our house windows to protect us from glass splintering from bombs. Air-raid shelters, personal and public. Gas masks, even though we thought them utterly ghastly, made us feel important and cared for. The novelty soon wore off and we carried combs and cosmetics in our cases, leaving the masks to gather dust at home.

We soon became cynical about these paltry measures. The philosophy round our way was that there was no protection; if you were going to go, you were going to go. If a bomb had your name on it, you were a goner anyway. So we gave up air-raid shelters. 'Who wants a corrugated iron coffin?' my grandmother wanted to know. 'Give me the dignity of my own bed to die in, if you please.'

So many people I've interviewed for this book felt exactly the same, even when they were in the thick of the bombing in London and Hull and Coventry and Glasgow and Plymouth and Kent.

We all looked up at barrage balloons and saw them as strange Disney-like creations. We were friendlier to each other. Everyone was grinning and bearing the shortages – and making do and mending! Some of us had better intentions

JUST A GOOD AFTERNOON'S WORK

than application. All through the war I was knitting the same balaclava for some soldier somewhere.

We all knew exactly what everyone else was feeling when we sang (altogether now), 'There'll be love and laughter, And peace ever after, Tomorrow just you wait and see.' Up in the balcony of our public hall at a dance, we watched a young woman in the arms of a chap in uniform swaying to the strains of 'We'll meet again, Don't know where, don't know when, But I know we'll meet again some sunny day.' The tears simply poured down our cheeks unashamedly as if we were in the pictures, for we'd picked up the grown-ups' feeling that life was uncertain. This dance could be the last of that soldier's life; or that civilian's, come to that.

For all its comradeliness, the war did not sweep away the common view of 'the little woman'. While we're still on the dance floor, listen to the publicity for the Blackout Stroll, the first specially invented 'war dance': 'You ladies called "wallflowers," fated to sit out all the dances because perhaps your face isn't your fortune, or you aren't too good a dancer, or your figure isn't the cuddly kind ... here's your chance to dance London's latest step and your godsend.' The reason it was a godsend, apparently, was that the lights went out during the dance and you had to change partners!

Of course this condescending attitude had to be modified (for the duration of the war, at least) once the shortage of men made women indispensable to the war effort. They kept the home fires burning – on 25 shillings a week.

Yet when women went into paid civilian work, they weren't welcomed with open arms. There was even some hostility and suspicion from the men whose jobs they were taking over. Men didn't want to believe that women could perform them with as much strength and skill as they had done; they were worried that a makeshift arrangement 'for the duration' might prove permanent. And they probably resented the fact that women were effectively releasing them from reserved occupations to face greater danger in the forces.

Even the BBC were wary about employing women as engineers. By 1942 their trained women operators were still forbidden to open up transmitters or to rectify faults.

One area where women organised themselves in an impressive way was in the newly formed (1938) Women's Voluntary Service and the older, ever-loyal Women's Institute. Their ability to organise might have been turned into big business except that it was all done on a voluntary basis. Take salvage collection, for instance. These women brought in a thousand tons of aluminium – gleaming mountains of saucepans, kettles, jelly moulds and artificial limbs – when the Ministry of Aircraft Production appealed for it. The WVS and WI (and my mother and I!) were asked to harvest rosehips, which were then turned into syrup, providing valuable vitamins for mothers and babies. The WI, with the encouragement of the Ministry of Supply, gathered medicinal herbs, nettles and foxgloves for drug manufacturers. The result was that British imports of herbs were reduced by 50 per cent in 1943.

Members were trained to can fruit, having first gathered it. Their mobile canning units were sent all round the country with priority for the produce going to hospitals and homes for children and the elderly. The Ministry of Food made over to the WI the administration of the entire rural side of its wartime fruit preserving programme. They distributed up-to-date fruit-preserving outfits sent from the United States, and there were grants to cover costs. But there was no inducement to the helpers, who weren't even allowed to buy fruit from their

own centre. Their sole incentive was to give practical help in Britain's struggle and, I quote from a history of the WI, 'a feeling that is peculiarly the country women's concern, to keep the nation's larder filled'. So it was that in 1941, despite a poor crop, 1,300 tons of fruit were saved from waste and over 2,000 tons of preserves were made by women volunteers. One figure that makes me weep is the fourteen hundredweight of fruit which came from the Kent coastal town of Hawkinge where, because of evacuation and bombing, the membership of the Institute was down to a resolute *five* women.

Again, without the care provided by the WVS and WI, the evacuation of children would have been even more tragic than, for the most part, it was. It was they who made up the deficiencies of a well-meant but ill-thought-out idea hurriedly cobbled together by the government.

They set up information centres after bombing raids, took canteens to emergency areas, distributed clothing, and 'womanned' the re-homing gift scheme for people who had lost all their belongings in air raids. The list goes on. They replenished garden soil ruined by air attack.They set up services' clubs and organised bathing arrangements for the troops in private homes.They took over the running of British Restaurants and National Savings schemes.

It seems to me that our willingness as women to undertake voluntary work – though it has its virtues – is one reason why we don't rule the world. It has too often suited us to be liked rather than to be admired. Gratitude has been enough of a reward. Men, on the whole, prefer to be admired, and that breeds competition. Which, in turn, means business.

In voluntary work, one feels needed. The war provided the perfect arena for the self-sacrificing, serving part of many women's nature. They emerged as a formidable workforce; but think how rich and influential they might have become, if only they had turned those voluntary hours into paid man-hours.

There's no doubt that the war helped to liberate women. Up until then even if a woman had a job, she rarely earned enough to set up house on her own. There was no break in parental rule between adolescence and adulthood. Father could still require his grown-up daughter to come home at a set hour; to dress in a 'respectable' way; to avoid any male company he found objectionable. The only release from this authority was to get married, which often meant changing one form of dependence for another.

Joining one of the services, however, made women financially independent. The wages were poor but everything else was found, and in the war there was little to spend money on. Instead of finding uniform irksome, most girls seemed thrilled to wear it. It was the outward sign of their freedom from parental constraint.

And after the war? Many women moved on to the next phase of their life,

War artist Laura Knight's painting 'Ruby Loftus screwing a breech-ring'.

which was to marry, keep house and have babies while their husbands went out to work to provide for the family. The natural progression, they thought.

Others had grown accustomed to being *head* cook and bottle washer while their men were away. Children had grown up without a father and were used to the undivided attention of their mother. Suddenly, here was this stranger laying down the law and competing for their mother's time. It made for ill-feeling all round.

Some felt lost and lonely after the company and excitement they had enjoyed in the forces. Also they felt diminished. They had been important and valued, but now they were expected to make way for the conquering heroes. They were required to forget that they had been capable of exactly the same work in the men's absence.

Soon, under the pressure of prejudice, it was almost forgotten that women, once upon a time, had been strong enough to fell trees, plough fields, drive tanks, work in heavy industry. That they had been up to flying planes and manoeuvring cargo-boats along canals, and alert enough to take down wireless messages in Morse for eleven hours on end. That they had been brave enough to land in France on D-Day and nurse the wounded, or even to smuggle themselves in as secret agents; and to dust themselves down and start all over again during the blitz. That at a tender age they had been resilient and survived the inexplicable separation from home of evacuation or internment. That they had proved that women were as tough as they needed to be.

Most of the women in this book have never told their tale before. Patricia Pitman showed a proof of her chapter to her children and they were sufficiently moved to ask why she hadn't said all this before? 'Because no one has ever asked me.'

It was now or never. The narrators of this book are mostly in their seventies and eighties, and two, May Lawton and Kathleen Hale, are in their nineties. Only they could have told the tales they had to tell. Time waits for no woman. These personal histories of women in the Second World War are recorded lest we forget.

Anne Shelton, 'Forces' Favourite', aged 15 going on 19.

ANNE SHELTON
The Forces' Favourite

*Anne Shelton, the 'Favourite' rather than the 'Sweetheart' of the Forces –
that was Vera Lynn – told me she wanted, very much, to be included in this
book. 'But for personal reasons, dear, it's just impossible to meet you. Do
you mind if we do it all on the phone? You can take as long as you like. I'll
set aside the time for you. But I just can't meet. There's just too much
going on down here' – 'down here' being her home in Sussex.*

*She was true to her word, and we had our telephone conversation. This
is it. Trimmed but not altered. It took place just two weeks before Anne
died unexpectedly on 31 July 1994, so for me it has a certain poignancy. It
also makes you realise that all oral histories are precious and urgent.*

I never had singing lessons. My voice was just a gift from God. Mummy had a
very, very good soprano voice but she was not allowed to sing – not
professionally. My grandma was very religious so she didn't think it was right
for her daughter to sing on the stage. Just in church in the choir. Both Jo, my
younger sister, and I got our singing voices from Mummy.

I always wanted to sing in public. I remember, it was in 1939 – the year war
was declared, which made no difference to me at the time for I was only eleven,
twelve that November – my darling Daddy, God rest his soul, came home and
said, 'They're giving auditions for *Monday Night at Eight*. Why don't we write
off for one for you?'

It was one of the radio programmes we all used to listen to. Anyway, Daddy
wrote, and I got the audition, and Mummy and I went to Bristol, to Whiteladies
Road. Ronnie Waldron, the producer (we became dear friends afterwards)
heard me, and put me on the air. It was marvellous. And about a week after that,
Ambrose, the famous bandleader, phoned Ronnie and said, 'I want to see the
girl that sang on that programme.'

Ronnie said, 'She's no good for you, Bert. She's only a kid, she's just twelve.' Ambrose said, 'I'd still like to see her.' So, I was invited to go along to the Mayfair, to do an audition.

I must have looked horrible. I had my school drill slip on when I went to meet Mr Ambrose and the orchestra. It was all rather plush, you know, the Mayfair. I mean living in Dulwich, we never used to frequent the West End.

He asked me what key did I sing in, and I hadn't the faintest idea what he was talking about. He seemed kind and to like me, so I was able to admit I didn't know. He said, 'Try this one on for size', and I thought, what a funny way to speak. He played a bar and I sang 'Begin the Beguine'. And he said to Mummy, 'She's in, she can broadcast on Friday.' It was as early as that – this was on the Tuesday, and he was talking about the Friday coming up.

He said to Mummy, 'Can you make her look a little older and more dressed up?' I chimed in and said that I'd got a very nice pale blue and pink party dress. But he said, 'No, no, we'll leave the dress to your mother.' And Mummy told him not to worry, that I'd look all right.

Well I've always been a well-made girl, so I was able to wear my elder sister Eileen's dress, which was a gorgeous tan colour, with a big white collar, and her high-heeled shoes. These were a bit wobbly, but I only had to go up a couple of steps so I was all right, just about. My sister dressed my hair back, terribly smartly. The only thing I didn't like was wearing lipstick. I found it like gunge.

My Mummy took me, because she really wanted me to sing. She thought it was a wicked waste, since God had given me a gift, not to use it. I mean if I hadn't – what was I going to be? A Professor of History at Oxford or Cambridge? Because I was very interested in history, and always got full marks. I don't think I would have been much good to the world, though. There's enough of those about.

Ambrose always put me down as four years or five years older, otherwise I should have had to get an LCC licence to work as I was under-age. Being on radio I wasn't seen, so my looks were fine. By the time they'd groomed me, which gave them a year, my hair had been made blonder and my eyebrows shaped.

My darling sister Eileen plucked my eyebrows, and I looked like Herman Munster because they swelled up. All kids have rather thick eyebrows, except my baby sister Josie. She had the most gorgeous-shaped eyebrows. They didn't have to do anything with her. But she was a natural, she sang exactly the same.

I didn't mind the war as long as we were together, and we weren't going to be evacuated. We knew there was a war on, oh yes, for we used to say prayers for the soldiers, and of course it hit home when my brother, who was in the Army was sent to Arnhem and places like that. And, as civilians we started experiencing the air raids.

I was thrown into it by doing shows for the Army, Navy, Air Force, Royal Marines, AFS, NFS, the whole lot. And I met some marvellous ladies. People like Evelyn Laye, and my darling Elizabeth Welsh, who I did my very first broadcast with. We still keep in contact. She does Buckingham Palace concerts for me. I'm Entertainments Officer of the Not Forgotten Association, which looks after the disabled men and women of all the wars.

By now, I was doing live concerts. I looked quite grown-up. In photographs of me when I was about sixteen, I think I look about nineteen.

None of us ever had any 'teenage', shall we say. I mean that was the pattern in the war. Do I regret that? I can't regret what I never had, I look upon it like that. You see, I still had a childhood because although I was sort of second top to Maxie Miller at the London Palladium, I used to go home afterwards and play with my baby sister, Josie. We had our childhood together, and we were always together.

This is why people are wrong to think that there has been any animosity between Vera Lynn and me, which I laugh about. She was given the title in 1939 of Sweetheart of the Forces, and people used to say to me, 'You should be the sweetheart of the forces.' I'd disagree. You can't have a twelve-year-old sweetheart. But it only took me, thank God, a year to become the Forces' Favourite … with songs like 'You'll Never Know', 'Silver Wings in the Moonlight', 'As Time Goes By', all the love songs.

Even then I had a very mature voice, I wasn't one of those light, sweetie little voices. When I sang, you'd think it was someone about twenty-one, twenty-two singing. That's why people think I must be about seventy-nine or eighty now! I don't really care, it's never bothered me.

I became well known overnight, but it takes a long time to learn to become an artist, you know, a good entertainer. I haven't got much of a thing for the word 'star'. To me a star is something that flashes in God's heaven. You just become a good entertainer, or you don't.

I learned very quickly, because I loved it so. I loved my work, and God blessed me with a marvellous father and mother, and my baby sister Jo, and my elder sister, and, of course, I had my brother. And then when I was seventeen I met the man I was going to marry.

I met David on the Solent. I was asked to do a show for this naval friend of my brother's, on board the HMS *Tormentor*, and I just looked at him – you see, I'd never been out with anybody. I had no boyfriends. I hadn't even been kissed, because I had no time. I was with Mummy, and that was where I wanted to be. But I just looked at him that night and I thought, that's the man I'm going to marry, and that was it.

He felt the same way about me. We had an extremely long courtship, because of being Roman Catholic, and he was in the Navy until 1948. Instead of going back home to Scotland, he came and lived in our house, and that was rather like living in Buckingham Palace. David was at one end and I was at the other end. We weren't to live together. There was none of that.

After the Navy, he became my manager, so there was David, with Mummy, Josie and me, and Daddy sometimes. We travelled everywhere together. David fitted in like he'd been there for ever. In all the time that we were all together – I give you my word of honour it's true – we never had an argument. The only time we had a disagreement was when I didn't want to go to Canada, or Hong Kong, or South Africa. In other words when I didn't want to leave home. That was the only time when David would say to Mummy, 'You know, she's wrong, Mum,' and she used to say, 'Yes David, she is.' So David would say, 'Go and talk to Josie and ask Josie.' And Josie used to say, 'I think you should.' I'd say well, all right, we'll go. And that was the only thing.

Perhaps the most direct war work I did was a radio programme the Prime Minister had given me to do. I had done a concert for Mr Churchill, and he told me after it that I had a warm, compelling voice. The next thing I knew, I'd got my own radio programme. In those days it was like having your own television series.

In the studio, Stanley Black – Cecil – handed me this tatty old piece of paper and said, 'That's your signature tune.' I had immediately thought of a lovely signature tune, maybe, 'In the Still of the Night', or something like that. And when Stanley Black played this awful piece of music which had no words, I said, 'I don't like that, Cecil.' And he said, 'Well darling, it isn't whether you like it or not. You're being used to counteract the Nazi propaganda programme Goebbels is putting out.' They had Lale Andersen singing 'Lilli Marlene'.

It went on for about six weeks, and it was beamed directly to the North African desert, which was changing hands a lot at the time. Tripoli, El Alamein, and all that Rommel crew, and Monty's boys, the Desert Rats. And then of course we took it, and the Germans started singing *my* version of 'Lilli Marlene'.

One day I was called up by the BBC and asked could I explain how a high-ranking German officer had my photograph. I thought here's me, a kid compared to them, and they're asking me. I said I didn't know, unless he had taken it off one of our boys.

And I said, 'Well, you can't get in touch or write to the enemy, can you? You can't send letters to a general, or a lieutenant, or even a private in the German Army, can you?' So they said, no, it's just been a mess-up. That was typical. I don't know how I was supposed to have contacted them. Can you imagine? I didn't even know any Germans.

You felt you'd helped the war just a little bit when you went round hospitals and you saw the boys. I think I was one of the first to do a show at the Guinea Pigs' hospital at East Grinstead where there was that marvellous surgeon Sir Archibald MacIndoe.

They took me into one of the rooms at the very first stages of skin-grafting. But strangely enough, it didn't have the effect on me that it would have done if I'd been twenty-five or twenty-six.

I had kissed the side of their faces, and touched their shoulders, and the young flight lieutenant who was seeing me out had kissed me on the side of my face to thank me and said 'You've no idea what part of my anatomy has just kissed you.' It was a graft from his buttocks. 'Oh you cheeky thing,' I told him and just laughed. My pianist felt quite faint, because he was much older, he was a grown-up man.

Well, I must be truthful, Mavis, I didn't notice it because I was singing to them. Sometimes they would be lucky enough to have a piano, or otherwise we would have an accordion or something portable like that. It was nothing compared with what they were doing for us. I mean I'd been on Biggin Hill when the siren went – they always used to wait until a quiet song – and the boys would have to fly off.

I'd be dressed up in a nice afternoon gown. Mummy was very good. Let's not be stupid, if someone wanted something, and if you went to the right shop ... I mean you were doing it for the war effort. No one had uniform in ENSA unless they were going overseas, and you had to be eighteen to go abroad, which I was not. So I did my concerts all over Great Britain; I used to be taken out to sea to sing aboard the ships.

We often carried on with a show through an air raid. The Germans weren't nice enough to bother about our concert. I remember I was singing 'Fools Rush In' at Finsbury Park, and just when I got to the nice quiet bit, we heard a doodlebomb, and it cut out. And I thought, oh no. I mean what can you do? You can't run off, you daren't run off, because you're a performer. I'd been in the business a few years and I knew this. And then we heard an explosion elsewhere, and the whole house rose to its feet and cheered. A man in the front shouted, 'Start it again, Annie, without those bloody interruptions,' which I did.

Their appreciation rolled in like a mist would roll in, or like the sun would shine. And I used to get loads of letters from the boys abroad. On little pieces of paper like those stick-on yellow pads you get now. Lord Louis Mountbatten told me what a wonderful job I'd done, and Field Marshal Montgomery, and our own Sir Denis Crowley Milling, and Johnny Johnson, and Douglas Bader. Great guys, really great guys.

It was a hard slog. You were often at remote camps in bad weather – walk-

Anne Shelton, new blonde hair, same big voice.

ing with your gumboots on underneath an evening dress, so your evening shoes wouldn't get wet. Walking through the fields to get on to the stage. At that age, I don't think it mattered. You just put your head down and that was it. ENSA was something that we were very proud to give our time freely to. I felt good about the work every moment of the day. You can't face a thing like that and not know that it's marvellous, and God has blessed you specially to help them.

I had a programme that ran through the whole siege of Malta, it was *Calling Malta*. We were the only link between our mother country here and Malta. A musical programme with messages. They'd ask would I sing a song with their Auntie Kathy, and sometimes Auntie Kathy was singing way up high in the sky, and I'd be singing way down low. And singing with young lads who were fourteen and fifteen, and then sending messages from Mum and Dad.

This was done from the Criterion Theatre in London. Every Sunday I used to come back from no matter where I was – from Glasgow, from Edinburgh. I made sure I was on the train, and they'd hold it for me so I could get back, because I had to be on that programme. I used to start it with my little whistle and say, 'Annie, calling Malta,' and then it would begin.

I did the order of the programmes. I'd say what I wanted to sing. And during this time, 1944, I met and worked with Bing Crosby. That same year, too, I met Glenn Miller. He asked me to go to Paris with him on that fateful last trip. Yes, he wanted Mummy and me to go, and he wanted me to sing because they were going to have a coast-to-coast hook-up to celebrate Paris being liberated.

'You'll have to ask Mr Ambrose, Glenn.' He asked, but was told that I had six *Workers' Playtimes* booked. He gave me the most gorgeous bracelet, which is in the bank, and told me that there was more gold in my voice than there was in that heavy gold bracelet. He said 'When we come back, when this is all over, you come Stateside and we'll do some records and things.'

You see, our blessed Lord looks after you in different ways, because I would have definitely been with Glenn in the plane. Daddy would have stayed home with Josie, but Mummy, who sort of dressed me, would have come.

I couldn't tell you how Glenn died. We'll never know until we meet the Lord God Almighty. The plane just disappeared. I did the show with him about three nights before, kissed him God bless, and said, 'Take care.' He said, 'You take care too.'

But it's no good brooding. I think you live the life that God gives you. You can't go on worrying all the time. I mean I had no idea on earth that my David would die in 1990, and I never thought I'd lose my baby, my youngest sister Josie, who was my whole life and soul. We weren't like sisters, we were like one person. And the most marvellous thing is that my husband knew, and accepted it. There was never any animosity.

Jo and David and I travelled all over the world; they used to call us the Three Musketeers. 'All for one, and one for Annie,' they'd say. It was rather like losing one's left and right arm, because we'd never been apart, never. But still our Lord hasn't made me bitter. I'm very thankful that they didn't die of cancer, or muscular dystrophy, or that awful Alzheimer's disease. I mean Jo was only – she was just fifty-three.

I was never given an award in the war. My David knew I had got my OBE in 1990. And he knew what I'd be wearing to the Palace because I had already bought my outfit. But he passed away before he could see me receive it. It was the one time he couldn't come to the Palace after he'd been coming with me twice a year for the last fourteen years to do concerts for them.

The war didn't limit my singing career. When I met the great tenor, Beniamino Gigli, after the war he seemed to think that I had missed out by not having my voice trained for opera. He told me I was a very naughty girl and that I would have made one of the greatest sopranos the world has ever known. He said, 'Your voice is far too good for this rubbish you sing.' And I said, 'Well it's very good music, Mr Gigli.' He said, 'No, no, you must call me Gigli like you will be La Shelton.' So I said, 'No, you must call me Anne.' Ignorance, complete childish ignorance again!

I was quite happy. I liked my music; I liked Cole Porter, Jerome Kern, Oscar Hammerstein, people like that. Of course, I also liked classics, but I didn't want to become an opera singer. No, no way.

When I look back I believe the war brought out, definitely, a much finer type of person. We needed each other, we helped each other. You'd never hear of anyone being beaten to death, and people not going outside to see what the screams were. If they heard anything they'd be out there to see what it was.

I feel terribly sorry that the war took away so many of our boys' days. It gave us their days so that we could have our tomorrows. No, I thank God for everything He allowed to happen.

The war gave me such opportunities. That's why I do so much for the boys. That's why I was so thrilled to take part in the D-Day thing. I didn't see it as something to celebrate, I saw it as thankfulness to God for letting us put our feet on that soil. And I did it for the boys – as well as the boys that come home, God bless them, the boys that didn't. It was a commemoration more than a celebration, and of course next year, please God, God willing, if all goes well, that will be the time for the big hurrah.

NICOLA HARRISON
Life Without Mother

Nicola Harrison CBE (Consultant in Education and Local Government) would never, she insists, have allowed a family of hers to be split up – war or no war. They should all have been evacuated to safety or have stayed, risking it together.

She asked her own mother much later in life why ever had she allowed such a dreadful thing to happen to a six-year-old? Her mother said she herself had been dead against it, that Nicky had absolutely insisted on being evacuated with her classmates ...

We were living in number 32 Keedonwood Road on the Downham council estate between Catford and Bromley when war was declared. I was three but I do remember the air-raid sirens and the shelters. We didn't inhabit our garden shelter very much. It wasn't safe because it had been put much too close to our house. So we shared the people's next door.

Victor and Betty made a hole in their fence and we'd run through and into their shelter further down their garden. And Victor was so scared that he used to jump down first and say, 'Don't worry, I'm helping the children down!'

I used to sit putting my curlers in, on the top bunk with the boy from next door, and my mother was always very concerned that, as I was at the top, I would get it first.

The war was a kind of a game to me, I suppose. We used to be able to get rings with a blue stone at the front with a head on it. Did you have those rings? I would take mine off and leave it on the mantelpiece at night, so when the air-raid sirens went off and everyone rushed downstairs, I would go into the room to find my ring. And the others would be screaming at me to hurry. So for a while it was a game, rather unreal, but then it became very serious.

Bombs dropping everywhere. I had a Great-Aunt Lou, who had a pub in Bermondsey, and we were a family that used to have terrible knees-up parties

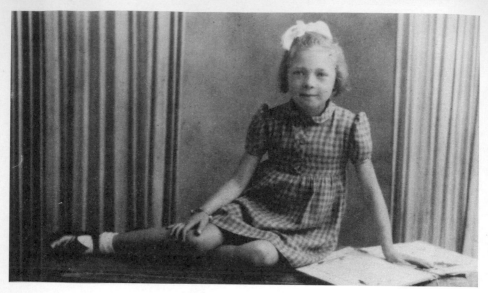

Nicky, an eager evacuee.

(I say terrible now but I think they were probably rather wonderful). Kids went to them because you didn't know about babysitters in those days. And there we all were in Bermondsey, by the docks, and the raids there were very real and very frightening. I guess it must have been about the time of the Battle of Britain.

The noise that still gets to me is the sirens. I was in France a couple of years ago, and every first Wednesday in the month, they turned on a siren – a fire alarm that they were testing. And I actually went cold.

The Downham estate was brand new. My mother was the first person to live in our house. Herbert Morrison was the architect of all this, Mr London, if you remember. And it was so vast that there were several schools on it – two or three secondary schools, and a lot of primary schools. It was like a town. In the middle of that estate was the main road, and trams used to go down from Grove Park into Catford.

We had all been rehoused from Deptford, and it was something for my mother to move into this house, which had a front door and a back door, and a front garden and a back garden, and also a bath! There was no running hot water, of course. A boiler, and you used to have to pump the water to get it up to the bathroom. But everybody was feeling that they were very grand, and then, God, there was this bombing destroying their new houses.

For a lot of the time we didn't know whether we're going to live tomorrow. I was young, and didn't feel it, but who knows how the older people felt – how women, of my mother's generation with young children, felt. Terrible.

A lot of mums worked at this time. And there'd be frightening incidents like when an odd rogue aeroplane came in. I remember that clearly: coming home on my own from school one lunchtime, and this plane flying very very low, machine-gunning the streets, and everybody diving into the hedges. Great panic and anxiety. It was a bad time, bad time. I think those women did awfully well.

I was evacuated twice. The first time was a family decision. My Uncle Ben was sent down to Southampton to do his training, so everybody felt – my mother, my Aunt Lil and my Aunt Grace – that they'd all move to be together. And within the week they'd bombed Southampton. It was flattened, and we all came back.

The second time was in '42, when they decided that our school – teachers and pupils – was going to be evacuated, but we were given an option. Either the kids went or they didn't. It was up to the parents. And I went. I always accused my mother of being really quite dreadful for allowing me to go. She said she had to let me go because I insisted.

I've thought about that. It could easily be true – my mother and father were getting on so badly. The marriage was quite violent as well, and I think I might have seen not just a way of getting away from the bombs and the sirens, but of getting away from the scenes at home.

So I went with my label on, carrying a bag with my very few things, and my gas mask in its little case. We were threatened with death if we lost our gas masks, so they were round our necks. And I remember getting on the trams, and arriving at a railway station, God knows which one it was, and then arriving, after what seemed to me such a long journey, in a place called Bury. That journey was just for ever.

I was with a boy called John from the same road. He was a year older than I was, and had been told to look after me. But even so that journey was vile. For the first time in my life, I was given my own toothbrush to take with me. I can't ever remember cleaning my teeth, well who would? I had with me as well a round green-topped tin of Gibbs toothpaste. I was very hungry, so I just licked this pad of violent-pink paste until it had gone.

When we got there, they took us to a church hall, and then the local people came to choose the children. Amazing. Throughout my adult life, I guess, I don't get many people wrong. But at that time I was obviously not too good at picking the main chance. A woman had seen John and me, and would have had us both, wanted us both. John said I had to go with him because his mum and my mum had said so, but I saw another woman with rather pretty dangly earrings and I chose to go with her. God, what a mistake.

John lived the life of Riley. The family were highly civilised, and obviously so much better off than most of the people in the area. Big house. Really nice. Mine was a two-up, two-down with this woman and her husband. I don't know why the husband was there, but he certainly wasn't in the Army. And their two kids. The three of us had to share one bedroom. They weren't cruel to me or anything, just completely indifferent. It was this indifference that was pretty bad to a six-year-old.

I had a camp-bed, and grey blankets and a pillow, I can't remember sheets. They had no curtains up at the windows, so when I was put to bed very, very early on light nights, I could never ever get to sleep.

There was their dreadful lavatory. I've never been so constipated in all my life. We all had jobs to do; one of mine was to walk up the hill and buy the bread. I actually peed myself in the bread shop – anything rather than go to that lavatory. Oh, it was awful, right at the bottom of the garden, and it smelt. There was no chain, it was a hole. It was the first experience I ever had of an earth closet.

I don't think I had a bath the whole time I was there. And I don't remember having my hair washed once. We just washed our face and hands in the kitchen sink.

Mrs M., however, made wonderful Lancashire hotpot. I've loved it ever since. She was a good cook, and I wasn't ever hungry.

I stayed there for about eighteen months. My mother didn't ever come to see me. Because things got so bad in London, she went off with my baby brother to Sheffield. Not for long. She was there, I think, for a couple of months, and then she couldn't stand it, so she went back.

I'm sure my mother and my father wrote to me, and I'm sure I was made to write back to them, but I forget, I've got so many blanks in that time. I was homesick like hell, but I'm not a great crier. In fact, I am quite self-contained, and I certainly wouldn't have shown them any of my feelings.

It must have been very difficult for people to take on somebody else's kids. But it was also a bit like 'The Londoners are Coming'. And as far as calling it the warm-hearted north – forget it!

To make things more difficult our school wasn't even integrated with the local school. Half the school building had been given to us, which meant we didn't learn side by side with the Bury kids. And we were greatly resented because we'd taken over so many of their rooms.

It was a joy to see John when I got to school. He used to come and sort me out. He really was so conscientious, and thinking back on it now, I really let him down, didn't I, by not going with him? We liked being with each other, but we didn't see very much of each other after school.

After about eighteen months, my father came to see me and took me to the fish and chip shop for lunch – no, dinner, it was called in those days. After a while, he asked me what I was doing. Well, what I was actually doing was pulling nits and lice out of my hair and cracking them between my fingers. It had become quite a habit.

I found them an enormous comfort. I remember lying in bed pulling them out and cracking them; they make the most wonderful noise. So I thought, not quite that they were my pets, but they were very much part of me and I loved them. My father sitting opposite me, watching all this, just couldn't take it.

He marched me back to Mrs M., and said he'd like all my things please, because he was taking me home. The first thing that happened when I got back, I was marched off to the cleansing station. My rather long hair was cut very very short, and there we were, back to normal.

I had mixed feelings about being back. Yes, I was very happy to be back with my mother, but the fights were still going on. It was all still quite dreadful. But now, happily for me, I spent a great deal of time with my grandmother, because I couldn't go to school as there wasn't one. I lost a lot of schooling, as many kids did of course. I didn't go to school for about a year. But even so I passed the Scholarship when I was eleven.

I adored being at my grandma's. It was – to me – just heaven. She had a transport caff, at the bottom of the Downham Way, and all those tram-drivers and conductors, and Dan the dustman, all used to come in for their food.

You kept hearing about the most dreadful disasters. A school in Hither Green, just down the road, was bombed and over three hundred kids got killed. It was tough, and I think we kids were pretty nervy, you know. A bit shot through.

I've always said I'd never let any children of mine go away as so many of us did in that war. Look at Northern Ireland now. Those families in Belfast, the families keep the children with them – at times with terrible consequences. But there's no mass exodus of those kids, and I think that's absolutely right.

No, I think it's one of the worst things ever, ever. And in Bosnia when they fly the children out and leave the parents there, I think that's really appalling.

About fifteen years ago I was working on an education committee, and I spoke up supporting the good work I had experienced as a child at my school in the LCC [London County Council]. I thought they'd given us all some very good schooling in very difficult situations. And the after-school clubs they provided, these were a great invention. With my mum always working, I used to stay behind after school, and for a penny was given a piece of bread and dripping and a cup of tea. Then they would look after us until about half-past five, six o'clock.

After the talk one of the officers asked me what school I was at. I told him the name, Rangefield. He phoned its head and told him that Alderman Harrison, chairman of Haringey Education Committee, was one of the old students of the school who had been evacuated. And the head asked me to come and give the certificates to these kids aged ten and a bit who were leaving. I said I didn't know whether I was strong enough to do this, because it had been a really bad time in my life.

He said, oh please, please come, and we'll try and find some people who were around at that time. So I asked a friend, Liz Murphy, to come with me. I couldn't face it on my own.

Anyway, we arrived at the nursery, where I used to take my brother in the morning and pick him up in the afternoon with his Mickey Mouse gas mask. As soon as I entered that vast, beautiful room with Delft tiles on the walls, I was back forty years. It was amazing.

There was a policeman who'd been evacuated with me in Bury. And there was John's mother, who had been a welfare assistant at the school. John, she told me, was now a doctor. And she said a funny thing: 'I always knew you two were special, you and my John, I knew you were going to get out of the Downham estate.'

All through the war and later, I was a latch-key child. And from an early age I had to wash up the breakfast things, either before I went, or when I came back from school, and tidy up a bit. But the washing up was the big thing. It was part of what was expected of you when your mother or the women running the house went out to work.

There were bonuses. I quite liked coming in and being able to have my own space (I wouldn't have known that word then). And, of course, there were the dog-ends in the grate. At the end of the evening all the ashtrays would be emptied into the fireplace. And next day, when I came home from school, I would hunt for them and smoke them. There were ways of cleaning them up. In those days cigarettes didn't have a tip. But even if they were a bit singed, it didn't matter, you could get a couple of puffs.

People say they had a wonderful childhood on *Desert Island Discs*, but I didn't. As a family we never went on holiday – no one did, I know, in the war, but we didn't afterwards either. Whichever family I was in – because remember I was in quite a number over quite a short period of time – there was never a day when we all left the house together, to say we're going to have a lovely day today, nothing like that at all.

In a funny way, I don't resent it. Everything that happens to you is part of your being, it is your make-up. I wasn't pampered, I've always stood on my own two feet. Always defended my brother. I find that still happens. Bossy sister.

I think I've always been, anyway on the surface, self-assured. I've always wanted to be in charge of myself. In control. And I've never expected anybody to look after me.

PAULINE CRABBE
Cutting the Apron Strings

If the war hadn't happened, Pauline Crabbe feels sure she wouldn't have gone into any form of public life because she had completely accepted her role as a housewife. 'I wore my pinny. I never thought of taking it off unless I was taking the children out in the afternoon.' It was the war that got her out of it for good, and once that symbol was removed she was able to move on to other things. 'When I removed that pinny from my body, I removed it from my mind as well.'

However, just at first glance her public work might seem to be somewhat attached to that apron. She worked for the National Council for the Unmarried Mother and her Child, for which she was awarded an OBE. But that was in 1969 – a long time after the year where she begins.

I came back from Jamaica about three weeks before war was declared. I had gone out with my parents who had longed to return there, and had finally arranged it. And now we – Geoff my husband and Gail my little daughter, who was about three – had just moved into a flat in Hampstead with packing cases all over the place, when we heard the news on the radio. And then the air-raid warning sounded immediately after Chamberlain's speech, and we thought let's get out. The flat was right on the edge of the Heath, so we climbed up Parliament Hill. The barrage balloons were rising because of the warning and we watched as London was covered with them. It was almost magical, although the implications were frightening. But it was just amazing to see it, to see these great grey shapes rising up. They had a children's story-book image about them and they were covering the whole – or so it looked – the whole of London.

It was not really an air-raid warning. I think it was probably done to alert people to the importance of what had happened, and I don't think that any of us at that time really believed that the Germans were flying over London and were going to attack us then and there.

Geoff and I had thought about war before this. Both of us wanted to protect Czechoslovakia. I remember marching down Whitehall with my small daughter and my husband. 'Stand by the Czechs,' was the cry. On that march we felt that we might really be going into war, but at the same time we were trying to prevent it. A day or two later they were putting sandbags around the children's clinic where I was regularly taking my two-year-old daughter. I remember going to help fill the bags, feeling that we must make our clinic safe for the protection of our kids.

In a funny sort of way, we really didn't have any knowledge of what was going to happen, so I don't think we were frightened. There was a little bit of what I call sick excitement, and I remember thinking how relieved I was that my parents had settled back in Jamaica. I was always very protective towards my parents. I would have been worried if they'd been here and I couldn't have been constantly with them. They wanted me to stay in Jamaica, when there were rumours of war, but I felt that my roots were here. It was where I'd spent all my childhood from the age of five. It was where my friends were, and most of the family – one of my two brothers and both my sisters were living in England. And now my husband was here, and at that time, although we didn't have a magical marriage, we had a marriage and we were together. I never intended to leave him.

Then there was a whole lot of excitement because of the uncertain future. Geoff was working for the Pearl Assurance company, and after the Munich crisis they decided to decentralise their huge London office. So within five or six weeks of war being declared we were sent up to Carlisle. That was something I had not expected, hadn't dreamt was going to happen. There was I leaving a flat that had not yet been made habitable, and just going north into a totally new life, which was an absolute revelation. And soon I was caught up with the extraordinary difference in the way people lived up there.

I had been living in Hampstead first with my parents, who were quite comfortably off until they lost most of their money, and even then we managed fairly well. After I married Geoff, we lived with them for a while until we got this little flat of our own. Now suddenly we were in Carlisle, billeted in a council flat with another family. The husband worked as a clerk on the railways, and his wife was totally and absolutely subservient to him. She never ate with him. In Carlisle at that time, the women didn't eat with their husbands – they waited on them. And although we had certain sort of Victorian values in our family, because my parents were still clinging to the old ways, life was so different.

They took my colour as a tremendous novelty. They had never seen a black person before. I think Mrs Bishop, who was a very meek and timid creature

Pauline Crabbe: wartime drama in Carlisle.

when her husband was there, now attained a certain status in the neighbour-hood because she had this black woman billeted on her. And she was wonderful to me. She taught me so much.

She taught me how to make bread. She was very, very surprised by these Londoners with their ideas of bought bread. Even shocked, really, and she soon put me right, showing me how to bake. It extended my own way of life, and later, when things got tough, I was extremely glad that I had once been billeted with her.

After a few months we got a house and our furniture was brought up from London. I sent the keys of our Hampstead flat to the same removal people who had only just moved us in there and told them to just bring up everything. And they did: absolutely everything. They even swept up the dust. I don't know whether this was meant to be a joke or not, but they put it in a little bag which I found when I was unpacking.

But, as I say, I learned a tremendous amount from Mrs Bishop about the way women were treated in Carlisle. No women went into the pubs, for instance. There was one very sophisticated place called the County Hotel, which had a bar for men, and a bar for women, and that was the only place you could go and have a drink. You just didn't go in the others. I was so shocked at that. But I found it a wonderful experience, Carlisle, and I made a lot of friends there, and all that was the background for my war. It was training me to accept a different sort of life – a life north of Watford – which I thought was really tremendous.

Before the war, I had simply expected to get married. It was the norm. My two older brothers went to university, and so did the two older girls – but then they got married. One at least completed her degree and married afterwards, but the other one got married after two years at college and left. Seeing all this happening, I thought it was the thing and so I thought well, why not? I decided I wanted a big family with six children. Quite mad. I didn't really want them when it came to the point, but that's what I thought I wanted.

We had been a very happy family. We were very close. I was just trying to repeat it. My mother and my father were devoted to each other, and they expected me to get married, though perhaps not as soon as I did. I was about twenty. I know I had to get my father's permission, so I must have been under twenty-one.

Geoff was called up in our first year in Carlisle, joined the Navy and went for training down to Devonport. That was the big watershed: I was quite shattered at being left. I'd had no preparation for it. In fact I had never been alone before. I had been with the family, very much protected by them, and although I had travelled out to Jamaica and back again on my own, it was just a trip. After that I'd lived with my husband, and it was shattering to find that I had the responsibility not just for myself, but for my child.

I was nowhere near my parents, who were in Jamaica. Nowhere near my brothers and sisters, because they were mostly still in London, with one sister out in Egypt with her husband.

Because I was in a house I was expected to look after evacuees from

Newcastle, which was supposed to be in the front line. And because I had a big house I was given three children. Two of them were sisters: nice, tidy, pretty little girls. We got on all right. And although I don't think that with all the books and pictures this was the sort of place they really wanted to be in, they made the best of it in a very graceful way.

Then I took on a boy who was far from easy in one way, and yet terribly easy in another. He was called Jack, and he never spoke at all to me. He wouldn't speak to the two girls either. He would only speak to my daughter Gail, who was then three. In fact I didn't know for certain that he could speak, until I heard him talking to Gail. Otherwise he never said a word. Then I met his mother, and I realised why. She was an overbearing woman who spoke for him the whole time. He was about nine, and she had obviously done it from birth.

They had asked me if I could take a difficult child, and very bravely I said, well I'll have a try. But he wasn't a bit difficult.He settled awfully well, in spite of all that. He was lovely. The girls moved out when they were fourteen or fifteen and reached school-leaving age, but Jack was with me right up until we left Carlisle.

As soon as Gail and Jack went to school – I don't know how they managed with Jack at school but they did – I went to work, partly because we were always short of money, since Geoff at first was only an Ordinary Seaman. When he became an officer things were a little bit easier, but we still needed money. More than that, though, I found a job because I had made friends with quite a lot of people in the neighbourhood, and many of the women were working.

I had quite a nice social life, in a way. I was running an amateur dramatic society which gave a performance every now and again, and which used to meet at my house because I couldn't go out in the evenings. Women in this group often talked about the work they were doing, and this got me interested.

I asked myself what I was going to do. The children were at school all day. I didn't want just to be the housewife and keep cleaning the whole time. It seemed an unnecessary waste. As I had taught myself to type, I got a job typing invoices in the Air Ministry. It was the first money I'd ever earned in my whole life, and I was so thrilled. By this time, too, I had learned how to take responsibility for myself and my daughter. If you've got a house and three kids, you have to work out the money, pay the bills, and make sure that the lights work – all kinds of things.

Members of the dramatic group had been a great help to me, and there were quite a few men who hadn't yet been called up, or were too old for the services. One was a conscientious objector and working locally on a farm. They taught me all these 'men things' that I had never done, like changing plugs and bits of proper gardening. They were wonderful, and they got a great kick out of teaching me how to cope with the things men usually cope with. And I just thought, well I don't really need a husband.

Geoff very rarely came home on leave. We still had, it seemed, quite a good relationship. Not my dream relationship, but then nobody ever comes up to that. My expectations had just been so ridiculously high, the happy-ever-after from the minute you got married. I fell straight into that trap, and of course it wasn't like that a bit. But we were still together, and it wasn't until he went out to the Pacific, and didn't come home at all on leave, that the marriage definitely began to break up. It took a very long time for our letters to reach each other. It was difficult to sustain any sort of marital relationship under those circumstances.

And there were lovers all over the place. In fact everybody was taking lovers. Me and all the women round me were taking lovers. Polish officers were in great demand. It was just happening, and that was the beginning of the end of my first marriage.

It was linked with a feeling of unexpected freedom. I had never really looked for any sort of freedom. I'd never been free of the family, my own family, parents and brothers and sisters. I'd never looked for freedom from them. I was quite happy to be still in the womb, as it were. But freedom's very heady, and when it comes unexpectedly I think it sort of permeates everything that you do. My freedom came when I actually earned my own money. Not that it was a lot, but I decided how it was spent.

I've certainly found that when you feel free you're a nicer person, and it's easier for people to like you. I appeared to be popular in Carlisle. Again that was a novelty thing, because there weren't any other blacks, and partly because I had a good speaking voice. And then running the amateur dramatics attracted a lot of people. I was also very alive and interested in what I was doing. They'd never had a drama group before. Everything had gone on in a very quiet sort of way in the little neighbourhood: it was a small suburban bit of Carlisle just on the edge of the town. So now they were glad to come because there was something interesting going on.

I never found prejudice there at all. I'd come up against one or two instances before the war. In one bar they had refused to serve my husband with drinks, which puzzled me at the time. I could not believe it was because of me. But I didn't encounter any prejudice at all in Carlisle.

I don't have any chips on my shoulder, and I think that's got something to do with it. It's partly having been brought up from the age of five in a white society. I was aware that there was prejudice – and it couldn't be ignored after the sixties – but it never really seemed to involve me deeply. And certainly Carlisle was a lovely experience.

The first black people I met in Carlisle were the American blacks. There was a contingent billeted in the town, and they saw this black girl, and I really had some difficulty. I had to make it quite plain that I was not interested. I felt sad about it, because it would have been so nice to ... but I really had to fend them off, and I didn't like that at all. But it didn't last very long.

After four years I left Carlisle. It was just before Geoff went to the Pacific, and was still on the corvettes which were doing convoys from their base in Weymouth. He said why didn't I come to Weymouth and join him? Our marriage had got a bit rocky. He had been having lots of affairs; he told me so. And I suppose the knowledge of that was why I began having affairs myself.

We both felt, well, this is silly. Let's have a go at making it work. We had this lovely child, and she needed both of us. She loved her father, she really loved him. So we did make a tremendous effort, and I gave up the house in Carlisle, which was a wrench.

It was also hard leaving little Jack, and I thought, however is he going to manage? The billeting officer couldn't find any home for him. But I did. I found a family of lovely people. The woman had twelve children, and they were nice children.They were very friendly with us. They used to come and play around Jack. Not with him actually, but around him, and they just took it for granted that he didn't speak. It was the obvious place for him.

I went down south quite deliberately to try and make a go of the marriage, and we had only about six months together. I got a little job in Dorchester. And it was all right, more or less all right.

Something that really stands out in my memory was the Normandy invasion in 1944. We had a flat that overlooked Weymouth Bay. Geoff wasn't allowed to tell me anything but everybody seemed to know that something was going to happen. We'd all been awake, the whole night before, cowering in a cupboard because of the bombing. And we were still up at dawn and watched this thing. The sea was covered in boats. The whole thing was solid. It looked as if you could walk over to France from boat to boat. And they all just went, and then came back in dribs and drabs.

Geoff went away soon afterwards, and I stayed on in the little rented flat until my sister Eunice, who was living in London (her husband was in India during the war) said, 'Well I've got this big flat, so you'd better come and live with me.' It was the greatest mistake of my life; it was a disaster. I thought it was a good thing at the time, because she had a child who was four, and I had Gail, who was seven or eight. I thought we could help each other. But no, she didn't approve of me at all. She didn't approve of my lifestyle, and my interest in all kinds of things. So very sensibly we parted and remained friends; if we'd stayed together, we would have probably had a big bust-up and never wanted to speak to each other again.

This was the time of the doodlebombs in London. They were very alarming. I didn't like them at all, but one just got on with it. I don't remember feeling fear, partly because I was so busy. I was working. I'd got the bee in my bonnet now that I could work, so I did an ordinary office job, nine to five, typing invoices. The same as I'd done in the Air Ministry, but it gave me a bit of money.

By now Gail was about nine, so I'm afraid she was a latch-key child. But only for about an hour a day, and we managed. My sister Eunice helped out and had her during the holidays. And Gail also made friends quite easily, so I usually found that she had a girlfriend with her.

We had to cope with the bombing, which was disturbing. I couldn't bear going into the shelters. When we were in my sister's house she had one of those Anderson shelters; she insisted on sleeping in this with her daughter and Gail. It was big enough for the four of us, but I couldn't stand it. I spent two nights in it, and then I said no, I'd rather have the bombs. So I went back to my own bed and left Gail with Eunice.

There was great relief when the war in Europe was over, but it was short-lived for me because of the shock of Hiroshima. I remember the news of that, and was just shattered by the horror, and what it was going to mean. It was just so, so awful. I had the most terrible feeling of guilt that this nation which I'd adopted had done this … well, it was the Americans, really, but still.

Deep down I don't think I ever believed that the war was ever right, and I had kept this in my mind all along. I had always, throughout the war, stuck up for the pacifists. I had been very angry with two older women in Carlisle who gave white feathers to men who had refused to fight. I found that so disgusting.

My husband didn't come back after the war. He'd got himself nicely tied up with a lady out in Australia. He could have got a passage back within a few weeks of being demobilised, but he hung around. Then he wrote and told me that he'd got somebody, and I just said, well that's it. We made a try, it obviously hasn't worked, so let's call it a day. By that time I had met Neville, who was acting in a play with me. And I thought he was the most beautiful man I'd ever seen.

I had always been involved in amateur drama, and when I came back to London I did a year's training at LAMDA – the London Academy of Music and Dramatic Art – hoping that I would have the nerve to become a professional actress. But there were no parts for blacks who didn't sing or dance – except as the coloured maid in any American play that came to London. I did all those in my family name, Pauline Henriques. But I never took it very seriously.

But by this time I had been lucky enough to get work in radio, and I was on a literary programme in the BBC called *Caribbean Voices*. I worked for a very long time on and off on this, doing all kinds of things, reading poetry and reading plays. I loved it.

And then Ken Tynan heard my voice, and chose me for the part of Emilia in *Othello*. He had this wonderful idea that Othello and Emilia had had an affair before the play began. It was typical of Ken. He always had these extraordinary ideas. He didn't change any of the lines, but he worked it in, right at the beginning of the play. It was a little scene that was only mine, in which there was a subtle implication that they had been more to each other than actually came out during the play. That was the most wonderful acting experience that I'd had, and it decided me that although I would go on happily working for the BBC as long as they wanted me, there was no way I could play an American coloured maid ever again.

Instead I looked around and said well, what is my other love? Working with people. So, to cut a long story short, I eventually got a job at the National Council for the Unmarried Mother and her Child. The general secretary who was running it decided she would like to have this black woman for her secretary. She just said, 'Out of the lot, I'll have that one.' I always thought she chose me because I was physically very strong. They kept spare prams in the committee room, and on committee day all of them had to be moved out. And I could do that, you see.

Eventually they had to get rid of her; she had gone stark raving mad. She'd not do any work at all. I would do it, just to keep the thing moving. And now I had to take over. It was absolutely unheard of, the trust they put in me. But I think the committee felt that I had handled it all when she was sick, and that here was somebody quite sensible. Anyway they made me acting general secretary, and I ran the place for six months.

They were embarrassed when they began to realise that they couldn't really have a black heading the organisation. I'm never quite sure, but I knew when they made me acting general secretary that they were not going to make me general secretary. I just knew that. Nobody ever said anything, nobody ever explained that to me, but they were ostensibly looking elsewhere. They said they wanted somebody with a degree. But I knew that they could not have a black. But do you know, they were wonderful to me. It was through their recommendation – I'm convinced – that I got my OBE, which I enjoyed immensely. It was very nice to get this public recognition.

Without the war happening, I don't think any of it would have happened. I think I would have been like my sisters – married, quiet, no public work at all.

Renate, right, *and friend with obligatory gas masks and obliging labrador.*

RENATE OLINS
Island Prison

Renate Olins is Director of London Marriage Guidance. In 1938, when she was six years old and Renate Steinert, she and her mother and father arrived in England as Jewish refugees from Germany. Their lifestyle changed drastically: from living in a large flat in Berlin to renting a small flat in London; from a comfortable middle-class life to one of genteel poverty and extreme anxiety.

We left Germany at the end of 1937, but stopped in Amsterdam to visit my grandparents, who had not been able to get visas for either England or America, which is where they really wanted to go. My father ran backwards and forwards between London and Amsterdam like a nesting sparrow trying to get the papers for us all to be allowed into England. Finally he succeeded, and we arrived in England at the beginning of 1938.

The experience of being Jewish refugees was not one my parents could accept in the kind of robust way that some people could. Being German and Jewish was always referred to very *sotto voce*. You didn't let on about it, and you tried desperately to become part of the community in which you lived. We would certainly have passed Norman Tebbit's cricket test.

I arrived in England without a word of English, and was sent off to the Norland nursery to begin my education. By the time war broke out I spoke very good English without a trace of an accent. I was seven.

There was a sense of waiting for a thunderstorm to break. If there was a war, then the next thing could be, couldn't it, that England might lose? That was the cloud under which we lived.

I dimly knew why we had left Germany. I can remember walking around Berlin with my mother, and everywhere I looked, there was a picture of this man with hair down one side of his face, and a moustache. To a child of five, this man in military uniform looked rather smart. 'Mummy, who is that man?' I wanted to know. And she looked wretched and agonised, and said, 'He is the Führer.' I said, 'Is he a nice man?' and she said, 'I hope so.'

We left Germany with what furniture could be accommodated in a lift van. We still managed to get furniture out. When we arrived in England we moved into a small flat in a little 1930s block just off Portobello Road. It's still there, Lancaster Lodge. A cousin of my father's had found it as a *pied-à-terre* while we settled down. Thirty-two years later, my parents were still living there.

In 1939 I was going to Kensington High School. My education was an absolute priority with my parents, that was the one thing they felt they had to give me. When war broke out, their anxiety was redoubled. German-Jewish refugees became enemy aliens. And because Hitler didn't want us, we were deprived of German citizenship and so we became stateless: a double insecurity. What I remember from my childhood is total love and desperate anxiety, always the two together.

In 1940, a regulation called clause 18b was invoked. My parents, in common with their friends and relations, were summoned to tribunals. They were set up locally, staffed by well-intentioned but often not very well-informed local worthies, who were there to assess what kind of a security risk you represented. All 'enemy aliens' were put into one of three categories.

Category A was for those considered 'high risk', and you were likely to be interned. Category B meant they didn't quite know what to make of you, and Category C was for those they thought were OK. With my parents' luck, we were classified as Category B, and my mother talked to me about the possibility that my father might be interned.

He came home as usual one evening, exhausted after a long day working at Seven Sisters Road, where he had set up a small factory making toilet products like sponge-bags and shower caps. There were two detectives waiting for him in our little sitting room. When he saw them there he went ashen.

I was in such a state of agony. Yet because I knew of my parents' own fragility, I wanted to protect them. I locked myself in the bathroom and cried, sat on the floor with my head on the lavatory basin. After a time my father's suitcase was prepared. My mother had got supper ready, but they couldn't wait for him to have supper.

I was asked to come out, and I kissed him goodbye, which was quite dreadful, quite dreadful. I was crying, and my mother was crying, my father was struggling not to cry, and then he was marched off, we didn't know where. The detectives didn't know. They were detectives from Harrow Road police station, what could they know? They wouldn't have known a real enemy alien at fifty paces.

So my mother and I were left alone, and there followed weeks of absolute misery, while my mother worried desperately about where my father was. We could get no news. And then one day, a couple of months after he'd gone and we still hadn't heard, I became ill. I got something like flu, and was in bed with a very high temperature.

There was a knock at the door, and there stood two more detectives, a man and a woman. They explained that they'd come to collect my mother, and that she was being interned. But they had no instructions about the child. I said, well I'm coming too.

My mother once again plunged into agony, and said, 'Oh but Renate, you're ill and what shall I do? Maybe you should stay with Aunt Inge' (who was her sister and lived nearby). I said, 'No, I'm coming with you.' And the detective said, 'This child can't travel unless you get a medical certificate.'

Our old doctor, another German-Jewish refugee, was summoned and he certified that although I had a temperature of 102, I was fit to travel. So we began to pack, and being the horrible precocious child I was, I said, 'We should take some books, Mummy, and it would be a good idea to take *Pears Cyclopaedia*, because it has a lot of useful information in it, and we don't know how long we may be there.' My mother was too punch-drunk to worry about such things.

Anyway, we were marched off, each with a little suitcase, to Harrow Road police station. I felt terrible. We were kept there for eight hours, waiting for instructions. They did give us a cup of tea.

Eventually we were moved to some kind of barracks where there were dozens and dozens of women, and a few children, and we were given camp-beds to sleep on. The next morning we were all herded into a train and set off north for Liverpool. There we were embarked on a boat to take us across to the Isle of Man.

When we got there, me with my raging temperature, we were dragooned into groups and marched off to the hotels and boarding-houses to which we were allocated in Port Erin. You just had to submit and do as you were told. We were mainly German-Jewish refugees, with the odd Italian shopkeeper or ice-cream vendor, and a few 'real' Germans. I mean Aryans, not Jewish Germans.

We went off to a boarding-house, run by a drunken man with a great bulbous red nose. He was never sober, and always had a cigarette hanging from his lip. Apparently he got a pound a week for each of his residents, so the less food he gave us, the more profit he made. And the jobs were shared out between all the women. Tuesdays my mother would peel potatoes, Wednesdays she'd help with washing the sheets, and Thursdays . . . there would be lots of rotas worked out.

There was a mortifying incident once, when my mother was working in the kitchen. A big German woman who had been working as a chambermaid in a hotel dropped a tea caddy and all the tea spilt out. It was loose tea, you didn't have tea bags in 1940, and I was sitting on a table swinging my legs. Being an imaginative little brat, I said, 'If this was the land of Araby, and I were a princess, I'd make you pick up every one of those little tea-leaves.'

There was the most dreadful silence, and my mother hurried me out of the room. I didn't know what I'd done. My mother then explained to me that I had just played up to the worst stereotype that some people had of girls like me. So I had to go back and apologise most humbly to this woman, who I don't think had quite understood what was going on anyway.

So that was life in the hotel. One of the women told fortunes, not just from tea-leaves but from melted-down toothpaste tubes. These were made of lead and you'd drop them into water and the shape they made would tell your fortune. A great deal of knitting went on, because of course people had a lot of time. My mother knitted herself a dress in a very pretty shade of lavender blue.

Port Erin was a seaside resort, and in the summer you could go down to the beach, and there were lovely places to play. There were rock pools and you could walk along the edge of the cliffs. I've never lived in such a beautiful place, before or since. And in the winter there were gales, real gales, which were very exciting because people literally got blown over, which when you're young you think is funny.

A wonderful school was set up by a very well-known educationalist called Minna Specht and I went there every day. She was very strict, and if I arrived late, I was sent home. But the school was excellent: when I got back to the mainland after a year and a quarter, they didn't know what to do with me. I was so advanced compared to what children of my age were doing back home.

All sorts of activities were organised in our group of exiles. They put on operettas and concerts, for there was such a lot of talent. I led quite a full life, but I missed my father dreadfully.

We did have news of him shortly after we arrived there. Around my mother's birthday, on 21 June, she got a letter from him – he was also on the Isle of Man, in a men's camp in Douglas. After many months a reunion was organised, and husbands and wives were marched off in long crocodiles under military guard to meet in a church hall for an hour and a half. My father was marched in together with the other men; it was a miserable business, miserable.

My parents sat clutching each other, and my father had managed to get me a couple of chocolate Penguin biscuits. They were very rare and special in those days, and I've always thought them rather special ever since, even though I never particularly liked them.

There were a couple of reunions for my parents during that first year, but I used to worry because my mother worried, and everybody else worried. What was in our minds was that if Hitler should win the war – which at that point seemed by no means impossible – he would find us all very neatly rounded up. We didn't have passports, we couldn't become naturalised until after the war, so during the whole of the war we were stateless, and certainly we would have been very easy to identify.

It was a most peculiar existence really: a combination of a benign prison and a seaside holiday. Quite strange. But the misery was the separation from my father.

The more I thought about it, the more anxious I was. My mother was very short of money. Every now and again I would get a penny or a halfpenny, and although I longed to go to the sweet shop, I hated asking her for money. She had a big pigskin handbag which she kept in the wardrobe, and which she used to get out from time to time to count how much money she had left. When she did that I couldn't bear to look. I used to turn my back on her, so that I wouldn't see how little there was. I remember telling her about that years later, and she was quite stricken; she hadn't noticed I was doing it.

I saw it as my job always to disguise the extent of my anxiety from my parents. I always felt they had enough to cope with, so I got a degree of satisfaction from not letting on. They weren't robust. They weren't built for the vicissitudes of life; you could feel them flinching with the blows.

After about a year a married camp was set up but that was only for about three months before we were released.

Released from the Isle of Man and its seagulls. The seagulls are extraordinary: they're absolutely enormous, and they were always wheeling and squawking. All that was certainly a great deal better than a small block of flats off Portobello Road. I wasn't confined, and the beach was wonderful. In those days it was totally unpolluted, and I learned to swim there, so it was a kind of bittersweet existence. But it wasn't quite real life. My father couldn't work. We used to go every week or more to the post office to see whether our name was on the list for a food parcel. People sent parcels sometimes and that was very exciting.

The point of interning us was that some of us might be fifth columnists. Most people on the island probably found it a bit barmy, and I should think that there might have been some local resentment. After all, we were being kept by the state, weren't we? Our keep was being paid for by the taxpayer, so I don't know how people felt about that. And the concept of being a refugee from Hitler wasn't something that everybody really understood. In those days, what did people really know about Hitler, about concentration camps?

I do understand why we were interned. It was totally ridiculous, it was grossly misjudged, and it was entirely understandable. One does these things in order to keep the public quiet; we all have our constituencies to mollify, whether at work or in the country. And if interning a few German-Jewish refugees will do the trick, well then let's do that. I mean you're not killing them, you're not torturing them, and to merely scoop them up and uproot them doesn't seem so very dreadful. And the feeling that something had to be done to distract the muttering populace, at a time when clearly the government hadn't got its act together, was … normal.

In 1941 people were beginning to be released. It was a matter of the process working its way through, because it was recognised that it had been a panicky and ridiculous measure to intern all these perfectly innocuous refugees. The Amadeus String Quartet was in my father's camp, except of course they hadn't formed themselves into a quartet yet. It was full, on the whole, of German-Jewish refugees who were either respectable tradesmen like tailors or pastry-cooks, or musicians or academics or businesspeople. As a way of scooping up fifth columnists, it was a pretty broad net.

And when we got back to London? The flat was still there. It had been lovingly looked after by friends and relations, and it was clean and sparkling fresh, and there were flowers, and food in the fridge, and next to my bed was a book for me to read, and a bowl full of vanilla and chocolate fudge. I had never tasted such ambrosia. I had never had fudge before, and I lay in bed in my lovely linen sheets, brought over from the continent, reading a book, which was all about the pleasures of London, and eating fudge. It was wonderful.

And now once we were together again, once we were this little tight group of me and my parents, anything could be faced and the waiting was over. I found it lovelier than I could have imagined to be back in my own bed, my own bed linen, and I've never lost that.

But the war was still very much on. There was a hell of a long way to go. It now left us free to worry even more about my grandparents. I haven't spoken of them. They had been left stranded in Amsterdam, and so that was the other great cloud of anxiety, worry about what was happening to them. In fact they were taken off to Belsen.

I remember all that very clearly, because at the beginning, when they went to Belsen, which used to be called Bergen-Belsen, they managed to get out a couple of Red Cross letters, so we actually heard from them a couple of times. In one of the letters they said please send food parcels. My mother looked absolutely miserable; she said it must be very bad for them to write that.

Of course, we didn't know just how bad it was. We tried to send parcels: whether they ever arrived or not I don't know. I can remember my mother composing little Red Cross letters to them – it was a very limited number of words you were allowed to write – to tell them about their grandchildren, that was me and my cousin David.

I have no idea whether that ever reached them. But they didn't come out of Belsen. My grandfather died on the first of April, and my grandmother died on the tenth of April, just before Belsen was liberated, just days before.They both died of typhoid.

Just a few weeks after the end of the war, when you could begin to get news again from the continent, a letter arrived. I had a friend staying when the letter came, and my mother opened it. And she read that they were both dead; it was just dreadful, dreadful. She rang my father, who left his office and came home immediately, and she was crying. I took the other girl off to the cinema so that we could be out of the way, even if only for an hour or two. When we came back, my mother had dressed entirely in black, which gave me a turn. And I remember my mother saying, 'They didn't even know the war was over.' Awful, awful; well, it's two of six million.

So you see my grandparents were interned, and I was interned, and you can't compare the experiences. When you ask, 'Is it still a thorn in your side?' well it doesn't even rate, doesn't even score on the register. There was no question that we wouldn't be returned in good condition as far as the British were concerned.

It does sometimes surprise people that one can be so charitable about it. But you have to see it in the context of what else was happening at that time, and what goes on happening. Really, you know, life is a risky and frightening business, isn't it?

I don't know whether the war changed me. You are what you are, and you have it in you. But I think the war changed me in that it made my parents, and therefore me, much more anxious, and much more aware of the fragility of everything. Yet paradoxically, it also intensified my love of things, and of the important people in my life. It instilled a kind of greediness, a kind of desperate and hopeless need to try and have everything with me. It made me want to have it all close to me.

I want it here, I want it now, I want it next to me, and I think probably – and this is not good – it has made me long very much always to be close to my children. Physically close, as well as emotionally close, because who knows, tomorrow might be the last day, or even today.

I think people whose experience of life has been more bland, or less frightening – and I appreciate that many people have far more frightening lives than I've ever had, but for me mine was frightening – are in some ways perhaps better. Better for themselves and better for their children.

You're not so emotionally caught up in things, you're not so enveloping and potentially devouring, which I see as a bad and restrictive thing. But it's also an instinctive thing, and of course it's a source of great pleasure. I get a lot of mileage out of my affections. I did with my parents as well, but it did always feel like us three against the world, and that's why to be ripped apart was so dreadful.

As a child I saw the war through my parents' eyes, and when they were anxious I was anxious, and when they were frightened I was frightened. And when they thought it was a bad thing to speak German in the street, which it certainly was during the war, I thought it was a bad thing. And if they thought that being Jewish was a dangerous and risky thing to be, then I thought so too. I remember my headmistress, who professed socialist beliefs, saying to me, 'Of course, Renate, it is particularly important that you behave well, because you are after all Jewish. People will judge other Jewish people from your behaviour.'

I was so taken aback that I was shocked in the real sense of the word. I thought, that's a dreadful thing to say. But at the same time it chimed in with what I'd been made to feel anyway, by my experience of life. So the war was a very very anxious time. I hoped that the end of the war would see the other longed-for reunion, with my grandparents, but of course that didn't happen.

PAT PARKER
The Rewards of Hard Labour

Pat Parker admits that in retrospect we always think life was better. 'But for us the war, with all its ups and downs, was the happiest time of our lives. All the Lumberjills will tell you that. I wouldn't have missed it for the world and sometimes I wish I could go back. I really do.'

She does not, for one minute, think it was more fulfilling than her later family life was (and is) with her husband and son. It is just that it was her time, and hers alone.

What I wanted to be was a nurse, but my mother talked me out of that, because she said they couldn't afford to keep me while I trained. There were three of us in our family: an older brother, a younger brother and me in the middle. We lived in a flat in Hercules Road, Lambeth North, London.

I don't think I ever had any bright ideas about what I wanted to do when I left school. We weren't supposed to leave until sixteen, but by the time I came to fourteen and a half, I was getting a bit bored. My friend was going to get a job at Odham's Press, and my father said, 'Well I'm in the print, let's take Pat out of school and give her the chance.' So to Odham's I went and earned two and six-pence a week and a box of chocolates at Christmas.

Just before war was declared our family moved to Streatham. On the Saturday an air-raid shelter was dug in the garden, the next day war was declared, and the next minute an air-raid siren started. My father in a bit of a panic said, 'Quick – outside, all of you– into the shelter.' We scooted out into the garden, and Tony my younger brother tripped over the piece of corrugated iron that was sticking up at the entrance to the Anderson shelter. He cut his shin – some two inches – and it went right through to the bone. My father picked him up and shot over to the doctor, and we all said my brother must have been the first casualty of the war.

It was ages before there was any sign of war after that. I remember my first experience of it. I went to help my father who was digging for victory up on Streatham Common, on our allotment right at the top of the hill. We heard an aeroplane coming over – flying only as high as the trees – and we were so surprised to see the black cross. It was a Nazi plane and it bombed Croydon airport, which we could see in the distance. But even that didn't frighten us, because it just flew over.

But then, soon after, the blitz started, and all the way along, the main road became a bombing run, from Croydon right the way through to central London. We used to sit at home at night in the kitchen listening to the bombs falling – my mother wouldn't let us go anywhere away from her. And if we had gone to bed and there was a warning we'd all have to get up and stay in the kitchen until we heard the air-raid all-clear.

We did get blasted badly a couple of times, and a bomb blew out the window in my little bedroom on one occasion. In the morning we found, where my head would have been, a large piece of glass stabbed in the pillow. I was lucky.

When I was eighteen I thought rather than be called up and directed into a factory, I'd join up so that I could choose which service for myself.

I was mainly thinking of the WAAF, since my elder brother, Eric, was already in the RAF. I didn't tell anyone, but one morning before work I went to the WAAF recruiting office near Victoria, but it was shut; it must have been about half-past eight. I thought, lazy lot; if I have to go to work at half-past eight, why can't they?

A few doors down was the Land Army office, open. That seemed a good idea. I'd sooner be out in the air – because I used to like to swim and play tennis – so I went and asked if I could join. I'd recently seen an article in the *Daily Sketch* about the Timber Corps, girls working in the woods. And I'd thought, that's a job that would suit me. I was at the age when I was reading romances, and my mind was full of pictures of strong men, hunky lumberjacks! They asked me what work I'd like to do. So, I told them the Timber Corps. 'You do realise,' they said, 'that you won't be able to go home for at least six months.' I said, 'well, it doesn't bother me, I'm pretty independent anyway.' (Well, I said independent. In those days, girls weren't at all independent.)

Anyway I joined up and was told that in a few days my uniform would arrive by post, along with my instructions and a travel warrant. Then I trotted off to work.

I got home in the evening and said to Dad, 'I think I'd better tell you now, I've joined up. I'm going in the Women's Timber Corps.' 'What the hell is that?' he said. So I told him. 'My God, it'll kill you!' he said. And I thought to myself, oh dear! what have I let myself in for?

Land Army poster.

My uniform turned up. I was sent a brown hat which suited me quite nicely, green pullover, cream shirt and a pair of breeches (these were something special, as it wasn't customary for women to wear trousers then). A pair of very solid, brogue-type shoes, thick socks. And a greatcoat with lapels. I thought I was really the cat's whiskers!

My instructions were to go to Fenchurch Street station. Mum and Dad came with me, and there was a whole group of girls standing on the platform. One came over and asked, 'Are you going to Culford?' I told her I was, and she said, 'Well why don't you come over and join us, we're all going the same way.' That lady, my mate Lily, is still my friend. More like a sister to me now.

The train came in – I think Mum was worried, but she didn't show it – and I hung out of the window saying, 'Bye Mum!' till she was out of sight. I sat down and thought again, oh God, what have I done? But the girls were talkative and we all told each other what we did. One was a hairdresser. There was a secretary, a salesgirl who worked in one of the big stores up in the West End, two or three office girls. And Lil, sitting opposite me. She had been humping sacks of coffee around in a warehouse. And I thought good grief, I couldn't do that.

At Culford we were taken by lorry into the camp, and we were there for a month. We were taught how to sharpen and use a saw and an axe, how to tell one piece of wood from another, one tree from another. And I can still remember all of that. If I see the leaves, I don't always know the name – but I do if I see the trunk and the bark.

Lumberjills at work: Pat and her best friend Lil.

The fun part was learning to chop a tree down. First, we were given stumps, believe it or not. We laughed about this because they were only about four foot high. One of the male instructors gave us each an axe and told us to have a go. Being daft and not knowing, we chipped away as though we were chipping matchsticks. We hadn't a clue. The instructor came back laughing and said, 'No, that's not the way. Let me show you.' Down swished the axe, then another chop and he cut a lovely V-shape in the tree. A couple of the girls swung the axe, missed the trunk and the weight of the axe spun them round full circle. We laughed so much in that first week, and our muscles ached. But the more we ached the more we laughed.

The next thing we had to learn was criss-cross sawing. We used a long saw with handles at both ends: Lily on one end and me on the other, pulling never pushing, to and fro and the saw did the rest, eating through the wood.

Then the instructor took us into the woods to cut our first tree. When the tree was ready to fall, we yelled 'Timberrrrrr!' and with a crack and a whoosh, down it came. We cheered. We'd done it. We were always very tired. But as we were such great pals together it hardly bothered us. We were a group of about fifty girls in the camp, and there were about ten or fifteen of us in the huts.

The only thing I used to worry about was undressing in front of everyone. After a while I got used to it. Nobody was taking any notice of me, so I just did what everybody else did.

After we washed it was out into the field to do the old physical jerks, about half-past six in the morning. Then we'd go and have breakfast. Pretty awful food: very plain and not a lot of it. We were given sandwiches in a big wooden box to take up into the woods for lunch.

A lorry took us up there, and after we finished work we were free in the evenings. We'd go walking down to Culford village. An army camp a bit further along had dances, but I only ever went to one. But there was a lady in the village who opened her house. All the uniforms used to come in, and she always had tea on the go.

At the end of the month's training, we were asked where we wanted to go. Lil and I put in for Cornwall and, typical Army, we got sent in the opposite direction – up Hereford way. We became general foresters: you name it, we did it. The measurers were the brains of the outfit. They did the paperwork. They'd find a wood, talk to the farmer and sort out how much it would cost, make the arrangements to get the timber out, and do all the measuring. They'd mark the trunks that would have to come down.

Lil and I were sent to an estate about twelve miles outside Hereford city. It belonged to a Lord – Cornwall, I think it was. Rings a bell because I remember thinking Cornwall was where we asked to go!

We had to work for a male foreman, and on the first day he said, 'Right, you two, see those logs there, well put them over behind that there stick.' He just left us to it.

You felt with a lot of the men you had to do twice as much to prove a point. You had to be a cussed sort of person – which I am – and say, well, I damn well can do it. I had no muscles whatsoever – the heaviest thing I'd ever lifted was an envelope – but I eventually got myself fit, greatly helped by Lil. She, as I said, used to shove coffee sacks around, and she knew what she was doing. She'd heave and I'd push until I got strong enough to heave, too.

This foreman of ours, Lil noticed, seemed to be out to separate any girl who wanted to work alongside a friend. And she said to me, 'Where I go, you go, where you go, I go.' Right, fair enough, and that's how we stayed. For the rest of the war Lil and I stayed together through several changes of billets until we ended up with a Mrs Davies. She had three sons, and Lil and I had to share the top bedroom and the same bed. They'd probably call us lesbians today because we slept in the same bed, but it wasn't anything like that.

There was no bathroom in the house so we'd go for a proper bath to the public baths – the swimming baths, I mean, for in those days they had hot baths on the sides. At home we'd get the hot water on and, as we used to say, wash up as far as possible and down as far as possible and leave possible to chance. We often washed our hair under the old pump in the back kitchen.

Some of my washing I used to send home to mum by post. She'd send it back with a packet of biscuits or something tucked inside.

Lil and I – on our bikes, which were supplied to us at the cost of one shilling per week – always got up to the woods early. We'd have a fire going for the girls when they arrived from the hostel. In the thick of winter it was bitterly cold. We'd leave the house wearing our big coats and as many jumpers as we could pile on. Then we'd do a bit of sawing and the coat would come off, and we'd be down to our shirt-sleeves by the time the girls arrived freezing after a half-hour's journey in the back of the open lorry.

The life made me practical. I learned a lot while I was away. I'd gone through all the usual things of being a Brownie and a Girl Guide, and joining the Girls' Life Brigade. But now, suddenly, I found I could do all those things that I wouldn't have thought of doing before.

I helped pull the timber out from the tree. I helped in the sawing and the loading of the timber, from four-foot-six pit-props, the first I ever loaded, to six-foot-six ones that went across the lorry. Then I graduated to nine-foot pit-props, the heavy ones.

Our driver and his mate made up our loading crew: two on the ground and two on the lorry to stack. To load logs two poles were placed from the ground

Proof of a day's work.

to the lorry bed. The logs were then rolled up the poles and stacked. Once the bed was full, we raised the poles higher on to the stack and this process was repeated until we had four or five layers, the last layer being the hardest. We then drove to the railway station, and unloaded them into coal trucks. Two, sometimes three loads a day. Riding on top of these loads was quite a thrill.

Charcoal loading was a filthy, rotten job. Nobody wanted to do it. As well as making us black as the ace of spades, it used to get into our clothes, and make us itch like mad. One day we were sitting on top of the load in a lorry, and all of a sudden there's a cloud of smoke blowing like anything at the back of the load. The wind as we went along had fanned it alight.

We made roads. It was the first job we ever did. There was a slope up into the woods, and in the winter, when the rains came with lorries going up and down, it would turn into a quagmire. Real mud, thick gooey mud, it was. The boss said we must get a road built before the bad weather really hit us. So we went to a sawmill and picked up slats of wood, like the outside carvings from a tree, and laid those all the way up. Then we chucked tons of sawdust over it, so that it would eventually work down into the ground.

Round the fire at lunchtime, we would stick our cheese sandwich (the everlasting, everyday cheese sandwich) on to a forked stick, hold it over the fire and toast it. Or we'd get a knob of cheese and stick that over the hot embers until it was nearly dropping, then wipe it on our bread quick. We ate more ash than cheese or bread.

I wouldn't say we were always hungry, but I lost a lot of weight. Yet it was one of the best diets going, wasn't it, the wartime diet? We were very fit.

We had Eye-ties working with us for a while. Italian prisoners of war. And they used to make beautiful coffee. I don't know where they got it from. We'd drink it out of jam jars – beautiful milky coffee. Some of the Eye-ties were naughty and some of the girls were naughty with the Eye-ties. And then the poor Italians used to get sent to what we called the bad boys' camp at Presteigne.

The group we worked with were nice, real good chaps. On my twenty-first birthday and on Lil's they gave us a woven basket each which they'd made. And twisted our ears, which they told us was an Italian custom. One of them was a jeweller and he made us rings out of a silver spoon we bought. Mine was lovely. It was a small square with an outer square on it. It was all beautifully chased round the edge.

And sing! Oh, my godfathers, could those Italian blokes sing? They were always singing. 'Sorrento' they used to go in for in those days. I think they were glad to be out of the war. Well, let's face it they weren't badly treated over here. They did pretty well out of it.

It was six or seven months after the war, I suppose, that I finally packed it in. Lil wanted to get married to Les, a local boy. Rooms were hard to come by, so she wanted him to move in with her. And my Ted, who I had been writing to, was coming home from his POW camp in Germany. So there was going to be a general shift round. The war was over and I'd got to go home.

Ted came to pick me up on the day I was leaving. I cried all the way along the road in the bus, and all the way home in the train. Ted said 'Well if you want it that much, go back, and we'll find somewhere to live up there.' But I said, no, I've got to go home, and that was it.

I'd been so happy there. No matter what happiness came after that it would never be better than those three and a half years. They were absolutely fantastic. They were complete freedom, where I'd never known it before. I'd always had my father standing on the corner of the street saying, 'You should be indoors.' This was nine o'clock at night. Imagine telling a girl these days to be in by nine o'clock at night. But that was the way it was. Dad had to go to work, because he was on night work, and if we weren't home before he went, he'd be standing on the corner waiting. And that went on until I was sixteen. Whereas being away, I could do what I liked. All of a sudden nobody was bothering me, my life was my own. It was really a marvellous time.

For all that freedom, there was still a certain amount of convention. Is convention the right word? I mean, these days it seems you look into each other's eyes and you're in bed together. Well it was nothing like that. It was a real courtship time. I think that sort of thing went on; it didn't happen to me, but I think it went on occasionally. Not as much as that expression about Land Army girls – Backs to the land! – would have you believe. We had one lady in the Corps, her husband was in a prisoner-of-war camp, who was having an affair with an RAF chap. The husband came home suddenly at the end of the war and caught them at it. That was the biggest scandal that ever happened, but other than that, no. It was just boys, girls, all mucking in together. I wish, I wish, I wish it could come back, the atmosphere and the feelings and the caring.

That was the main thing: people cared about each other so much. I can't exactly explain it. You could talk to a complete stranger, and if they wanted help, you'd say, 'Of course, if I can, I'll help you.' Almost as though there was a thought in the back of your mind: I might not see you tomorrow.

It was Dickens in the opening lines of *A Tale of Two Cities* said, 'It was the best of times, it was the worst of times,' talking about the French Revolution. Our war was the best of times, and it was also the worst of times. I mean, people were being physically hurt, being hurt by losing someone, being hurt emotionally, children were losing their parents, and parents were losing their children. But the spirit of the country was so terrific. I know people say it's jingoism, but we were going to win this war. We weren't going to let it get us down. I wish I could have bottled it so we could now say 'Look, this is what it was like, why can't we get back to that?'

It's funny, it's only in the last couple for years that people have begun to realise that the lumberjills existed. The Land Army didn't take to us during the war (and have more or less ignored us since). At the dance in the village hall, when they'd call out, 'Land Army only. Step into the middle for a special Land Army Paul Jones', we'd join in at first. But we soon gave up, for they made it clear they didn't like it. I think it was because they had such lousy hours and we had an eight-to-five job. Yet our work was mucky, like theirs. We didn't have to get up at four to milk the cows, like they did. But we did just as hard a physical job – in all conditions. Perhaps it was because they didn't have our nice green berets!

After the war ended I went back to my old job. I was going to the office in my Land Army overcoat, because I had no clothes, I had nothing. I just had a few coupons, but no money to spend. Fortunately my mother was a needlewoman, and made me a lot of things when she could get the material. But I kept that overcoat for a couple of years after the war.

Ted and I got married in 1947. In those days married girls had to leave their jobs, but I was allowed to stay on until I was pregnant with my son. From then on I stopped work altogether for a while. We had three rooms at Peckham until we got enough money together to move into the house we've got now.

When my son was about twelve, I went back to work full time in the classified ads department of the *Evening News*. I found it a bit tough going back into an office, and at weekends I'd be off and away. I had to get out. Even now, if I've been ill or bad weather has forced me to stay indoors, after a while the walls seem to close in on me and I have to get out. I just go and walk.

Lil and I were only two of the 4,000 to 5,000 women who worked the woods throughout the UK. It was a marvellous experience and we have wonderful memories. She and I have always kept in touch. I don't see her quite so often now, because it costs such a lot to get up to Gloucester from south London where I live. And it's the same for her. But still, we see each other a couple of times a year, and we write every couple of weeks.

Lil is the sister I never had.

MARY FEDDEN
Work Suspended

It's hard to imagine that anything would have stopped Mary Fedden becoming an artist. She's such a strong, resilient woman. At seventy-nine she works office hours every day in her Hammersmith studio and sells everything she paints, mainly still lifes. She is a member of the Royal Academy, which she loves, finding it not at all as reactionary as it's portrayed, and her social life spreads beyond this to a great circle of friends of all ages. But for the war she might have moved seamlessly on from student at the Slade to professional artist, never moving out of that world. What it did was to give her another set of experiences as a Land Girl, WVS helper looking after the victims of bombing, exhibition designer for the Ministry of Information and, after D-Day, driver in France and Germany for Naafi, the universal provider of tea and comforts for the troops.

It was an adventure being abroad, and being in the Land Army was an adventure, too. But the WVS and painting murals for propaganda, they were boring. And I hated the war. It made no sense. It didn't do anything for anybody. Personally, I felt what a waste of four years, when I wanted to be a painter. I didn't paint at all during the war, and it made me four years later in getting going. But that was a purely selfish personal feeling. And of course on top of that I felt what a terrible waste of all those people, of every race involved. And materially what a waste, all those cities smashed. But funnily enough, when I was in France driving those beautiful cars, with a rather nice boss, superficially I had a rather jolly time. You can have a jolly time and yet hate the thing that causes you to be there.

I was staying in Wimbledon when war was declared. I had a great friend, Maisie Meiklejohn. We had been at art school together, and we'd shared flats and houses for ages. Her family lived in Wimbledon, and I remember quite well when it was announced on the radio. We'd expected it for so many months and her father said, 'Well, that's that, now we can have lunch in peace.' I was absolutely appalled, feeling, this is the end of the world.

I was twenty-two and I knew straight away that I would have to do some sort of war work. I was such a coward that I chose to be a Land Girl. I thought, I'll be on a farm in the depths of the country and I won't be bombed. As it turned out, I was put on a farm in Gloucestershire, next door to the Filton aeroplane company, and we were bombed every night for a year. Served me right.

If I'd had the courage I think I'd have been a conscientious objector. But I was rather young. I felt patriotic in that of course I wanted us to win, but in principle I hated war so much that I didn't have any sort of flag-wagging feeling that I'd like to go off and fight for my country. I sympathised deeply with conscientious objectors. I went to court for several of my men friends and spoke up for them as conscientious objectors. They weren't cowards; they were men who thought killing was evil, as we mostly do, and they weren't prepared to go.

I did only six weeks or so at an agricultural college called Seal Hayne in Devonshire, full of young men, mostly farmers' sons, all learning to be farmers. And that was very jolly. One funny thing happened when I was there. I had a little Brownie box camera, and took photographs of my friends on the farm, and somebody took a photograph of me with a newborn calf. I took the film to the chemist in Newton Abbot, where the college was, but when I brought back the photographs, I found that the negative for that photograph of me with the newborn calf wasn't there. So I went back and told the chemist, but he said, 'Oh no, I sent all your negatives back.' Well, there was nothing I could do. But when I came up to London ages afterwards, there was a ten-foot-high poster of me on a hoarding, with the newborn calf, recruiting girls for the Land Army. He'd pinched it, and he made thousands out of that photograph. Wasn't he clever, that man? During the war, you didn't send films away. He did them in his back room, and he saw a little bit he could make on the side.

From the college I went to a farm north of Bristol, near where I lived. And the farmer was absolutely dyed in the wool, and thought no woman could be any use on the farm. He had to take me because his chaps had gone to the war, and he had only two old men. So he had to accept me, and he gave me all the toughest jobs he could find to try and prove I was no good. I was determined to prove I was OK, and I worked terribly hard, because we were battling it out. His wife was incredibly nice and very much better educated. She knew that he was overworking me – though I don't think she ever knew how he bullied me.

It was a funny life. I got there at six in the morning, and about nine we all had breakfast in the farm, and we had lunch together – and I was paid twenty-eight shillings a week. The farm was quite a rough place. But I lived with some

Mary and newborn calf: the missing negative which turned up as a Land Army recruitment poster.

friends in an enormous house, a mile away, on the next estate. These people had known my family always, and their daughter was one of my best friends. So in the evening we had lots of talk and music.

The daytime was pretty rough. There was one rather strange thing I used to do. There was a pen, a little shed, where calves were put when they were taken away from their mothers. They were half-grown, usually five or six of them. And when the farmer was beastly to me I would go into the shed and sit among the calves, and cry. They were so warm and comfortable and cosy, and we used to snuggle together. I always imagined they cried too. I just sat on the ground on the straw, among these calves, and howled.

I spent hours of every day harrowing a field with horses. We had no tractors or anything. Or I might spread dung on a field all morning, or cut hay. It could become very boring. So every night in bed I learned a poem, and then I would shout it to myself the next day. I ended the war knowing a lot more poetry than I'd known before. Things like 'Ode to a Nightingale' and 'Ode to the West Wind' and those romantic sort of poems. I had little books of Keats and Shelley.

I was always exhausted. But the loveliest thing I used to do on the farm, was when we were haymaking. It was all very primitive. You cut the hay, then when it was dry you had to scoop it into lines, and finally bale it up. We had those things called hay rakes. You'd sit on a high seat with curved tines and scoop up the hay. And when you pulled a lever, it dropped the hay, which you had to leave in straight lines across the field.

There was a sort of low-mentality farmhand called George. I think he probably wasn't fit to go the war. He wasn't old, thirty-five or so, but he was a silly old thing. We had two hay rakes and two horses, and we used to have what we called chariot races, to see who could get to the end of the field first. We had these horses cantering across the rough ground, and we were sitting up on these little iron seats, and pulling the lever when we got to the line of hay. It was fun.

The farmer did ease up in the end, when he realised that I could do the jobs he gave me, and he became quite nice. The food was rather good on the farm; we had eggs. And at night I had my old friends. So I didn't have a rough time, really.

I was on the farm for about eighteen months but then my mother, who was by herself in Bristol, and being bombed every night, got ill and so I gave up the Land Army and went to live with her. My sister was in the ATS, and my brother was in the church. He was a conscientious objector. Being a parson he didn't have to come before a tribunal, but he stayed on in the slums of Bristol all through the bombing.

My mother was in the WVS, the Women's Voluntary Service, and she drove a canteen for the troops in the docks at Avonmouth. There were American troops there and all sorts, and one day there was a huge urn of boiling water on the floor, which had to be lifted on to a stand. An American soldier outside said, 'Oh don't you do that, ma'am, I'll do that for you.' He heaved it up and dropped it, and it went all over her legs – ten gallons of boiling water. She nearly died. She drove her own canteen back to Bristol from Avonmouth. He stockings were stuck to her flesh, and all the flesh came off her legs.She was in bed for weeks and weeks.

But she recovered. She had very tender legs for the rest of her life, but she could walk around. Anyway, that was why I went home. The branch of the WVS I worked for was collecting clothes and finding places for people to live who were bombed out. Bristol was badly bombed; the whole of the centre of Bristol was shattered. So it was fairly harrowing.

Air raids I found very frightening. When I was in the Land Army, living in this beautiful stately home, we slept every night for a year in the basement, all of us – the farmhands and the cook, and the old lady who owned the house, and my best friend. We all slept on mattresses in the basement for ages, being just next door to the Filton aeroplane works. In Bristol we just got under the kitchen table, we hadn't any shelter. And I remember lying on the floor behind the sofa, hoping for the best. I was very frightened when the sirens went in the middle of the night, and listening to the bombs falling.

Curiously enough, I didn't come face to face with any bodies in the street. It's amazing: you could live in a city that was being absolutely smashed, but unless you were an ambulance driver or something like that you didn't actually come across ghastly scenes, or houses on fire and dreadful shattered houses. I was in an office sorting clothes, helping people, taking down addresses. And then, after perhaps a year of that, my mother was better, and she had some lodgers in the house, so I came to London.

It was because my friend Maisie was in London designing and painting all the sets for the Arts Theatre in Great Newport Street. In fact she was Alec Clunes's right-hand woman. She desperately needed help, and I liked working in theatre. So we got a flat in Redcliffe Road, off the Fulham Road, and I was taken on by a firm who were doing exhibitions for propaganda – recruiting for the Land Army, and stopping people showing lights at night, and all that sort of thing. It must have been run by the Ministry of Information. I was painting murals at Harrods, who had given over a section of the shop to propaganda. So I was painting, which I had wanted to do since I had left art college, but they were pretty ghastly paintings.

We sometimes spent all night painting scenery for the Arts Theatre. We worked terribly hard. I never remember the Arts Theatre closing, though I suppose it must have done sometimes during the air raids. We went a lot to the

Players Theatre that's now under the arches at Charing Cross. Then, it was in Albemarle Street or Dover Street, and if there was any bombing, there was a basement. And the chairman – it was Victorian cabaret – used to say, 'There is an air raid, ladies and gentlemen. You can all stay and eat and drink and dance as long as you like, until the air raid is over.' So often we used to stay most of the night. We were thrown together so much with people, and the times were full of happiness and fun. A marvellous sort of camaraderie.

Another place we went to was the Ivy, because it was round the corner from the Arts Theatre and they couldn't charge more than five shillings for a meal. Though you had to have enough ration coupons. It was the same for all restaurants. The government wouldn't let them profit by getting food on the black market and putting on expensive meals that some people couldn't afford. Of course they put on cover charges and things, so you didn't pay exactly five shillings, but that was what you were supposed to be charged. It was so lovely after painting scenery all night in a cold shed in St Martin's Lane, scrubbing your hands and going off to the Ivy for late supper, with all the most famous actors in the world round us. There was John Gielgud, and Laurence Olivier and Edith Evans, all having meals there after the theatre.

I don't ever remember being hungry, but the food in those days was jolly boring. There were shortages of onions, and sometimes you waited a fortnight to take up your meat rations, so that you could have a little joint, and it would all turn out to be gristle. There were some things which weren't on rations, sausages I think, but then you had to queue for an hour for them, and was it worth it?

Eggs were almost non-existent. At one stage one got about two a year, and it was a great occasion when egg time was coming up. After six months I went to the grocer and got two eggs for myself and Maisie. We were thrilled – eggs, you know – and we decided to fry them. But I broke one into a frying pan, and it was bad. Addled, completely. Then I broke the second one and it had a double yolk. We thought that was the luckiest thing that happened to us in the war. Little things like that seemed miraculous at the time. We had dried egg, which was disgusting. Dried egg to make into scrambled egg, but it didn't taste like egg at all. And the thing that was really horrible was dried potato powder which you boiled up with water or milk into a great mashed potato.

The shortage of clothes didn't really affect me. Well, everybody in London was so shabby anyway.

There was a community feeling, especially in London. People were so kind and loving, it's true, they were. It's a shame that you have to have a war for people to be nice to each other. But I think you had the feeling when you were talking to someone that they might be killed tonight, and it might be the last time you'd see them.

Also when people were in love, and one or other of them was in the services – or even just living in London – you felt this might be the last time. There were a lot of partings. You met people in the most wonderfully casual way, and became passionately fond of them in a short time because everybody was flung together. The meetings, the partings and the comings together were wonderful.

The songs of the time reflected it. They were so romantic, so sentimental, and yet they meant such a lot. When I was at the farm college, I didn't have an affair with any boy there, but they were all terrifically loving. There was that song, 'We'll meet again, don't know where, don't know when', and we all sang that on the night I left, with everybody in floods of tears. Although I didn't really in my heart care about any of them, we thought, we're never going to be together again. In fact, I never saw any of them again. But it was very powerful, the feeling of togetherness and then parting.

I had quite a lot of boyfriends, but I didn't have any attachments. It was much easier that way, I think, because you kept on losing people. If you'd been passionately attached to one person, it would have been a series of miseries, wouldn't it? To have been engaged or lately married in the war must have been agony. It was quite difficult to make a firm attachment during the war really, because you were never in one place for very long. I got engaged once during the war, but I knew it was a mistake and I ended it pretty soon. And I did have one or two rather serious affairs, but thank God I didn't marry anybody. I just had boyfriends where I was stationed.

I knew a lot of people who died in the war. Not any lovers or really close friends, but lots of other people. Nearly all the boys I and my sisters went to parties with were soldiers. They were all the right age for it and a lot of them were killed. But a lot weren't. I mean it must have been far worse in the First World War.

Anyway, I did my propaganda painting for another year or so and then the recruiting department at the War Office decided that propaganda wasn't necessary any more. Anybody who could be was already involved with the war, I suppose. This was about 1944. They said I must do something more profitable for the war, and they suggested a driver in the Naafi. The Navy, Army and Air Force Institute ran bars, cafés, restaurants and dance halls for the troops. Wherever the forces were, there was a Naafi depot.

So now I went abroad. We arrived in Paris and were sent up to Brussels, where I drove lorries for a bit. Then there was the Rundstedt Push, when the Germans came back through the Netherlands, having got pushed back to the German frontier. I think Rundstedt must have been a general in the German Army. So we were rushed back to Paris again, and it was there that I became a

Mary with the NAAFI, in Germany, 1945.

staff driver. I liked it better, because the truck driving was terribly tough. It was also dangerous. I mean, the roads were not full of potholes, they were full of craters, and there was a lot of bombing.

For the next two years I drove the deputy head of the whole of Naafi for the whole of Europe. I don't know why, I was just given him. And we had the most wonderful cars, because we had to race across Europe all the time. Once we drove from Brussels to Marseilles in one go. I think we stopped in the car and slept for two hours or so.

Something I remember well is driving my boss to the coast in Normandy; we had lunch in an officers' mess. A more delicious meal than usual, and rather smart chaps in uniform, nice company, and we all sat through it with guns roaring quite close to us. I hadn't been near the front for some time, and I was frightened. But they simply didn't notice; they'd been under fire for so long, these chaps. They just went on talking about films, or landscape, or places, and there were these deafening guns.

As a driver I earned probably even less than the twenty-eight shillings a week I got in the Land Army, but I didn't need it. Everything was provided abroad in Naafi: your digs, your clothes, your food. If you wanted a new toothbrush, you had money to buy a new toothbrush. But you had nothing else to spend it on except bars of chocolate.

There were no ranks in Naafi, but we weren't allowed to wear brown leather belts, we had to wear canvas belts, which meant we were other ranks. So there were slight problems. I had a lot of friends who were officers, and there was trouble if they took me to dances in the officers' clubs. So several of us bought Sam Brownes – leather belts – and put them on, and we were caught once or twice. That sort of thing was a bit tiresome. There was a hierarchy which you had to stick to.

We never had to go on parade or anything like that, and I was driving around most of the time, on my own or with my boss. There was discipline in that you had to make sure the car was in good condition, and have it serviced, and be ready for this very jolly man whenever he wanted to drive off to wherever. We chatted away like mad in the car. I wasn't ever regimented.

Very often I was back in the digs for two days when my boss didn't have to go anywhere, so I got to know all the girls. By the time I was in Naafi I was twenty-six or twenty-seven, and some of the girls were only eighteen. Saturday night there was always a sergeants' mess dance, which they spent all the week looking forward to. Usually I didn't go to it. It was a wonderful occasion to be in the digs by myself, wash my hair, write twenty letters, and read a book. But one little girl said to me one day, 'Do come tonight, Mary. I know you're too old to dance, but you can sit and watch'!

I was in Lille, in the north of France, when the war ended. There I was in digs with a lot of girls, all the other drivers. We knew the war was coming to an end, and suddenly we heard somebody on the radio say, 'Peace is signed.' We all raced about and roared. My boss said, 'Let's go to Paris! Lille's not the place to celebrate the end of the war.' So we jumped into this great Packard, and raced off to Paris.

Soon afterwards we moved up into Germany, and I stayed on there another year doing the same work with the British Army of the Rhine. It was horrible there, I really hated it. We went to Cologne, and it appeared to me that the only building standing was the cathedral. It was a flattened city.

I suppose I felt hostile towards the German nation, because they had caused the war. But I felt terribly sorry for every individual I met. The plight of the civilians, well of everybody, was awful. They were hungry and wretched and living in awful conditions.

I didn't know any German at all, and several of the other drivers wanted to learn as well. This man who came to our digs to teach us was terribly thin and pale. During the lesson we used to provide coffee and sandwiches, and he always asked if he could take the sandwiches home for his wife because she was so hungry. That sort of thing was awful.

Not that we met many German civilians except the ones who were servants in the clubs – they were put to work doing things – and the ones whose houses we stayed in. We requisitioned houses in the towns, and the people who owned them had to have us as lodgers. They were mostly polite, cold, rather subservient. I mean they were a conquered race, having never expected to be a conquered race. It was a painful relationship. I couldn't imagine it would happen, but they've rebuilt fantastically. They must be a gutsy people.

At the beginning of the war I wished I'd been a conscientious objector, and at the end I think I felt the same. Perhaps more so. I felt the war had been pointless, and disgusting and cruel, and no matter how badly the Germans bombed Coventry and London and Bristol, we killed almost every inhabitant of Dresden, for instance, and Cologne. There was nothing to choose. Once the war was going, there was no right on any side.

I didn't come back to England until the end of '46, and in a way life was more difficult because people had to get jobs. The winter of 1947 was, I think, the coldest there had been since Elizabethan times. There was no fuel, and there was still rationing; it lasted for about three years after the war. We just froze to death. My flat in Redcliffe Road had one coal fire, that was the only heating, and there wasn't any coal. Yes, it was a very bleak time. But as soon as I came back, I started to paint.

In 1948 I again met Julian Trevelyan, the artist and engraver whom I'd know since I was seventeen. On holiday in Sicily, we decided to get married, but I worried terribly about breaking the news to my best friend Maisie.

We had just bought a house, a whole house in Redcliffe Road, and I was in tears because I didn't know how to tell her. When I arrived back, she was in floods of tears too because, she said, 'I'm getting married tomorrow, and I didn't know how to tell you.' It was absolutely perfect: we both found our fate exactly at the same moment. I have been terribly lucky in my life, things have dropped into place. The only awful thing that happened was Julian's death five years ago. But otherwise, my life has been so lucky.

Recruitment poster for the Women's Auxiliary Air Force.

PHYLLIS WILLMOTT
Met Girl

It's remarkable how many veterans can instantly recall their service numbers from half a century ago. Phyllis Willmott, who was in the WAAF, produces hers without hesitation – 481200. But perhaps it is less surprising that she can do so. A writer and former lecturer on the social services, she has kept her memories in good repair in a series of autobiographies, the third of which was called Coming of Age in Wartime *(Peter Owen, 1988).*

Seventeen when the war broke out, Phyllis Noble, as she then was, found herself stuck for the next three years in a reserved occupation in the City of London. Only in 1941 was she able to exchange it for the comparative freedom of answering to that number.

I don't think I had patriotic feelings about joining up and serving my country. I was much too self-centred. I would just have thought of it as romantic, and much more interesting than the life that I was leading.

Most of my influences were literary. I was a bookworm and thought that living in a Bohemian, independent way was what I really wanted to do. I wanted to travel, I mean that was for me an expression of freedom, to be able to go to wonderful exotic foreign places. In fact, I wasn't brave enough to do any of these things. Without joining up I couldn't easily have got away from home. And I think for an awful lot of women that was true.

I left school early – well, as soon as I got Matric. The school wanted me to go on to the sixth form, but by then I hated it. It was so boring and restricting, and that wasn't where life was. I hadn't any doubts that there was a world out there waiting to welcome Phyllis Noble. It was a real shock when I found that it wasn't a bit like that. Phyllis Noble was just a little bug, whose only claim to charm was her youth and her looks. That's what I could get attention for, not for any brilliance of mine.

I did have some notion early on that I'd like to be a writer. But again it was all rubbishy romanticism. I remember I went up into my parents' bedroom with my notebook, and started writing. And I kept a diary from very early on, which was my outlet. I also did pen portraits of my friends; if anything, I saw myself as an artist, a painter, not as a writer. I didn't want this ordinary life of going to work, and getting married, and having children.

It's funny when I look back. I had virtually four brothers – two brothers and two cousins, but all in the same house – and it was clear that I was the most academic of the group. My parents recognised that; so did my grandparents. But it was as if that was of no importance really, because in the end she's going to get married and have children.

I was allowed to go to the grammar school, and stay on after fourteen, because my parents made the sensible decision that it might help me to get a better, more secure job. For as soon as you could, you were expected to start earning and contribute to the household income.

I started work at a private library, the Times Book Club, which was quite an interesting option. But it wasn't up to my expectations. I thought it was outrageous that you should be expected to work from nine till six every day – and Saturday mornings, don't forget – with only a fortnight or three weeks' holiday a year.

After nine months I was very fed up, and looking for another job. I must have read about this job at the National Provincial Bank headquarters in Bishopsgate, and at the interview they gave such a marvellous impression of the work that I thought, yes, yes, yes, I'd be willing to do anything. It turned out to be training to be a ledger clerk, which was doing customers' accounts on big calculating machines. And when war was declared three months after I got to Bishopsgate, banking immediately become a reserved occupation, and I was caught.

I had tried to join up. After work one day I walked through the City to the West End looking for a WRNS recruitment office but couldn't find one. I did find a WAAF recruitment office so I decided to enrol there, but I got a letter from the Ministry of Employment saying that I couldn't join the services as I was already doing work of national importance. Then I was called into the office because papers must have got back to the bank somehow, saying that I'd tried to join up. I thought that was wrong.

But as the war went on, the government was needing more and more people, and was widening the conscription net. Eventually they set up a committee to look into the reserved occupations and see whether they could be squeezed again to provide more recruits. And that's what happened. The National Provincial Bank lost several hundred of their staff, mostly men but some women, and I was one of the three women released from the head office.

I was thrilled, delighted, because I'd been longing to get out of the bank for so long. I'd been there all through the blitz, when things got a bit more interesting. It was an adventure. It's rather a joke really, because I was so terrified of air raids when the war broke out. But when the blitz actually came, I never had any fear at all. I was an air-raid warden, though not a very good one, because when the siren went, it was absolute agony for me to get out of bed. I was a very heavy sleeper and so I was always waiting for the all-clear, hoping it was a false alarm. It had to go on a very long time before I dragged myself out of bed.

When the conscription papers arrived, telling me I had to join the WAAF at Gloucester, my parents thought it was jolly lucky that I'd been kept in a reserved occupation for so long. They were obviously nervous for me, but what was amazing in the war was the way everybody really accepted that we'd got to do it. And my mother probably thought, now she'll really learn how spoilt she's been and what a good mother she has. She'll soon be wanting to come back home.

When you're called up, they kind of put you into purdah for the first fourteen days. It was very difficult. You couldn't have letters coming in, though I think you could send them. At Gloucester we lived in very, very large wooden huts, because there were big intakes of girls on each occasion. A Tannoy woke you in the mornings, and the first few days I woke thinking I was ill. I felt so absolutely awful, I really thought that I must have some serious illness. It only gradually dawned on me that I was homesick. It was like a physical pain.

I felt miserable enough when I went to sleep. We had the sound of lights-out on the bugle in the evenings, which was a pretty depressing noise. But somehow the one in the morning was even worse. Probably because it was six o'clock, and I had never got up in the morning without being woken with a cup of tea. My mother always called everybody in the house with a cup of tea. And here I was just woken up by this ghastly noise, that was a terrible shock.

We'd been picked up at Gloucester station, and taken by lorry to the camp. It was remarkably like all displaced persons' camps. It was closed in. You went in through a barrier at the entrance, and there were all these horrible-looking huts with a parade ground in the middle. And just by the entrance there were four or five telephone boxes which were your only contact with the outside world for the first fourteen days.

And then we were put through this business of being measured, and having our hair inspected for nits, and, I think, a medical examination. And we were given an intelligence test in this big hall so that they could decide what were suitable trades for us to take up. And we were issued with our kit, and given grave warnings about what would happen if we didn't look after it. To my astonishment they issued me with two pairs of corsets – well, not exactly corsets but pretty near, with sort of bones in, incredible things.

I suppose they assumed that everybody wore corsets, and perhaps some of the girls did. But mine always stayed in my kit bag and got filthier and filthier, which was always a problem when I had kit inspection, which was practically every fortnight. We had to lay out our kit, absolutely precisely, on the bed, to show that we'd still got our two pairs of lisle stockings as well as the ones we'd got on, and so many shirts and all the rest of it. And I used to get accused of having neglected my corsets.

Sharing living quarters with other people I didn't find too difficult. But that may have been because we lived rather hugger-mugger in my own home. I suppose a middle-class girl, who was used to having her own private room and shutting herself up in the bathroom, would have found it a problem, but I'd always washed over the kitchen sink anyway, so that didn't affect me. I didn't like going outside to the ablutions, the wash basins and lavatories which were in a central block. That was unpleasant in March, when it was pretty chilly, but there was plenty of hot water.

We were treated as the men were – we had route marches and a passing-out parade like they did – but in a sort of moderated way. And we used to go into town, not just Gloucester but wherever we were posted later, and have teas out. Because out in the sticks – and this was quite a revelation after London, where you could get nothing – there were always places where you could get fried eggs and bacon and beans, and things like that.

I had thought I might have liked to be a flight engineer, working on the planes, but at the trade test what I put a tick against was meteorological observer and that was what I was allocated to. This meant taking a six-week training course in London where we were put up in Chelsea in a very nice block of flats which the WAAF had taken over. The only thing that troubled me was the mice which overran the place. These were blamed on the girls bringing food in, but it was horrible. You'd lie in bed and they'd be running over your sheets.

From there I was posted to Woolfox Lodge, an airfield in Rutland where bomber crews finished their training. We were in Nissen huts there, and they were always mixed; you weren't just with WAAFs from the Met Office. There were five of us Met girls together in the same hut. But then there were also girls who drove the lorries out to meet the air crew when they came back, and cooks and clerks, and they came from all over the world. That was lovely.

For the first time since I left school I found myself doing work I really enjoyed. What we did was make hourly observations of the weather and draw up weather maps. I loved it. The Met Office was like a club, always full of people popping in and out, it was tremendous fun. It was a satisfying job. About

370 stations had to be plotted with these symbols which gave the wind direction, the wind speed, the temperature, the amount of cloud, the visibility and so on. Then you drew in isobars on very big maps, and these had to be done more than twice a day, as the weather changed.

Most of the observations were taken with the naked eye. But we had barometers in a sort of beehive thing, so we did get accurate bar measurements. And sometimes we sent up balloons if we weren't sure about the cloud level. We'd assess the visibility at forty yards, eighty yards, a mile, ten miles; thirty miles, we'd say sometimes. We developed a sort of skill at it, and we were kept on our toes by the forecasters, who were officers. They would check and say come outside for this, what height do you think that cloud is, then? Oh, 1,500 feet? Have another look.

On top of that we had to send in hourly reports by teleprinter to group headquarters who put all the messages together and sent them out again to other stations. Then, after we decoded them, we plotted them on to the map. Between doing all this we were making coffee for the air crew as they came in and out, and talking to them about the weather. Because we were only observers, we weren't supposed to do any forecasting, but inevitably we did. The air crew would come in to ask, say, what the weather was going to be like up in Glasgow, and of course we'd tell them as far as we could.

We went on making these observations every hour in all weathers even after flying had stopped for the day. There were always WAAFs in the Met Office, which was downstairs, in the flying tower. There was somebody in charge of the flying tower upstairs, but he went to bed. Quite often the only people awake on the aerodrome were the women. If there were any flights out, it would be the girls who were the drivers in the trucks waiting for the men to come back. And if it was a very long flight, the men in the flying tower would have more or less gone to sleep – or were dozing anyway, while the girls doing the Met were still going out, backwards and forwards, all night. Really it was very strange. And they drove those huge lorries, too, little tiny bits of girls.

The reason they didn't mind was they felt that they had a greater freedom than they'd ever had before. I noticed this particularly with the Scottish girls, who'd often come from very rough, poor backgrounds. They probably had much better food than they'd ever had in their lives. They had quite a wardrobe; it was a uniform admittedly, but they had plenty of clothes. They had baths with masses of hot water – a much higher standard of life, strangely, than they'd had in civvy street.

The jobs were more interesting, too, I suppose, even if you were in the cookhouse. You were cooking for large numbers, and there was a lot of joking and laughing. And to me, working in the Met Office was much more interesting than

Waafs Phyllis and Doreen, who went AWOL.

being a ledger clerk in a bank. There was more going on, and you felt you were doing something worth while.

Then after a very happy eight months, they decided to close the Met Office down. The forecasters were posted elsewhere, and the Met WAAFs were left to wait for instructions. We were made to do odd jobs – picking up all the paper in the camp – and I was so fed up that I 'deserted', and Doreen, my corporal, came home with me. It was only for four days but the Air Force takes a rather dim view of takers of leave – otherwise known as deserters.

We were summoned to the awful presence of our head WAAF officer and individually marched in (minus hat!) under escort, and charged in the usual long-winded manner; ending as we knew it would, by being remanded to the CO. He, the big-bug of the station duly examined and condemned us while we were surrounded by one person of equal rank as escort, one corporal, one station adjutant, one station warrant officer, one or two WAAF officers, and the Great Man himself – all this for two miserable WAAFs who went home because they had nothing at all to do.

If I'd been a man I would have been in real trouble. Instead, Doreen got a severe reprimand, and I was put on fourteen days' jankers, which meant being confined to the site – you couldn't call it a barracks, because we were just in a field. But before the fourteen days were up, I was posted first to one, then after a fortnight, another station in Lincolnshire. Then in May 1944 I was posted on to North Creake in a remote part of Norfolk. It was a bomber station but they weren't doing bombing raids. They went out in advance to drop strips of aluminium foil which sabotaged the German radar.

My main feeling when the war ended was one of uneasiness. I was uneasy because I couldn't see then what it meant for me. Selfish, you may say, but I suppose most people are. You had to be pleased that the war was over, but where did that leave you? What was going to happen next? There was a sudden great yawning gap, because you just didn't know. Was I going to go back to the bank? Horrors. I couldn't bear the thought of that. What was going to happen to the station? It all became quite meaningless. We were on this Air Force base, but there was no point in going on making hourly observations of the weather, because nobody needed them. We did go on doing them, of course, but it was finished.

ATS AT THE WHEEL

Ceaselessly new vehicles roll off the production lines.
Army units await them, the ATS deliver them

Recruitment posters like these for the Auxiliary Territorial Service tempted Christina.

CHRISTINA KIRBY
How to Park a Tank

The woman driver who can't park her car is one of the stock characters of male folklore. And perhaps there was some truth in it in the days before women began to run their own cars – and run their worse-for-wear husbands home from parties.

Christina Kirby, five foot and a promise in her khaki socks, parked heavy-duty lorries in confined spaces before power steering was thought of, drove tanks up high ramps every day of her army life, no sweat!

I'm not surprised that I loved driving all makes and types of vehicles in the Army. I used to drive a milk cart with three churns in the back from the time I was eight. The farmer's wife would start selling the milk at the first house, and I'd drive the donkey right the way into the town of Dungarvan.

It was an idyllic childhood in Ireland, down the fields when they were cutting the hay; in the sea cockling and discovering how to open the cockles and eat them raw. And then when I was thirteen we came to England. It wasn't that I didn't like it in Ealing, I just didn't want to leave the farm. I came in 1934 so I'd hardly got used to it when war started.

I left school when I was fourteen, or just before, when we broke up for the holidays. My first job was helping my mother in the house. When I was fourteen, she got me a job in the laundry, which I didn't like. We were getting paid seven and fourpence a week, and for long days.

Then I started thinking about other work and ended up in the Odeon as an usherette, and I thoroughly enjoyed that. It was meeting people. I got two free tickets, for my mother and brother. And we had a cinema organ there, and I loved singing. When the bombing started all the customers would rush out of the cinema to the stuffy, smelly shelter in the park. The staff had to stay behind and shut down, before we could take shelter. I was nervous but I can't say I was frightened to death.

I can't say I was patriotic, either. But I thought, I am living in this country, so one day, I asked my mum did she mind if I joined up. She said, it's up to you, girl. I wanted to drive and thought the best chance of doing this was in the ATS. I enlisted at Guildford, and then went to the Royal Army Ordnance Corps depot in Greenford, and took driving lessons there. I started off learning on a 30cwt Bedford, and then I went for the driving test with my friend, Violet.

The sergeant testing us drove up Harrow Hill. Now that's a really steep hill. He got out and put a Swan Vesta matchbox behind the wheel of the car, and told us, 'If you go over that, you're out.' Luckily I went forward, and passed, but my friend went over the matchbox, and failed.

For a while, I worked for the railway transport office. Stuff was coming in, tanks, all sorts of things, food, goods from all round the country. We had to take a check on what was in each wagon, so that it could be unloaded.

One night, a young soldier and I were working late, and we had to go down to the railway track. It was pitch blackout, and we hadn't got a torch. While we were checking the trucks I heard the roll of an engine. A train was coming. We didn't know which line it was on. What were we going to do? If we ran we might run into it. I said, 'Why don't we take a chance and lie between the lines?' We did and the train came so close we could feel the wind of the wheels on us. Somebody must have been watching over us at that moment.

Then I was posted to No. 1 VRD at Ashford, one of the biggest vehicle depots in England, and I thought, oh! at last. I quite enjoyed it there, living in a girls' school, all together in one room with twenty-one bunks. I didn't mind it a bit once we got to know each other.

I was never really homesick, because Ashford wasn't far from Ealing. I used to ride home on my bike through Hounslow, and take my mother my bit of weekend rations.

She used to love to see me coming because she knew the butcher would give me extra meat – which I shouldn't have had, to be honest. People were like that, kinder to those of us who were in the forces. Instead of giving me two sausages, he'd give me a dozen. A big piece of beef, where normally you'd be lucky to get a piece as big as a chop. Of course I paid for them out of my money.

It was at Ashford that I got into driving. That's where I had the fun. The depot was huge, three miles around, nothing but vehicles in it. All sorts – tanks, and amphibious ducks that went down on the river. I'd get to the depot in the morning, and the officer there would say there's a hundred Bedfords to get ready for when the soldiers come to pick them up. I would get them petrolled, make sure the tyres were all right, move them to the place where they'd be collected, and line them up. I went from these vehicles to moving tanks, and then, towards the end of the war, jeeps.

Later, I found myself taking vehicles up on to ramps, really high ramps, so the men could work underneath. I moved all these different kinds of vehicles up on them and I never went down the side once. It was hard work. Climbing into a tank wasn't easy, nor some of the huge lorries!

I also drove smaller vehicles. There was this Lord – Rock of Gibraltar, he was known as – and his car came back to our depot. The first time I moved it, they'd just serviced it in the REME workshop. And as I got into it and turned the engine on, I thought, Jesus, Mary and Joseph, it won't start. I looked at the exhaust, and saw it was running. The engine was so quiet, I couldn't hear it.

One day with a friend, I was putting antifreeze in the engines for the winter. We'd been at it all morning, probably about a hundred vehicles. After a while she said to me, I'm dying to do a wee. So I said well, we'll have to walk a mile back to the lavatory, we might as well do it here. We pulled our trousers down and were doing a wee, when all of a sudden there was a load of clapping and booing and shouting. What we didn't know was that in each vehicle was a soldier, sitting in the cabs, watching us. We had to laugh!

We worked long hours, and once or twice I did feel too much was asked of us, especially when the winter came and it was raining. They'd have us up at six, then down for breakfast. The food wasn't too bad at all. Sometimes you'd get a rasher of bacon, and a couple of slices of bread and a mug of tea, or perhaps a bit of toast. Then we'd start work about half-past seven, and work on till six.

I had to learn how to take a tyre off. That was hard work, changing the wheel of a lorry. When I went on a vehicle course to Ashby Castle, Northampton, I saw the Queen. I'd taken the written test, then they put us under the car for our practical, and that was the day the young Queen came. I didn't know she was coming. I just looked up from underneath and she was looking down at me sort of nodding and smiling.

I didn't do badly at all on that course. I wasn't the best, because I wasn't good at writing. I didn't read English when I came to this country. I could read Irish, and one of the nuns in the Catholic school in Ealing asked me to read aloud the Irish book I'd brought with me to the other children, and to translate it into English. I could do that, yet I couldn't read English. Once I had lessons, I learned to read in two months.

From that depot, every now and again, I used to drive a three-ton lorry to the brewery to pick up beer for the camp, mostly for the officers. The first time I went there, a girl called Laura B. asked if she could come with me.

We went inside and a couple of nice middle-aged men invited us to see how it all worked. At the end they offered us a drink of beer. I had never touched beer, so I just tried a drop but Laura had a glassful. Then we filled the lorry, and Laura, after her drink, was a bit tired, so I said why don't you go and lie down in the back?

As I was driving along there were people on the pavement pointing. I wondered what's what with the lorry, so I stopped and looked at the wheels, and then I looked in the back, and there was Laura with several empty brown ale bottles, and I don't know what else. She was pulling faces at all the people going by. She was well and truly tiddly!

I met all sorts at Ashford. Once, I asked one of the girls, who wasn't mixing with the rest of us, why she was in the Army. She said, 'I've been working in London for years as a prostitute, and I joined up to try to leave it all behind me.'

I have seen all sorts of things. One night I got into my bed, and after lights out I could hear the bunk of the girl sleeping opposite me creaking. The noises went on. I thought perhaps she's ill, so I got up and walked across in the dark. You could hardly see. She said she was having a baby. I was frightened. None of us had had a clue that she was even pregnant.

The others in the room began to stir and I said I had to put the light on. Doreen was actually giving birth. I had to go downstairs to the guard, and tell them about it, so they could phone the hospital. I ran back upstairs, and went over to her. I didn't know what the hell to do. What annoyed me was three or four women at one end of the room blasting her, calling her all sorts of names including whore, and none of them would go near her to help.

She was a lovely girl and she had a lovely little fair-haired boy. The old fellow married her, and they invited me to the wedding. She didn't come back after that, but for weeks I couldn't talk to some of those girls. The things they were still saying were terrible.

I knew about attitudes like that, coming from Ireland. I always used to play with the barefoot gossoons – the children who couldn't afford shoes. They lived in the poor part of the town, where other girls weren't allowed to go. People didn't mix with them, but I did.

I got married in 1942, to Art whom I'd met just before the war at a friend's wedding. We were in uniform, for we couldn't afford anything else. I couldn't borrow my sister's clothes, because she was only four-foot eight.

As soon as we married we were apart. But he'd come home on leave, and stay at my mother's, and I used to cycle back to join him there.

We got married in Ealing, in the Catholic church, because my mother was Catholic. I'd given it up when I was fourteen – there were things I just couldn't stick – but when I was getting married, you know what mothers are like ... My father didn't say much, but to please my mother I said, oh, all right, what does it matter. But they asked me to swear that when I had children, I'd bring them

Lorry driver Christina marries Art in 1942.

up as Catholics. I said no. It's up to them to make their own choice.

I was three months pregnant with Pat when I was due to be demobbed. I was still driving tanks and everything but one thing they would not let me do. A whole lot of new army motorbikes had just come in. The officer said you can check them but you can't ride on them. I lost interest.

I left with only the uniform I was wearing. The demob centre said, 'You can have your army overcoat, but you'll have to pay thirty shillings.' That was a week's rent, so I said no.

There were times when I really did hate the war, there's no getting away from it. I had come from a troubled country, and my father had been badly wounded in the First World War. I'd seen enough of that sort of thing. Once I was walking along, and I came by this church, and I felt so sad. It was the first time I'd felt like that since I was younger. I walked in, and stood at the back and started singing with them.

I don't think the war changed me. I knew where I was going all the time, really – although perhaps I wouldn't have learned to drive. And ever since, I have always kept up my interest in cars.

Barrage balloonist Ann marries her RAF rear-gunner, George, 1944.

ANN FOX
Ack, Ack...Beer, Beer

If you were the oldest child in a large and poor family you had to leave school as soon as ever you could: find work to eke out the family's finances.

If you were the oldest girl, the best job you could hope for was in service, to live in somewhere as a maid. Then there'd be more room in your over-crowded home. And somebody other than your mother had to feed you.

Ann Fox was both a girl and the oldest in her family. So she had to move out as soon as she was fourteen with no dreams of a future other than the one she saw stretching ahead – of drudgery. What on earth else could she possibly do, however bright she'd been at school?

I was born in Llangynog in mid-Wales, the oldest of eight children. And as soon as I was old enough to leave school my mother had to tell me, 'Well, you must go away to work.' So, I went into service in Old Colwyn. And that's where I stayed.

I wasn't too homesick because there were plenty of young people I'd meet at Urdd (the Welsh youth movement) and so on. And I wasn't on my own in this private house where I worked. There were four maids. Ivor Novello's mother used to come to stay there. I waited on her many a time. And Henry Cotton, and all these friends they knew. It was quite interesting, that way.

But I decided one day I'd had enough. It was hard work and boring, too. I went to Colwyn Bay and volunteered for the forces. I was about eighteen or nineteen. After passing our flying flea inspection, as we called the medical, I was accepted into the WAAF. I don't know why the WAAF – I just fancied it.

I went home and told them I had been called up. Well, they would have wondered why I'd volunteered, wouldn't they? So off I went, to war.

I didn't know what it was all about. I didn't really, although my father had been in the First World War and used to tell me tales when I was a girl. I did my training near Bishop's Castle. We used to march every day, didn't we? And my feet felt it, I know. And then I took an extra passing-out parade, they called it, at Stanmore and I thought, oh! never in front of all those people. But anyhow I passed that. And felt quite proud.

Everybody was posted away. I was posted to Dyce in Aberdeen as a waitress in the officers' mess. And I found the officers very down to earth. None of them was stuck up. I think it was because what they were doing meant a lot, didn't it?

We were never really short of food. We didn't have a ration book, and the food was good actually. Yet in some places you could see through the bacon, you know. I was billeted out with a Mr and Mrs Williams. And oh dear me, I didn't understand a word they said. They were so kind, very very kind, but I couldn't follow their broad accents at all. (I went back to see them after the war.) But I was so homesick up there. On Sunday nights we'd have hymn-singing on the wireless and I cried and cried.

Anyhow after a while, seeing these pilots going over the North Sea – and you didn't know whether they were going to come back or not – I got to feel I wanted to do more. To be more involved. So I volunteered to go to Cardington, to join the balloons. They were looking for balloon operators. And my God, when I landed up in Cardington, I realised that this was where the R101 went from – the airship that I had heard about at school – from this hangar where we were now. I thought, well, I never thought I'd get to that.

At this camp we learned to splice wire and splice rope. Oh, we were good at it, too, and I learned to drive a winch. I've never driven one before or since.

After all that good training I was posted to Sheffield, on a balloon site. And there, of course, we had to know about wind changes, and how to move into the wind. Fill the balloon up with hydrogen; thirty big canisters, it took. And then flow it up about 500 feet to get the air into the stabilisers. And then put a parachute on the cable, and fly it up to a thousand. If an aircraft hit that balloon it wouldn't get back to Germany would it?

We had to do guard at night, and if the weather changed we had to turn this thing off, round and round to change its direction. Hard work, really. Heavy work, because we were shifting concrete blocks around. But that didn't matter, because I enjoyed it.

It was important work. We were doing men's work, weren't we? I don't think the men were very keen on the idea, because we were doing it just as well as they were. While I was at Sheffield I was promoted to corporal and could now be in charge of a balloon site. Afterwards I was posted to Trafford Park in Manchester, and Stretford. Wherever there was a balloon site there was action, bombing. It went on all the time, for we were in the cities.

The worst place I was posted to was Hull. I was in charge of that site. But, oh dear me, it was rough. The planes kept coming over and once a submarine came up the Humber near us but we didn't know anything about that until after the danger was over.

One night a field next to the site was on fire but I had to stay to get the balloon down, with flares coming from the aircraft. That was a time – the only time – when I was scared. But you mustn't leave your post, must you?

It said on my release book after the war: 'A good and conscientious worker. Proficiency superior' – but that was in 1945, my date of departure. Before that, in 1944, I was married. George lived in Llanrhaeadr, a village near where I was from. But we met I think in Llangynog, and that was where we were married.

I had to ask for leave, and I was scared of it being cancelled. And he didn't know whether he could make it or not, because he was up flying, but we made it. And we had a reception in the village hall. There was everything you could think of there. It was beautiful. The best man, a Canadian, brought all kinds of things for the kids. No one was short of anything, and they couldn't get over it, the people at the wedding, seeing all these sweets, and all the rest of it. Everyone was commenting on how very smart we looked in our uniforms. After the wedding we went to Colwyn Bay for a few days, and then George went back to Lincolnshire and I went back to the balloon site.

When the balloons were finished, which was before the war ended, we had to do something else. So I had to go clerking. I was on overseas postings then, near Market Drayton. On my release they signed a certificate of recommendation for civilian employment in clerical duties. And this was something I did – clerking in our village for thirteen years. It was great fun.

I took my forces life seriously. I never went to dances. We seemed to have lectures every day on not to bother with men and all that palaver. There was very tight discipline kept over women – more so than over the men – because of different diseases and things like that. The women I knew behaved themselves. Some got into bad company but on the whole, no.

When I left the forces at the end of the war George didn't come out of the Air Force straight away. He went to Nicosia in charge of landings – even though he'd been through D-Day and all of that as a rear-gunner. And I used to feel when he was eventually home, oh! he's making a fuss about this and that, but it was real, wasn't it?

I saw some of the reality of it, in 1987 when George and I were asked by our nephew, Edward, if we wanted to go round the Normandy beaches. George had flown thirty-one bombing missions in the war over Germany and France – and had never been back.

We drove down in our nephew's Mercedes to Hampshire in the awful autumn of the devastating storms in the south of England, and all the trees were blown down. The ferry we had booked on was cancelled, but having eventually reached Portsmouth we were able to make the crossing the following day.

When I landed in Cherbourg I was terrified. The place was in darkness, and you had to drive on the right, didn't you? Anyway we got to Bayeux by half-past ten and when I woke in the morning I thought: I've made it to France. I couldn't believe it.

We went to the cemetery first, where we both had a weep. The men who died were so young and that hit me to start with . . . We went to the Pegasus Bridge and found that there wasn't a Pegasus Bridge now – they'd taken it down. We went everywhere that George had fought. And it was lovely. We realised how lucky George was to be alive after so many missions – though he has suffered as a result from terrible headaches – for the rest of his life.

When I came out of the forces I was absolutely lost. There was nothing doing. Nothing at all. That's what life is all about, isn't it? Anyway, it's all over and we're home now.

PEGGY TERRY
A Neapolitan Romance

Peggy wrote home to her parents, still scarcely able to believe her luck. She was in Italy and swimming in the Lido di Roma, where the wealthy Romans had relaxed before the outbreak of the war which had brought W/257930 Pte Cotterill to this country. Her letter described the contrasts of her situation: 'the most beautiful sculpture I have ever seen or probably will ever see again – the masterpiece of Michelangelo's Virgin Mary supporting the body of Christ,' yet at the same time, 'the terrible bomb damaged places, German graves at the roadside, and an arrow to the British and U.S. cemeteries'.

Italy also turned out to be the setting in which she fell in love.

When war started I was eighteen and working in a transport office. I'd always wanted to be a nurse but my father didn't want me to do that and in those days you did what your father said.

It was quite a good job, but as it seemed likely that war was coming along, I took the opportunity to join the Civil Nursing reserve, which you could do part time. I went at weekends to the Children's Hospital. My father didn't object, as long as nursing didn't become my full-time job. He'd had a long illness when he was young, and people often got these bees in their bonnets about hospitals and nurses, and the hard life and the low pay.

With the advent of war, because I was now an auxiliary nurse, I was called up to work on the ambulance train. The day before war was declared, I was sent to King's Norton station, from which we had to evacuate an old people's home. Then it took us from half-past three on the Saturday until half-past three on the Sunday morning to get from Birmingham to Cheltenham. That was because of the blackout, and we had no lights, only torches.

I spent the night learning more than I'd ever known in my life before, because we had a ward full of men – thirty-two per ward per carriage – and I'd never nursed a man, only children. I didn't even know what a bed-bottle was. The men caught on that I didn't know; they thought it was hilarious, and of course they teased me.

It was a terrible night. All the lights went out, and the smell got worse and worse. It was hazardous carrying bedpans on a moving train with a torch in one hand and the pan in the other. It really was a night to remember. We were so concerned about the people on the train: they were so uncomfortable. They were lying on these stretchers that we called toffee squares, for they were just like a cake rack. And they had to lie on these for twelve hours.

We arrived in this great big kitchen in a great big house in Cheltenham, where there were two cooks – they were sisters, and they were huge. Both in uniform, and they had buckets of tea, which I think they'd been watering for the last twelve hours ready for us. It was awful. It didn't matter, it was hot.

That night, I think I grew up a bit; life wasn't quite as easygoing as I'd thought it was before. One old lady was blind, and she clutched my apron – we were wearing starched aprons – and said, 'Will you give me something? I don't wan't to go on living like this. I don't know where I'm going.' That was awful to me. When you're young you can't imagine people wanting to die. And there were other old ladies. You'd take their skirt off, and they'd have about nine tweed skirts on underneath, and wet pants.

In one old lady's hand, after she'd died, I found a bag of sweets clutched so tight they'd gone solid, and her little glasses were embedded in them. They were all so frightened. They didn't know what was happening to them, and when you're old, to be suddenly uprooted . . . and they had memories of the First World War. A lot of them were in absolute panic.

This frantic initial urgency went as fast as it came, and all we were left doing was cleaning brasses and counting the blankets. There was no movement after the first two months of the war.

A boyfriend I had at this time was in the Supplementary Reserve. Like a lot of lads, he wanted a motorbike. His parents couldn't afford one, he couldn't afford one, so he joined the Reserve really to drive a motorbike. And of course the war came, and he was in immediately, in uniform in the barracks at Hall Green. Three weeks after I saw him there, he was in France.

He came back from there, but ultimately he was sent to Italy and didn't return. At the time he was killed at Arezzo I didn't know that I would be going to Italy too, but when I did I went to visit his grave.

But things happened so quickly at the start of the war that we didn't take it seriously at all. We had no idea at this stage. It was just something different instead of going to the boring office every day.

After nine months I couldn't stand the idea of cleaning brasses for the rest of the war, so I applied for other work and landed myself in the Food Office.

I don't think we young people worried about what might happen to us. My mother used to panic because she was going through the menopause, and she was in an awful state. The day my young sister was evacuated, my mother just left it all to me. That was just how she was. It was as though she wasn't really with it all. I had this list of all the things my sister had to take, and then I took her to the station. By now it was night-time, and I'd got to go to stay at my aunt's, which was the other side of town. You couldn't see. There were no street lights at all. I got off the bus at the terminus. That was easy. But then I had to feel for the names of the streets – they used to have raised letters. I remember arriving on my aunt's doorstep. I was supposed to be taking her a bunch of flowers. They were just stalks, with the flowers all gone by the time I got there.

I found my work at the Food Office very repetitive and I wanted to be more actively involved in the war so I applied to join the medical section of the WAAF. It didn't work out that way. The ATS was the only place that had vacancies – this was 1943. Then they gave you tests for this and tests for that, and from them they decided what you were best fitted to do. No question of you choosing. I was, they decided, to be a technical clerk. I didn't even finish up as that. I was simply a company office clerk and sent up to Pontefract, to the York Barracks, a big, old-fashioned barracks, and a bit of a shock that was.

The ATS had the reputation of attracting the riff-raff. I was told by some soldier we were camp followers. I wasn't amused by that and said we had a lot of work to do, saving men from doing it.

My father accused me of being uniform mad because I'd been in the Guides and St John's and now here I was proudly sporting my khaki. He did calm down eventually. My brother, much to his disgust, couldn't join up because he was in a reserved occupation, so I was the only one representing the family. My mother was frantically worried all the time but my father was more concerned about my staying the same girl I was when I went in. He assumed, as many people did, that you were going to come out of the forces scarred for life. In actual fact I was twenty-five when I got married and my husband laughed his head off because I knew nothing whatsoever. He thought it was funny. I mean, I was so naïve, I didn't know *anything*.

Lots of us were the same. We used to hear dirty jokes and we really didn't know what they were on about. But I used to laugh; everybody else was laughing.

After I was posted to Italy, I was standing one day on the balcony of the office in the Via Roma, which was a notorious street in Naples. (I didn't know that.) I saw an old man in a white suit, chatting to the troops as they went by, and I said, 'I wonder where that old man takes the soldiers. He keeps chatting to them, and off they go up the road with him.' Of course the men roared at that, and then thought it was hilarious, that I'd never even heard of prostitutes. But that's the way we were.

I suppose I half knew, because I'd done biology at school, and I had a sort of vague idea. It's a natural thing, I think, that you know, but you won't piece it together. I was always of the belief that sex and love were the same thing. I thought those two were interwoven, which these days they're not, which I think is a great shame. I suppose the war did free women sexually a bit, because we used to have quite a few people playing the field, and what have you. But in those days, in the forces, if you were having a baby, you were discharged immediately.

My first posting in the Army soon got too claustrophobic for me. Our office comprised a couple of sergeants, a corporal and three girls. The married men started to get a bit interested. I didn't expect to go abroad, but I asked for a posting because I didn't want things to get out of hand. You started off going with a group to the pictures and then one of them asked you on your own, and that's the way it starts, isn't it? And I could see it wasn't a good thing, so I decided it was time to move on. I said I should like to go on the coast, if possible. I didn't mean the coast of Italy! But that's where I finished up.

I didn't know at the time, of course. They don't tell you where you're going. We were sent to a transit camp in Bristol. And I wasn't at all well. I'd got a terrible cough, but I'd been to see the doctor, and she was very uppity with me, and said, 'There's nothing wrong with you. You're just trying to get off going.'

So I travelled to this transit camp, which was a big old orphanage. And the thing that worried me, I know it's silly, were all these long dark corridors, and these deep stone steps and I visualised all these little children ... You know, these things that cross your mind at the time. It affected me a lot.

One night at nine o'clock we were told to get our kit ready and at twelve o'clock we'd be moving off. And we found out we were going to Liverpool by train. I stayed awake all night in the corridor so that I could see Birmingham as I went by. Yes, silly – but you're always homesick a bit. Not that you are wanting to go home all the time, but you think about it, especially if you've come from a happy home.

We got to this boat. I didn't know boats were that big. It was a very old one, I heard later on. We were allocated table duties: we were supposed to lay the tables on certain days, and so forth, but when we started sailing the girls were going down like flies with seasickness as soon as the boat began to roll. I wasn't sick, except that I didn't feel well with this cough. I went down to the doctor to have some jabs and I passed out. I'd got pleurisy. So they popped me into bed, which was an experience in itself, being in bed on a ship with a male nurse looking after me. It was all back to front.

They told me I'd got to have hot seawater baths every day. The little bathroom was off the ward, and a medical orderly used to stand behind the door and say, 'Shall I come and scrub your back?' I didn't know whether he was going to come in!

I was very peeved, because everybody was having marvellous meals, and I was on this flaming steamed fish every day. I didn't get up until we got to Algeria. And all the time the senior commander kept coming to see me. I met her again later when I was coming out of the sea at Sorrento after a beautiful bathe. She told me I had been giving them heart attacks with my pleurisy. 'You girls were the first batch to be conscripted abroad and there was a whole lot of hoo-ha in Parliament about girls being allowed to go abroad. They thought you might die on them, and that would really set the ball rolling.'

I wondered at the time why she was so concerned about a little private like me. I remembered the OC I'd left in Stafford, a regular soldier he was, being absolutely livid about girls going abroad. Dreadful. It was a soldier's job, not a girl's. My father wasn't very happy about it either.

On VE night all of the women were confined to barracks. Not because of the Italians but because of our own troops going mad, getting drunk. It didn't matter to us. Nothing mattered to you in the Army except the orders you were given.

You could go out in the day, but in the evenings you couldn't go out to a dance or anything unless you were escorted there. If you left the barracks in the evening, you had to have a man sign the book, and sign you back in again, which was very difficult. My husband always maintained that they used to check back 'nine months' to see who had caused it!

By the time I was in Italy the hostilities were up in the far north by the River Po. The Italians were very friendly. Our offices were in a large block of flats overlooking the Bay of Naples. Beyond any imaginings I'd ever had.

Food was short for the Italians, but not for us, though we didn't have food like the Americans did. They had beautiful food. We never had proper milk in our tea, always tinned, that sort of thing. But you got used to anything in time. We didn't think about it. If there was an egg for breakfast, news got round and everybody used to stick their battledress on over the top of their pyjamas, and down. And of course we used to get free cigarettes. Our issue, which came in circular tins, was about a hundred a week. Everybody, it seemed to me, smoked a lot.

When we had leave, we couldn't go home, of course. So, I made up my mind to see as much of Italy as possible while I was there. I went on my first leave to

Rome with another girl. We could wear civvies, but the men had to wear the uniform. We stayed in nice hotels because all the hotels were commandeered but they still had some of the staff. One in particular still had a little three- or four-piece orchestra. We thought we were very grand. These hotels would normally have been quite beyond our scope.

I decided that I didn't need to have a man with me to go round Rome. It must have been safer in Rome, I think. And also if you got a man who didn't want to go and see art and all that sort of thing, you'd be stuck. And I wanted to go and see what there was to see.

Well, the very first day we were there at the hotel, one of the NAAFI girls on the desk said, 'Two RAF boys have left a message for you.' I didn't know any, but this other girl with me said she did. 'And they want to know if you'll have dinner with them.' I agreed to have dinner but that was going to be it. I wanted to see Rome.

Well, my husband-to-be walked in. And that was it. He wanted to see the Rome that I wanted to see. We went off together in spite of my resolutions. The other two didn't like each other. I don't know where they went. But we went everywhere we could possibly cram in the next few days.

He was stationed near us in Naples, and when we went back 'home' again, he came to see me. From then on we went out with each other, and we were really good friends for about four months. Then I thought to myself, I've got to really know where this is leading me. I'm getting older. I was twenty-four by then. It would be silly to keep going on with the same person if there was no future, for when you got home there wouldn't be any men left. Which was true, there weren't.

I'd asked him in the first place what I always asked boys: if he'd got a girlfriend at home, or was he married or anything? And he'd said no. Well, I put it to him, and it turned out he'd got a girlfriend in South Africa. That did it. Out. But he came back about a week later and said he'd finished with his fiancée, so would I go back? So we started going out again. Then, when he was sent home, and without telling me, he visited my parents, and sealed the bargain that end, before I even had the chance to argue about it.

We had both made up our minds that we shouldn't get married abroad. You don't really know each other that much and you're in funny circumstances. We felt that we'd both like to meet each other's families, and really see what we were about.

In uniform you're not an individual, really, you're sort of part of a whole. You're RAF – or blue jobs, as they were called. Or you're ATS – known as brown jobs! When you are about to be demobbed you start to wonder if your family (and their family) will approve. And that was a very big thing in our day:

Peggy in wartime Rome, where she fell in love with Eric.

that your family approved of who you liked. They could make it very difficult if they didn't think you'd chosen the right person.

I think by this time we were longing to get back to living a normal life. Of course we didn't know that we were about to face the difficulty of jobs and houses and all that. I was still preoccupied worrying if, when I first saw him and he saw me, we should like each other. You were about to give your whole life to someone you'd met in the romantic setting of the war. But when Eric came to our house, we just took one look at each other and that was it. We were quite all right.

I'd met his parents by now. I'd had a horrible feeling – he was very tall and thin, you see – that he'd have a very tall, austere mother. Would I like her? We went down there, and this lovely dumpy, rose-cheeked lady said, 'Come in ducks, you must be tired.' And I thought, oh, I'm all right. And his father – I couldn't do wrong. Eric had warned me his dad objected to women smoking, so I had been sneaking outside to have a cigarette. But his dad piped up, 'Eric's a bit mean with his cigarettes, have one of mine.' I was in!

You can't compare the war with anything else. I mean our children think that it was all honey and roses, because we met and we were happy with each other, but there were many things that were awful. But you don't want to remember the dreadful things that happened. That's why, I think, when people – soldiers especially – talk about the war it's about some funny incident that happened in the desert, not about the terrible battle when they saw all their mates being killed.

I was out one night with a man – he was in the Irish Fusiliers, I think. And we were sitting talking, having a drink, when all of a sudden he went off. And it was just as though he was in a nightmare, screaming. He came to, and he was perfectly all right again. And I thought, what sort of horrors has he seen? Those sort of things, you don't tell the children. That's why everybody seems as though they had a wonderful time in the war. They didn't really.

I certainly did nice things that I would never have done, but it was rare. Oh, I'd forgotten about my stay in Perugia too, in what was called a Formation College for girls. I don't know if they had them for men too. They were for women who had got married or had spent their growing up years in the Army. If they wanted to learn to cook and run a home, they could go for a fortnight to this Formation College. And you'd be surprised how many girls didn't even know how to boil an egg.

I was sent there as the clerk to this college. It was in a beautiful house, a countess's house, just outside Perugia. We had all the furniture that belonged to the countess, beautiful long oak tables. Trained staff teaching how to lay tables properly, how to cook, and all the rest of it. It was the cushiest job I'd had in all the time I was in the Army.

You do get comradeship in wartime, for there was that element of 'you may not be here tomorrow, so be nice while you can'. That was partly to do with it. Lots of people still write to people they met in the forces. I mean, after all this long time I still ring up my ATS friend in Folkestone.

She was with me at Stafford. She didn't work in the same office as me, but we were both in the same billet in Dunstan Hall – another beautiful big house. We got ourselves a tiny room, a servant's room up two little extra flights of stairs. Just big enough for our two beds, and our boxes. We painted the boxes, and we polished the wooden floor with shoe polish until you could see your face in it. Funnily enough we never went out with each other, to the pictures or anywhere. Just shared this little room and took a pride in it.

I haven't seen her since Robin, my first son, was nine months old. He's forty-two now! We talk as though we'd just met. Because we were so close when we were young.

Propaganda photograph to show that working in the blitz had its glamour.

HELEN BROOK
A Late Developer

Lady Brook – Helen Knewstub as she was then – was born suddenly and unexpectedly in 1907 during a private view at her father's Chenil Galleries in King's Road, Chelsea. Her mother, who was barely seventeen and couldn't account for the pains she was having, was rushed to an upstairs room, and so Helen, as she puts it, 'shot into the world in the middle of the smell of paint and turpentine on canvas'.

Brought up in a bohemian middle-class family, she was educated at a Roman Catholic convent, becoming religious and quite convinced that she had a guardian angel. 'I went on being young for a very long time.' That period included an early marriage which failed, two years painting in Paris, and a second, enduring marriage two years before war broke out.

It was living and coping with a young family while her husband was away at the war, she believes, which brought her maturity. 'By the end of the war I knew that I could run my own life, and though I would not have wished, and cannot imagine not sharing it with my husband, if I'd had to be on my own I could have done it. I had grown up. I was self-reliant. I could now say no to people.

'If it hadn't been for the war, I would have gone on painting, and entertaining for my husband, and gardening, and enjoying my blissful life. That's all. But I'd have been frustrated, because I have this energy . . .'

There was one memorable product of that energy. Helen Brook went on to become in 1964 the founder of the Brook Advisory Centres which offered contraceptive advice for the first time to unmarried women and eventually to girls under sixteen.

In 1937 I married Robin Brook, whom I had fallen bang in love with at first sight. It was the first and only time I've ever been in love. I was twenty-nine, coming up to thirty. I had been married before, very young at nineteen – I suppose, really I'd been brought up to be married – and I had a small daughter by my previous husband, George Whitaker. A musician, a violinist and pianist who played Schubert brilliantly. I don't think I married George, I married Schubert.

By 1938 everybody around us was preparing for war, and learning to do all sorts of things: how to run for shelter, what to do with people in gas masks. We were making preparations all the time – turning an underground larder into a shelter just in case. There was such a lot going on. We had the filthy blackshirts marching around. It was quite horrible. I don't know of anybody who wasn't making preparations, making preparations to leave England if necessary.

It was getting worse and worse. In our house in Devonshire Place, we lived on the top two floors, and the rest of the house was let, mainly as consulting rooms to refugee German Jewish doctors, who were coming over to England, fleeing. There was a great feeling of disturbance in the air. You were very aware of it from 1937 onwards.

I must tell you about our first air-raid warning. We hadn't much money but we'd just bought a lovely china candlestick and a blue china clock. They were our most precious possessions at the time. When the siren went off following Chamberlain's speech we ran and grabbed them and then dashed down all these stairs. I can't tell you how many stairs there were from the top of one of those tall houses. We got into the air-raid shelter, and when we looked at each other, we had to laugh.

After the all-clear, I rushed off to D. H. Evans and bought so many toilet rolls, they lasted us until well into peacetime, about the middle of the fifties. And I also bought a huge amount of soap and an even huger supply of cod-liver oil, because I thought if Robin's going to be in a trench he must take cod-liver oil with him. Well luckily eventually Boots took back that cod-liver oil from me. They were, funnily enough, quite glad of it.

Immediately after war was declared my daughter Christine's school was evacuated to Berkhamsted. Two days later people like me were evacuated nearby. But at dawn after my first night there I caught the milk train back because I didn't want to be separated from my husband. He'd gone to his office by the time I arrived home and I trailed down Baker Street and volunteered to become an air-raid warden. And, by some glorious mistake, signed on full time.

I ought to have got a Victoria Cross for this, I can tell you. I'm afraid of the dark, you see, or I was then, and to have to walk on my beat around those streets in the pitch black ... Devonshire Place, along Devonshire Street, and right round by the crescent and all the way back. My refuge was a cellar just at the end. I could go down the area steps and shelter there when the bombs dropped. I wasn't afraid of people, I was afraid of all the things that were round … mysterious things, like ghosts, which is what being afraid of the dark is, really.

I was dressed up in wardens' gear, with the trousers miles too long for me. I had to roll them up, and the sleeves. And I had a blessed whistle, and a rattle, and a tin hat.

We had a retired naval officer, Captain Donovan, as our boss though he made us keep naval hours and have dog watches. And that was totally ghastly. My husband would be there in bed with me, and at two o'clock I'd have to get up and dress up in all this gear, while he stayed in bed. For two hours I had to go on walking about the street. I thought this really was winning the war. It was very funny because, of course, we never had any air raids, all the time we were marching around.

About this time I found I couldn't become pregnant, which was very, very important to me, because I thought that any moment Robin was going to be called up. He hadn't immediately become a soldier, because he was in a reserved occupation. I saw a specialist, Gladys Hill, from the Royal Free Hospital who was in Harley Street, just round the corner from us. And she said I had to have a little operation, like having my tubes blown, which in those days was considered fairly hazardous. So off I bravely went and had this job done, when she said to me, 'Now go home and do your duty.' So I had to rush off home and say to Robin, 'Come on, it's for England.'

Fortunately I became pregnant. By then the Battle of Britain was starting, and we went off to Godalming. We took a furnished house there by Charterhouse School, where Robin's Eton tutor was headmaster, and Robin travelled up to London every day, but of course he was getting bombed on the way. It was a very hazardous time. The aeroplanes were having tremendous battles in the sky; you could lie down in the field and watch them, and almost forget. It was an extraordinary time.

And then Christine went off to Charmouth in Dorset when the term started again, and I went off to stay with Robin's uncle in Wakefield.

By this time my husband had joined Hugh Dalton and Hugh Gaitskell at the Ministry of Economic Warfare, which also covered SOE [Special Operations Executive]. It was all tremendously hush hush, and from those beginnings this is how we won the war.

Robin was doing all sorts of things in London, including learning to drop from aeroplanes by parachute, because all of that had to be learned if you were going to be dropped into France. And although he never did that, he had to know what the training was for all those brave people who were going to be doing it. I felt isolated, of course, but there was a lot for me to do with the new baby – my second daughter, Sarah – and I had Robin's mother, who was also liv-ing up there, to keep an eye on.

Robin's uncle had a factory which made all sorts of optical things. He was a real old master of the ancient kind when the poor were kept in their place. But I'd never been in such an environment before, all the back-to-back houses with communal lavatories. And the people were very, very poor, and everybody was made to work to the last drop. I started talking to Uncle Robert, and he thought of course I must be a socialist, a communist, I don't know what I was meant to be. I thought I was just being a Christian, and that you should really think about other people a bit more when their lives were so horrible.

So he and I didn't get on awfully well. He thought that I looked like a little piece of Dresden china, which he then found I wasn't. My character was begin-ning to show. I'd kept it somehow tucked away up to then. And it was here I began to feel this need really to understand how other people were living. I think the north of England taught me a lot, I hadn't realised people lived quite so dif-ferently.

After a few months – by then I'd collected six hens – it was time to go nearer to Robin, and to join my friend Mary in Daisy Farm, Didcot, and be a PG in her house. She had a little girl called Willow, and I had Sarah, about a year younger. So together we hired the most conventional nanny you ever saw. All starch. And oh, such a nanny. Nanny Harris. My goodness, she wouldn't do anything in the house. Mary and I had to wait on her hand and foot, but she did know how to look after the children.

Mary had a little car. I couldn't drive in those days. She tried to teach me but I wasn't awfully good at it. Anyway Mary and I became VADs [Voluntary Aid Detachment], so we had a lot to learn, and it was quite tough work.

VADs were voluntary nurses and had to do all the dirty work. Clean out the bedpans – we were always in the sluice. But when there was nobody else at hand we had to give injections and help in operations. So we had to know an awful lot, and yet be absolutely prepared to get down to the lowliest things, which the VADs did cheerfully. We had a nice smart uniform, and that was rather fun too.

At this time, Mary's husband, Bill Morrel, was away looking after Queen Mary at Badminton. I never knew what that was all about. I think she rather liked having what you might call manly-looking men, full of sex appeal, around her. He often arrived home without any warning. On one occasion Mary and I were practising bandaging to pass our exams. I was lying on the floor and she was busy doing my leg or whatever it was, and a gun came through the window. This was Bill coming home, hoping to catch us out, because he always suspected us of having lovers.

He called us Arty and Crafty, because I was all into the pictures and art, and

Mary was Crafty of course, being his wife. In fact, Arty and Crafty didn't think of being unfaithful to their husbands. All the nice men had gone anyway, and there really wasn't time. There was always such a lot of work to be done.

We did do all sorts of funny things, like putting the gramophone on every morning with the record, 'Say little hen, when when when, will you lay me an egg for my tea?' That was so the chickens would be encouraged by it. We buried tins of baby food in the garden to be prepared in case of shortage.

Mary and I made great plans in case there was an invasion. Should the parachutists drop on us, my job – we'd got it all organised – was to crawl out on my stomach for help all the way to Didcot, which was miles away. While Mary, being Welsh, would entertain the troops. She'd got a stock of condoms (french letters, we called them in those days) in her drawer at the ready … it was really quite funny.

I caught flu once (you couldn't afford to be ill in the war) and when the doctor came, I was in bed with my sunshade up because the roof leaked. But even if the rain was coming through you couldn't find anybody to mend your roof. You had to put up with it.

There was a lull in the raids on London. I was pregnant again and Nanny Harris, baby Sarah and I moved back to London. But on 15 May 1943, just as I went into labour, the bombing started again. It was a great old raid. And as I gave birth, the all-clear came.

Those days in hospital were really awful. We had raids all the time. My baby was in the basement and I was up in a ward far removed from her. It really was nerve-racking. So much so that I was quite unable to feed my third baby, Diana, as I had the others. I had the most horrible abscess in my breast. Just nerves, I suppose.

I was dead nervous about the baby being on a bottle, because I didn't think Nanny would give her the proper vitamins. She didn't really like girls. So I was always sniffing the bottle to check. Anyway, Nanny Harris went off eventually because she got a job with somebody who had a baby boy.

So I was left with my husband, two babies, a houseful of Free French and a marvellously eccentric man called Patrick Hancock whom I saw go off one morning to the Foreign Office with two bowler hats on his head by mistake.

Then Robin was posted to North Africa, from which he returned with a most vicious illness, jaundice type B. Later we learned that most of the people who had got this type of jaundice had died. Our doctor said on no account was he to be moved from the bed he was in, which was up at the top of the house: 'He's got to stay there. If you move him, it is unlikely he will survive.' And night after night we had the most awful raids. The fear was the incendiaries that shot through windows and set your house on fire. My two babies couldn't be in the air-raid shelter because the two caretakers had turned the cellar into their bed-room. So we had to shelter just underneath the main staircase. So I'd be running up and down the enormous flights of stairs making sure about Robin, making sure about the girls. This went on for some time. However, we survived and, the most glorious miracle, my husband survived.

Robin was always in the know about what was going to happen in the war. He was amazingly self-controlled – you couldn't even mention the weather; nothing was spoken about. But one of the things he knew was that we were in for another attack from the flying bombs. Of course he couldn't tell me this, but suggested that Mary and I should get out of London. Mary knew South Wales very well, and found us a bungalow on the coast at Porthcawl. And so we went off just before the end of the girls' school term. The bigger ones – her daughters and my Christine – were still away at boarding-school. We just had the three little ones with us, my two and her Willow.

Off we trailed by train, and by that time I had a dog, six hens and two chil-dren and two bicycles with me. But the hens always laid an egg on the way, and when you got there you had a new-laid egg if you needed it. Somehow we arrived in Porthcawl with all this lot, and settled in.

A lot of troops were stationed in and around the bay – mostly American and they were forever calling in on us. It was a bit of home life that they were miss-ing, and it was wonderful for us too. They were so cheerful. And then I heard

Helen Brook washing the dog.

from Robin. He told me to go with Mary the next day, very early, and stand down at the seafront. That magical dawn. We stood and leaned on a railing and watched and waited.

Gradually it grew lighter, and then came the first ship, then another, and as we watched the ships come slowly, slowly, one by one, down the Bristol Channel on their way to France. Mary and I felt we were the only two women in Britain to see the beginning of that great, great day. And as they came, neither of us spoke. It was all quite silent except for seagulls. It was ... I don't know how to explain it, I suppose you'd have to put it into poetry really, to explain that great emotion that came up in you. It was almost a religious experience, it really was. See, I am crying at the thought. Those soldiers we had known so well who were always dropping in and playing with the children – so many of them died on that day.

After D-Day, Robin became a real soldier. When he was in the SOE he was always in mufti, you see. Then he went over to France and was in uniform and became a brigadier, and with him being away for a long time, I took over running everything.

What I did was really very startling at the time. Our friend Kenneth Cohen, who lived in Hampstead, had let it be known that he was moving from his house, Chestnut Lodge, which I had been half in love with since I was about twenty-two. I'd seen it then and thought, that's where I'd like to live, bang on the edge of the Heath. I knew every blade of grass on the Heath for I used to go there with my father when I was little, and it really meant a great deal to me. I had a beautiful idea. My friend Margaret Flower whose husband was fighting in France (in fact he got the Military Cross) had returned to London to find their house had been bombed, so she had come to live with me. My idea was that she'd take over the whole of our flat instead of half of it, and I'd move into Chestnut Lodge, which I did.

The end of the war was not a great relief for me. Robin was in France, and he didn't come home straight afterwards. Instead he went on into Germany. He was among the first into those horrible camps. He saw terrible things, and he was in Germany for quite a time. So my war went on, I always feel, until 1946 when Robin eventually returned. And when he did come back, he was really quite upset to find that his home was now in Hampstead. He wasn't the Hampstead type at all.

My painting friends and my musical friends, and Hugh Gaitskell and Douglas Jay, were all living in Hampstead and all practically next door, and it had been the most glorious time. I really enjoyed every single minute of it. But Robin couldn't stand living in Hampstead, and although I was immensely blissful there, I gave way. We went back to Devonshire Place.

I felt despair when we moved back. I totally hated it. Then one morning early in 1952, when I'd gone along to Cullens to give my order, a woman I knew a little, Nancy Raphael, came into the shop to get some coffee. We'd only shaken hands before but never really had an intimate talk. But as we were buying these things she said, 'I don't suppose you want a job, Helen, do you?'

Well at that moment, when I'd never been so depressed in all my life, I said yes. She explained it was only voluntary work. 'You come up to Islington on Wednesday,' she said. 'I'll teach you how to be an interviewer.'

'Interviewing what?' I asked. She said, 'Oh, women for family planning.' Well I didn't know what family planning was, but I turned up, and I sat with her all afternoon, and at the end of it I was an interviewer. But I couldn't say the word … you know, I called them french letters. There were a lot of things that were difficult to actually say. But, after I'd done it for three or four Wednesdays – I've always had the most frightful curiosity – I found myself totally interested in family planning.

I wanted to do more than just interviewing. Nancy asked if I'd like to come on the clinic committee of the Family Planning Association. I'd never been on a committee, and I was thrilled. But I said, 'Before I can do that I want to know exactly what it's about. I must come and see how you work at central office.' At first she refused, but in the end I was allowed to go down to Sloane Street, where I saw the famous toads. If it was thought the patient might be pregnant, the toads were used for testing the urine.

After about six months, I was certain that the FPA, with its determination to open clinics for women seeking family planning, was the cause to which I could devote my energy and imagination. I was in my fortieth year and was ready, as so many women are at that age, for a new life. I had no higher education, and you find many women of my age really had no chance at all. Many of my friends were brighter than their husbands, brothers, lovers but shorthand typing was their lot. There were few openings though they were capable of becoming doctors – or anything else. Now I became aware that all this could be altered if women could know their rights and then appreciate that they had to learn about equal rights for equal sexual partners.

Personally, I emerged from the war as a fully equal human being so that when my husband returned from Germany he found me a force to be reckoned with. This force was applied to the Marie Stopes clinic, where in 1960/1 we opened the first sessions for the unmarried woman – secretly because of the general opposition. This experience led in turn to the establishment of Brook Advisory Centres with separate sessions for the under 25s for whom the service was critical.

The whole world's changed in my lifetime. It's been marvellous.

DENISE AYLMER-AYLMORE
Courses for Horses

The war did Denise Aylmer-Aylmore a bit of a favour. In 1942 she was eighteen and due to be called up. The Land Army was her only bearable choice; at least it was out of doors. But her overriding passion, as she aptly put it, was working with horses.

Just at the crucial moment when she was going to have to choose, her mother sent her an announcement cut out of a newspaper, that the Remount Depot in Melton Mowbray was taking on girls for the first time because the young men working there were being called up. 'Do you want to apply?' wrote her mother. Denise replied, 'For goodness sake, I hope you've already done it.' Her mother had.

My application came back: yes, come for an interview. But I think this interview was just a formality. If you'd done enough, you were on. I can remember the adjutant saying, send your bike and your luggage up by rail. We'll keep them here and help you get them down to the digs, which we'll find for you.

Nobody had any transport, really. We did everything on bikes, which we were permanently losing because the troops, who were late out of the pub, were always nicking them to get back to their barracks. The police would find them the next day outside the gate. Nothing ever disappeared for good. It just meant you had to walk two miles to work the next day, which was a nuisance. But of course, when you consider the blackout, if you wanted to pinch things, it would have been terribly easy. But I don't ever remember any rape cases at all, and yet we were always wandering around in the blackout, unable to see anything much.

Denise, right, *mounting Cheeky at Melton Mowbray Remount Depot, 1945.*

All the traffic, the army lorries and our bicycles, had metal visors like louvre-boards that sent the light downwards so you could only see a few feet ahead. But you adjusted to it. I don't remember having many problems getting around in the blackout.

We went into the Remount Depot as groups, and there was no guarantee that we would get any riding to start with. We were employed as strappers. A strapper is somebody who grooms and looks after a horse. For this work we were paid the large sum of two pounds six and eightpence a week, out of which we had to pay for our digs.

It was a reserved occupation, rather like munitions work, and provided you kept your nose clean and didn't do anything disastrous, you were in for the duration. Anybody that liked horses was sitting pretty, thank you very much. It couldn't have been better for me.

Did I feel patriotic at eighteen and a half? I don't know. I was glad I was doing war work, and I certainly would have gone on to the land if I hadn't been at the Remount Depot. I would have absolutely loved to be a pilot, for I was already in the Air Training Corps. But I wasn't good enough mathematically – I've always erred more on the artistic side rather than the scientific.

You weren't given a uniform at Melton. We were issued with overalls, boiler suits basically, khaki ones. There was nothing special, the only thing that had been specially made for us were black riding jackets. All the rest was ordinary army issue. Dispatch riders' breeches, which were made of very heavy khaki cord with fans out at the sides, of course, for there were no stretch breeches in those days. They didn't come in until well after the war. And army puttees, which half the girls flatly refused to wear anyway. You weren't compelled to, you could ride in what you liked. Most of us wore leather chaps over our slacks, or whatever. And mostly people had their own jodhpurs. They didn't provide us with hard hats, but obviously anybody who rode had them anyway.

How some of the girls didn't kill themselves, I can't understand. Some really could barely ride, and although as grooms they weren't required to, we did have a strappers' ride each day, which would be twenty girls all going out together led by Major Catley, the equitation officer. I think he was frightened of the ones who really didn't ride very well. Once we got out on to Ashby Pastures, which are Leicestershire grass fields that run for a long distance, he used to say, 'Right, we will now canter.' But of course it didn't stay in a canter for more than a very few yards. The whole lot used to take off, and it was generally only a large Leicestershire bullfinch, which is a high hedge, that stopped them when they got to the other end.

But I think they only had one girl killed, and that was before I was there. An army lorry hit the GS wagon she was on and she got pitched off. The lorry hit them, the wheel went over her and she was killed instantly. But that was the only big accident. People broke legs and so on, but that's a fact of life if you ride horses, I'm afraid.

My digs were with a Methodist lay preacher and his daughter. Their house was cold, of course, for central heating was not very common. They were all right. I had enough to eat. I mean you handed your ration book over where you lodged. I can't remember being particularly hungry – any more than anybody was throughout the war.

Homesickness never occurred for me. My mother told me that when she took me to boarding-school at ten I just about kissed her goodbye before I rushed off with the girl who was going to look after me. I had wanted to go to boarding-school, though I said I wouldn't go unless there were horses, which was why I went to Stonar.

I'd always lived away from home. I was an only child and Mother was quite determined that I wasn't going to be hanging on her apron strings. I was sent off to my grandparents or to my aunt, just for holidays, you know.

I don't exactly know why I've always loved horses so much. When I was in my pram, which was one of those Silver Cross high ones, Mother used to attach an old weight on a strap to the handle of the pram. If she didn't, every time a horse went past – and there were always horses passing by: milk horses, brewery horses, coal horses, you name it – I'd start bouncing vigorously up and down and topple the pram over.

We used to start at the depot at eight o'clock in the morning, having come in from our various digs. Latterly, they did have some girls actually living on the depot, but there wasn't really accommodation. The grooms' bothies over the main yard were inhabited by ex-cavalrymen who were too old to go back into the Army, and a lot of ex-racing lads, called stable rats in those days, lived in vast dormitories on the place.

They employed girls because the Veterinary Corps were all fighting overseas. It's a very small regiment anyway because it's so selective, and even then it was getting smaller. The cavalry had virtually turned over to tanks and light armoured vehicles, so they weren't using war horses as such, but they were using pack animals in Wales to train Indian troops and British troops. There's a lot of skill in packing packs. They've got to be balanced, not to rub holes in the horses' sides.

There was a big Veterinary Corps depot at Doncaster. It was on the racecourse because they had the stabling facilities there, and spent the whole war producing serum for the troops. They used the horses as serum horses, so they were rather well fed. They had to be because of the quality of the blood. Every three weeks or so they had a drip stuck in the jugular, and they took about three litres of blood for the troops. This was before the days of antibiotics.

I don't know that there were any girls there. I think it was all staffed by men. We went visiting once or twice because they used to run horse shows, and invite all the people from the depots within a reasonable distance. We all went up to Doncaster by train. I've still got a certificate somewhere showing that I won the mule race.

Our day's work began by collecting the feeds from the feed sheds. The men put them up into individual metal bowls. We didn't have anything to do with that. They were elderly men, all of them, and quite cheerful.

We just collected feed bowls for however many horses we were looking after, and went and fed our horses. Tipped it into the manger and took the empty bins back again. After that we mucked our horses out, collected straw, put in fresh bedding, took the hay nets down, and round to the hay shed where we filled them. Then we brought them back and hung them outside the doors, because they'd have them at night, not during the day.

Then, if you were a strapper, the strappers' ride went out, at about half-past ten. It depended on when we'd finished sweeping up the yards and everything. After the ride, we'd groom whatever horse we'd been riding, feed again, and go and have our own lunch.

After lunch we'd strap all our horses, or get other animals ready if there were people coming in from outside: a whole lot of Americans from the big American air base at Cottesmore, say. Some of them could ride, cowboy fashion; some couldn't ride at all and thought they could. But we used to tack up horses for them. And when we'd groomed, we'd clean the tack, the saddle and bridle, and the horses were fed again, about five o'clock, and we'd put the hay nets in. If it was winter we'd rug them up, if they were wearing rugs, and we finished about half-past five.

So by the time we'd cycled back to our digs and had supper, it was quite late. But then there was no question, in wartime, of regular hours. As far as the horses were concerned, we were fairly well able to keep to a timetable, but if you were doing war work in a munitions factory or wherever, and they needed it, you went on. They worked shifts; we were lucky and didn't.

We did, however, have line duty guards. There was a rota. We had lunch early and while everybody else had lunch our duty was walking round to see that the horses were all still on their feet, and none were ill. None had got out and were disturbing the rest. I mean we had stabling for something like 300 horses, and there were a whole lot more out in the fields. At one time we had something like a thousand head, I seem to remember. And there were from sixty, possibly seventy of us girls.

It wasn't any good saying you weren't going to do the work asked of you. If you did, you found yourself pitched into the forces, or into munitions factories, which were worse. I don't think there was any query. There was a war on. If you were going to survive, you were going to have to work – unless you were a spiv, and went into the black market and made a fat living selling stuff that you couldn't get on ration. Because after about 1941, I suppose, everything was rationed. There were clothing coupons and we had to make do and mend. Fortunately with horses you don't need a lot of decent clothes because you never get the chance to wear them. As I say, most of us did have overalls from the Army, but they still wanted clothing coupons for them, the devils.

I was there from '43 to March '46, when they gave us a pat on the head and a little slip of paper saying we had one month's notice, thank you very much, goodbye. And that was that. We knew it was coming some time before, because some of the Veterinary Corps came back after Monte Cassino. They had been using pack animals to get the ammunition forward because the mountain roads were so bad. Horses and mules could get up when the wheeled transport couldn't. Then, of course, gradually as the war progressed, they were hardly using horses at all. Towards the end of the war we used to take a lot of redundant animals up to the old Elephant & Castle horse repository to be sold. It started in 1945, I think – 'the world's largest horse auction'.

I didn't mind this, not really. Apart from one or two that you possibly had an affinity with, because you competed on them, horses were always being issued and brought back again. The population was floating. The only horses that stayed there all through the war were the Household Cavalry horses, and the officers' chargers that were left over from the barracks at Weedon.

Pack ponies made good prices because they'd been corn-fed all through the war. You couldn't get any hard food for horses, only hay, for like everything else, it was rationed. If they were working horses, draught horses, you could get a small corn ration for them, but a lot of riding horses were put down simply because their owners weren't there. They were abroad in the forces, both men and women, and you really couldn't keep horses lying around doing nothing, and with nothing to feed them on. And I suppose we ate some of them – certainly some of the London hotels and restaurants were feeding horse meat. I mean, they disguised it as steak.

I haven't mentioned the fund-raising shows we did for Army, Navy, Air Force charities, you name it. There was a 'Salute the Soldier' event, a week where we were fund-raising in various ways, and we paraded the pack animals for that. We also did musical rides: working the horse to music like the Household Cavalry do, but we did it with thirty-two little pack ponies, about fourteen-two they were, not very big. You can't have anything too tall to put a pack saddle on, because they carry about 240lb, which has got to be balanced equally on both sides. If it's too tall, you can't lift the stuff off or on. Not even the troops could.

You didn't need horse-boxes much, unless you were wealthy people hunting with the Quorn, you know. We weren't allowed to hunt Army horses, so we didn't get any hunting, but Sir Nigel Coleman had a pack of basset hounds, and we used to go out on foot with the bassets every now and again. And Sundays, our day off, we didn't do very much. There wasn't much to do, quite honestly. I played quite a lot of tennis at a local tennis club which let us come in at Army rates. I played a bit of badminton too.

I used to go to the cinema two or three times a week; mind you, it only cost a few pence. They always had second features, plus a Movietone, plus adverts. It was good value. The cinemas at Melton were rather odd, because they both belonged to the same company. They were side by side, and one was slightly bigger than the other. They would put the major film on in one cinema at the beginning of the week, and by about Wednesday they'd swap it over to the other one, and put another one on.

But there was nothing much else to do, except go down to the pub with the current boyfriend, who might be there for two weeks or might not. I made many girl friends, whom I still meet. Quite a lot are still in horses, so we bump into each other at conferences and shows. The horse world is relatively small, in a way, and you suddenly see someone that you probably haven't seen for years.

Looking back at Melton, I had a very peaceful war. I'm afraid that if you work with horses you tend to get a little bit self-centred, retreat into a nice little cocoon. Certainly, we had a lot of fun. Melton only had one stick of bombs, which was from a Jerry running for home with some fighters on his tail.

An Abram Games poster which was banned for glamorising the Auxiliary Territorial Service.

JOYCE CARR
Just Like William

Joyce Brien – the only girl in a family of four boys – used to try to hang around with them, but they'd have none of it. Her brothers used to say, 'We're all going into our room to have a meeting. Girls can't come in,' and shut the door in her face.

Her experience of the forces was like that. When, eager-beaver, she volunteered at the beginning of the war, she'd expected to be up there fighting with the boys. If they had to risk their lives, why not girls too? Instead, she found herself stuck at first in a safe, mundane job.

In the December after war was declared, the friend I always went around with and I decided we wanted to help our country and have some excitement. We joined the Army.

We were told we'd get word when to start, and since we'd never been away from home before, we were glad to be spending Christmas and New Year with our families.

In the January, we were sent to the ATS training centre at Neville's Cross College, Durham. We were shepherded around as if we were still at school – queues of girls getting issued with clothing. I didn't mind the uniform. It was the thick stockings and heavy shoes that I hated, because I'd never worn anything but fine silk stockings and high-heeled shoes. I was very fashion conscious, when I was young.

We were called volunteers in those days, and got a service number. Do you know it's funny, all the people that I've met since in the ATS Association say your number is something you'll never forget. I did. I really was a bit bolshie about the regimentation. I didn't like to be pushed around.

They interviewed us to decide where to put us. My friend told them she'd never worked. She'd lost her mother when she was fifteen and had stayed home to look after her father and little sister. Right, they said, you can do kitchen work. I felt really sorry for her. She'd hoped to have an interesting war job not just more of the dreary same.

They said I could go into an office, which was also what I'd been doing. At least we were both sent to the same camp: the big one at Catterick – the training battalion of the Royal Corps of Signals.

We were given a little house, where regular soldiers had lived, and with some of our own things from home it was very comfortable. I enjoyed it at first. We were free from parental care, but though we thought we'd go mad, we didn't. We weren't allowed to. The Army kept us under strict supervision.

There was all this regimental thing. Saluting, addressing the officers: men to be called sir, women, ma'am. There wasn't any drill or marching, but we had to parade into the mess for all meals, and when we went to church on Sundays.

We always needed a pass to leave the camp. We used to walk over the hill to Leyburn, a pretty village where there was a little café that still had hens. It was lovely to go there for a bit of ham and a real egg, and have a linger.

One week, my friend, who was working in the officers' mess, got two invitations and our passes to go to one of their dances. We were on the floor dancing, when, all of a sudden, one of our senior officers beckoned us with her finger. She told us, 'You're on a charge. You're just volunteers. You're not supposed to be dancing or mixing with officers.'

It was awful. We felt terrible. And angry. If we'd been in civilian clothes, we could have been invited. Why should we be banned because we were wearing uniform? But that was the thing. You didn't fraternise with officers. We were put on a charge, and we had to stay in the camp for a week.

But that sort of thing aside, life was very peaceful in the countryside. In fact there seemed to be no war going on at all that first year. We didn't want to go home, because when we did there were blackouts and raids. At the same time we both still wanted to feel we were doing something for the country.

We were in a cinema once when the Military Police, the red caps, came in and said, 'Out, back home.' We were transported back and confined to camp for about a week. They said there'd been a rumour of a German being dropped on the moors – and if we'd met him, and he was dressed ordinarily, we might have given information away. What information could most of us have given away?

After the first year, conscription came into force. Life changed. More restrictions, and we were put in barrack rooms with about twenty or thirty people in each. There were more drills, gas lectures, and gas masks to be carried at all times.

If a dance was held at any of the other camps, we had to queue up to get on to the bus, which dropped us outside the dance hall. Once we were in, we weren't allowed to go outside.

We used to dance around with our young man, but if we fancied him we couldn't give him a goodnight kiss or anything. We used to argue about all these restrictions – then we'd get put on a charge for speaking to the officers in this way. We thought we should be responsible for ourselves.

When the conscripts came, life was very different. The girls came from strange backgrounds. Some of them did not know how to use knives and forks. Once a girl ran away, and I went with an NCO to Glasgow, to the Gorbals, to bring her back. The first time I'd ever been there, or heard about it – and we had to bring her back forcefully. I thought, my goodness, life was like a palace in the camps compared to where she lived.

And the foul language some of them used! Quite a lot of them I don't think had ever seen nightwear before. When they were given pyjamas, they put them on over the top of their vest and knickers and went to bed. They got into trouble an awful lot. I felt sorry for them because they were just ignorant of these things.

You did realise that there really was a war going on when, after they'd had their training, the troops couldn't tell you where they were going. None of them were told. And some never came back.

I had a young man – a short little affair of three months – who was sent to Singapore, and was reported missing. He is to this day. So I felt suddenly just sick of not doing anything serious. Without qualifications there would never be a chance of me going abroad. But I saw they were asking for Ack-Ack volunteers. It didn't matter what your qualifications were, they wanted to train you. I thought, right, I'm going to try for that.

I thought, I must be going to see some action at last, if I'm going to be on guns. The training was at Anglesey in North Wales. We all had to learn aircraft recognition, and how to work out what height the planes were at. The planes that trained us had to fly across the sea off Wales, and they pulled a sleeve behind them. Once we had worked out their height, we gave a message to the guns and they would fire. Sometimes we had a competition between us to see how many sleeves we'd hit. At first we might go the whole week and never hit one, and I used to think, what's it going to be like when we're really on the guns, and defending a town? But when we left we were able to hit every sleeve that went flying past. I was now a trained height-finder.

Anglesey was a bleak island in late November and December. We were very high up from the water and below were great big black rocks. Looking down on to them, I used to sometimes think – I was so miserable – if I just dropped in there I'd be dashed against the rocks. I really got very low there, for there was nowhere to go. Everybody had told us that if we were stationed near a town,

Joyce at home on leave with her parents.

people would invite the girls and the boys home for the weekend, or for the night, or to have a meal with the family. But no one spoke English on the island, only Welsh, and they never tried to get to know us at all.

After training, we went to an army camp at Birkenhead. It was mostly women on the plotting and men on the guns. I'm afraid the Germans did bomb Liverpool post office just after we went there. They blew it to pieces, so we must have let that plane in. We worried, if we were to blame. I comforted myself by thinking that the ones on the guns were not hitting the things properly. But you couldn't think like this. There were so many planes coming over you were lucky to hit one. And anyway another one would drop a bomb at the same time.

I didn't feel I was hard-worked at all. The hours were reasonable. But the adrenalin was running all the time – oh my God, what if I make a mistake! You just had to be calm and do what you could to make sure they got the message right. It was frightening.

At the end of 1942 I met my husband to be, Tom Carr, who was home from the RAF. It was love at first sight, really. A pilot sounded so romantic and I liked his Air Force uniform. I was sick of looking at army men. They looked very drab after a while, though I felt sorry for the soldiers. Their uniform was unfair – those awful hairy shirts, and they never had collars and ties. And there was the RAF with nice revers, a blue shirt and navy tie – so much smarter.

Tom and I got married very quickly. I'd had my baby by then. So, of course, I'd had to leave the ATS. There were so many in this situation. Both of you were just home on leave and you didn't know whether you were ever going to see each other again. Tom and I were madly in love. And it happened. At that time it did seem terrible. It's nothing now. But then, people's idea was that you shouldn't have sex for the pleasure of it.

I was worried about breaking the news to my mother but she was quite calm about it. She said, 'Well, you've done it now.' And his mother was all right about the baby, too. They were two staunch Christians and knew each other in the WI.

I had my baby at home with my mother. We were in a very vulnerable part of the country, and there was a lot of bombing. Oh, I hated it. In fact my little boy used to wake up and scream when the sirens went off. We had to pick him up and put him in this horrible gas-mask. I used to worry all the time because the baby was lying in a cage thing, and you had to pump the air in. I thought, what if anything happens to me, or I don't pump properly? In the end I just didn't put him in it. We just cuddled together and if we were to go, we'd go.

My father was an air-raid warden, there was just the dog, my mother, me and the baby, sitting shivering in a shelter in our wellies, frozen, with water round our ankles. And our stupid dog used to sit there panting, terrified, all the time. As soon as ever my mother opened the back door for us to go in the shelter, whoosh, the dog was in first.

Tom didn't see our baby for nearly a year. My little boy was delighted when he first saw him because he'd been looking at photographs and saying that's daddy, that's daddy.

After he returned to camp, I kept worrying that he'd never see the baby again. Tom was flying Lancasters across to Berlin. I heard this Lord Haw Haw on the radio one night telling us that a thousand planes had gone out, and only two hundred had come back. It was a terrible night, and Tom could never tell me about his movements, so I didn't know whether he was in one of those shot down.

I did go and stay on the camp for a while, but I didn't see Tom much. He was working all the time. I used to hear the planes leaving, and I couldn't get to sleep. You'd think about it, and then the next morning you'd hear the planes coming in. You were counting them in. Well, of course, quite a few didn't come back. Young girls I knew were married to these fellows, and when they're gone there's nothing you can say to them.

Tom used to tell us stories of coming back from the raids. You'd go down to breakfast after being out all night, and if one plane had gone, that meant seven men were not sitting with you. Some men broke down, and had to come away from planes altogether. They called it lack of moral fibre or something awful like that, and they were dismissed from the services.

I never worried about killing when I was on the guns: I wasn't actually killing the Germans, I was killing those that were flying with their bombs. I thought that was good, I really felt that. The only thing Tom worried about later on was when he saw how much damage he'd done, and how many people were killed. But in war the innocent do suffer, don't they?

It wasn't until he came out in 1946 that we were together as a family. When Tom got demobbed, there were no jobs. The place where he'd worked didn't want him back. Quite a few of his friends were in the same fix. They had to change their lives. I think they felt let down, cheated. The people who had stayed at home had made an awful lot of money. Now the others felt what fools they'd been for joining the forces.

Anyway, Tom worked hard to become a teacher. He had to work during the day and do his degree at night. Eventually he got to be senior lecturer in building in a technical college. And he was very, very well liked.

I had worked in an office while Tom was away. My mother was happy to look after my child, since all her sons had left home by now. But when Tom came home, he didn't want me to go out to work. I accepted it because I'd always loved children. I thought the happiest time of my life was to see my three little boys growing up.

EVELYN JONES
Living Through the Blitz

Evelyn Taylor married Jack Jones on his return from the Spanish Civil War where he had served with the International Brigade and been wounded on the Ebro. Her first husband, following the same idealistic path, had been killed in Spain.

In the late sixties Jack was to become general secretary of the country's largest trade union, the Transport & General Workers'.

At the beginning of the war he was on his way from his native Liverpool to take over as district then regional secretary of the TGWU in the Midlands.

Evelyn shared his socialist beliefs, and during the war was an active trade unionist herself. But, having lost her home in the Coventry blitz of 1940, her uncomplaining account of those times centres more on the struggles of a bombed-out family living almost as refugees in the heart of their own country. Evelyn remained philosophical throughout. At least she still had her family. So many people all around her had lost far more than their homes.

We were moving house on the day war was declared because Jack had been appointed to the district office in Coventry. We were going by train from Liverpool and heard about it as we waited in Broadgate station café.

That evening when the removal van arrived to unload our goods, people were shouting, 'Put that light out! Put that light out!' There was I with a seven-week-old baby, trying to bath him, to feed him, to sort out the home.

In fact we only lived there for about a fortnight, because it was one of those modern little houses with rooms so tiny I couldn't get my living-room furniture in. It was terrible. So eventually we found a flat in Chester Street in the central area of Coventry. It was in an old stone house that had been converted into four

flats, and that was where we were when the 1940 blitz hit us.

If we hadn't had a cellar – and the night of the raid was the first time we'd ever used it – we'd have been dead, because a bomb fell in the back garden, demolishing our kitchen, and the blast brought down the ceilings. We were in chaos.

It was a brilliant moonlight night. Most of the other occupants of the flats were away. A young couple had fixed up the cellar with bunk beds and a rug, and an electric fire and goodness knows what. But they had decided that the raids had got too busy, and had gone to stay with the girl's mother out in Kenilworth. So there was Jack and I and the baby – he was a year and four months then.

After the first half-hour I said to Jack, I think you'd better go upstairs and bring the headmistress down. She was occupying the other flat and had a friend staying with her. The four of us sat gossiping. Jack kept going out, helping to put fires out in the area, because the incendiaries were coming down pretty heavily.

The raid didn't let up for about twelve hours. We heard the bombs whistling down. They were just round balls of metal with fins on, and as they came down they burst and set fire to things. A factor that many people don't appreciate is that the casings for these incendiary bombs were made just outside Coventry before the war, and they were exported to Germany. A macabre detail, isn't it?

It wasn't until after midnight that our bomb dropped, and we spent the rest of the night in the archway at the bottom of the stairs. That was the safest place to be. Young Jack, he just woke up and went to sleep again. I wrapped him up in his eiderdown.

This bomb that fell in our garden was a big bomb. If ours had been a modern building it would have collapsed, but because it was an old, well-built stone house it withstood the blast. The great big window-frames were out, and the

Polyfotos of Evelyn, before she was bombed out of her Coventry home.

laths and the plaster in the ceiling were down, and the new kitchen and bath-room which had been built on the back, they were destroyed.

The noise was tremendous. But we thought it was just our part of Coventry that was being hit. It wasn't until the next morning we realised the extent of the damage. There were so many people leaving the city, just walking out. And later we learned that sixty-odd thousand homes had been destroyed.

Anyway, I don't think I've ever had much feeling for possessions since then, because at least the next morning we were still a family. We were not destroyed, and that was important. So many people that night had been killed. Eight hundred people. Next morning when I went down to look at the town, the gas works had gone, and a woman was asking me did I know where her children were? They'd gone to stay with friends that night. The house had gone.

The raid had started quite early in the evening. This was November time and it was already dark. It was about half-past six when the incendiaries began to come down.

My younger sister was living with me at the time. On the night of the raid she had gone out to the cinema with her boyfriend, and I didn't know until the next morning that she was all right. There were so many dead people being carried out of their homes that day.

Later, after I'd cleared up, we were able to salvage some things – mostly books – out of the rest of the flat. The bedroom at the front, although the windows were out, was intact so eventually we were able to put things in there and cover them over with matting. People could have thieved all our things from it, but although I was away for a good many weeks, nothing was touched. There was no water, no gas, no electricity, so that we had to have somewhere just to exist.

Jack's colleague, who was regional secretary at the time, came into Coventry by car. He was one of the few people that they let in, because by that time there was martial law. Although they let people out, they weren't letting people in. And he took me and young Jack and my sister out to the station in Birmingham to get a train.

By this time we were absolutely filthy. We couldn't change, for I'd had to find clothes for an Indian father and his four children. His home was destroyed, and he was in the shelter by the canal. The water had come in and they were all wet. Imagine that, in November. I found them what I could, but he was about half Jack's size, so you can imagine.

We were glad to get on the station. When we got to Manchester, there weren't any trains running down to Knutsford, where my mum lived, so we had to wait at one of the YMCA places where there were Australian and New Zealand troops. They were very good to us. They found us mugs of tea and some food.

We got the early train out the next morning. I can remember opening the door – Mum's door was never locked in that village – going and sitting down on the stairs, and I just wept. I was exhausted, and I was also relieved to be home. I can hear my mother calling out, 'Is that you Tev?' That was my family's special name for me.

It was a full house at my mother's, for my elder sister with her three children were there. They'd been evacuated from Eastbourne. And my younger sister, who'd come with me. So there were all of us in my mother's very crowded house for several weeks.

The night we left for Knutsford, Jack also got out of Coventry, and walked ten or twelve miles along the railway lines to see some people in Nuneaton. There he found us a place where we lived for about eighteen months. Then we got a house back in Coventry. The council just put names in a hat, for they only had a few places. The building had concrete stairs and a concrete roof, because they hadn't got any timber. But although it was a bleak house, it was a good home for our family to grow up in. We lived there quite a few years.

Later we moved to a prefab in Solihull. It was down a little lane which we had accidentally come across. We had put a notice on one of the doors to ask if anybody wanted to swap council places – people used to do this at the time – and someone came running after us down the street. They said they'd been trying for ages to get a place in Coventry. And so we ended up living there for eight years. There was a bluebell wood not far away. It was a lovely spot, really.

Because we lived on the outskirts of town and we were friendly with the farmer we were lucky about food. The milk came in an open can and was ladled out. And when I wasn't there the farmer used to come in and leave extra milk.

So I got more milk than I was allowed, and a few extra eggs, which did help the rationing.

I used to feed the boys in the evening and they'd think I'd be eating later with Jack. Jack would think I'd eaten with the boys, and so quite often I'd make do with the end of the cheese or whatever. There were lots and lots of other women who did the same thing. I became very anaemic after the war.

For a short time I worked mornings making aircraft at the Standard Motor Company, while my neighbour worked in the afternoons. This helped to keep the job going until I became pregnant with my younger son, and after a few months gave up working there. I could only work as long as I did because a day nursery was opened for the older children of pre-school age. Jack used to take young Jack and Lee there before he went to work. After a few weeks my older son said, 'Mum you always come and collect me at lunchtime, and I miss the story.' So I was very grateful that he could stay and listen to the story, because it meant I could go home, whip round and make the beds, do a few jobs, light the fire, get the house going ready for when the boys came home.

During those years you didn't have much leisure. I used to work from the time I got up in the morning until I went to bed at night, because I'd now become the secretary of my trade union branch. And this branch grew. Partly, I think, because I had enthusiastic support from a Welshman called Jack Adams who went round the factory during the day, distributing union forms. He used to bring me the completed forms at work in the daytime, and I'd give him the membership cards the next morning. So between us we built up a big branch of the union.

I was drilling metal, and working in a horrible screaming noise. I think the factory made cars before the war, then aircraft in the war and reverted to cars afterwards. But it became a very militant factory, and by building up our union, other unions were strengthened. Coventry became a recognised trade union city. In fact when the men came back from the forces, they learned they'd got to be a member of a union to get a job, which was good. The women in Coventry were militant, too. One of the first big strikes after the war was by the women machinists who were making covers for cars.

I had left home in the early thirties, largely because I disagreed politically with my dad, and went to work in an engineering factory where women were very lowly paid. The top rate was twenty-four shillings a week, and by the time you'd bought your overalls and travelled to work you were no better off than if you were unemployed, when you got fifteen shillings a week. It's the same today. Many people can't afford to take a job because they get more money with Income Support, so it's crazy.

Many women went to work in the war who had never previously bothered going. They were directed to labour, for one thing. They either had to go as farm workers or factory workers or join the forces. There was no option if they were a certain age and didn't have children under fourteen. If they had a child over fourteen they were considered capable of work.

We had to fight our corner, just as much during the war, to get equality. But we didn't get as much equality as women have today. The Equal Opportunities Act has been passed largely as a result of women fighting to have that right. Mind, they're still treated badly when it comes to it. Now people are afraid to lose their jobs, and because of that, trade unions have become weaker.

I had to make a conscious decision at the time whether to be like Jack, fully involved, and let someone else bring up the children. But in the end I think I made my contribution by helping to make it possible for Jack to do what he was doing.

KATHLEEN HALE
A Tale of Two Wars

Being ninety-six, Kathleen Hale can describe her life not only in the Second World War but in the First, when as a recent art school graduate she was pitchforked on to the land and ended up delivering vegetables by horse and cart at dawn each morning to Covent Garden.

Having the sort of mind that invented Orlando the Marmalade Cat, who wears a wrist-watch on his tail, her artist's and writer's viewpoint of both wars is crystal clear and zany.

Orlando, renamed Mish-Mish, in fact was part of this last war's effort. Kathleen was commissioned to write an Orlando series for the British propaganda programme which was sent out to Arab countries as a monthly magazine. And since marmalade was unknown in these countries he was called Mish-Mish meaning apricot, the same colour!

Kathleen had her first son in 1930 and decided she couldn't bring up children in a town. She used to put Peregrine, just born, on the roof of their flat in London for his airing and he would come back covered in smuts. At first Douglas, her husband, did not want to go to the country 'to pander to cabbages'. But eventually he was moved to a laboratory of the Lister Institute near Elstree. So all through the war they lived nearby at South Mimms in still-rural Herefordshire – in a house which, as it turned out, lay directly in the flight-path of the German bombers.

At the beginning of the First World War I had been doing art at Reading University. The whole place was taken over by the Army Air Corps. Just officers. All these marvellous uniforms and splendid men, some of them. They were not allowed to fraternise with us, and we were not allowed to fraternise with them, but it was still a very glamorous kind of environment.

All the same I wanted to live in London, so I sold my bicycle, which just bought my railway fare. Mother had told me the facts of life, which I refused to believe. She also frightened me about white slavery, which I knew meant abducting young women and sending them to brothels or something. So when I got to London I was feeling, oh my God, I shall be in the middle of the white slave traffic.

I decided that the only safe place to go and live was the YWCA in Baker Street, which I did. Well they hadn't got room for me, but they found me a room in a house nearby where this woman took a fancy to me. She used to take me out every evening, walking up and down Baker Street. I thought this is funny, the same place all the time. And why does she suddenly disappear? Well, she was obviously a harlot, and using me as a decoy. So that was the YWCA.

The war enabled me to run away from home and I was also fighting against being like my mother. She was a woman who could never show affection. I never sat on her knee, she never read to me, I don't remember her kissing me, she never came to say goodnight to me, she just nagged at me. But she was amusing and beautiful. A lady of great courage and independence, and she brought up three young children with no free health service, no free education.

I don't know, to this day, why my mother nagged me, but when she was dying – and I didn't think she was conscious – she said, 'You were such a dear little girl, and I did so go on at you.' They were her last words, so it's true.

The principal of Reading University found a job for me in the Ministry of Food, where I was employed to add up the statistics on how much meat the country was eating per week. I can't imagine how I was given the job because I couldn't even add. Well, eventually, or rather soon actually – as soon as the figures were published – it was discovered that these statistics didn't hold water.

They decided they didn't want to sack me. I kept people amused. So they put me on to the map department, and I had to fill in counties in different colours. For some extraordinary reason, although I was an artist, I could not keep the colours within these little tiny sections. So they found a typist who could do it far better than me.

I was kept on with nothing to do (as contributing to the Morale in Wartime) and was rather bored. I really wasn't earning my keep. What was I doing? So, I joined the Land Army. Not for patriotic reasons, because I was a pacifist, but because I wanted to have a horse.

I was crazy about horses, a lot of youngsters are. I couldn't bear hoeing vegetables but by registering with the Land Army I was able to become a carter to a market gardener at Barnes – an enormous area, acres of it, just beyond Hammersmith. Every night somebody on the farm had to drive up at midnight to Covent Garden. My turn was once a week.

I was supposed to get there just before five o'clock in the morning, but I was

Working on the land in World War I, drawn by Kathleen Hale.

usually a bit late because things happened on the way. At one point, at Hyde Park Corner, Prince and I jack-knifed the wagon. Fortunately there was a coffee stall there, with people always lounging around it, and somehow they managed to straighten the wagon. The horse was used to being given a bun there – though I didn't know this at the time – and he just decided to cross over the pavement to the stall. That's how the thing jack-knifed.

Another time, drunken young men in top hats and evening shirts climbed on to the wagon and tried to make love to me. I had to push them off. Then there were drunken soldiers about. Those I encountered when I was sleeping on the sacks in the porch of a church in Covent Garden. Once I found a soldier getting on top of me. But the thing to do is laugh, you know. That withers everything.

You were completely in charge of your horse. And I didn't realise what was happening for quite a time. Prince got rather thin. Then somebody told me what old Bodger was up to. Bodger was the old one-eyed ex-soldier who had a horse in the stable next to mine. He was getting up before I did, and stealing some of my horse's ration. He was an old rascal. Anyway, it worked out all right. When I knew, I got up even earlier.

I learned to plough. When I was told to plough, first I thought, what on earth do I do? Then I remembered somebody saying that if you can see the trace of the previous furrow go straight beside that and you will be all right. So I did, but it was a very old-fashioned, heavy wooden plough, which all the people on the farm called the 'man-killer'. I soon learned why when it turned and knocked me over at each turn. I was terrified the other workers would see me, so I scrambled to my feet and continued. This went on all the time, and in the end I couldn't use it.

The Land Army supplied an awful uniform. Do you remember footballers wearing long shorts to their knees, how drab, how awful they looked? Well our uniform wasn't cut short at the knee, but it had that same sort of dreariness. A sort of khaki overall and puttees, a word which nowadays nobody understands. And we had a badge, and some awful kind of felt hat with no shape. But a cousin of mine had a pair of riding breeches with smart suede knee patches and they fitted me. So when I was off duty I used to go up to London and dance at the Berkeley and places like that in my chic uniform.

The first time I was taken to the Berkeley hotel, they wouldn't let me in. A chap I was with, a Scottie wearing tartan trews, made a fuss. 'You let me in, so let her in. She's in uniform like all the services.' They did at last, and of course I was much admired for my patriotic war work.

We all loved dancing; very few didn't. There was dancing all the time. The men coming back from the trenches on a week's leave, they wanted to do everything. There were plenty of girls around. Before the war you had to get to know the family before you knew the girl. Now all the girls, the munition workers and everybody were all around at dances. There were hysterical attachments made, people got married on the spot. People went to bed together, and the girl was branded if she had an illegitimate child. But it wasn't the climate for serious, knowledgeable relationships. I enjoyed it so much but I was so ignorant, and innocent and po-faced that friends nicknamed me the curate.

When the Armistice was declared I was absolutely devastated rather than in party mood, thinking of all the past carnage, the horror of the trenches, the misery of the war. We had stifled this feeling but it was there all the time we danced.

I was on the farm that day. Everybody else went up to London for the celebrations. Nobody thought about me. I had a load of parsley in a tip-up cart, and the men who were on duty jokingly pulled the pin out, and tipped me and the soft parsley on to the ground. And that was for celebration. But I was absolutely in tears, over the four years of nightmare, the reality of the war.

In the Second World War I was like everybody else with a family. The whole time I felt a basic thread of anxiety. You couldn't get away from it. It was an awful strain wondering when and if ever the bombing and killing and destruction would stop. The daily anxiety of whether husband and children would come home unharmed from work and school.

Kathleen's sons Nicholas, 6, and Peregrine, 9 – the undersized home guard – with their Uncle Julek.

I tried to distract my sons, Nicholas aged six and Peregrine aged nine, from fear of the war they were to experience; I made imitation khaki uniforms for them and rigged them out with tin helmets and toy rifles. After school they would ambush and parade and present arms in the lanes and fields around us. A neighbour remarked to his wife one day what an undersized lot our Home Guard was. She replied, 'You soppy date, those are the McClean children.'

Douglas had no physical fear. He went up to London during the blitz to medical meetings and those of the Association of Scientific Workers where he much enjoyed arguing. He didn't understand how terrified I and the two boys were during the nights when the doodlebugs clattered and juddered low over our roof – waiting for the dreaded moment when the engines stopped, meaning that the 'bug' would fall. Night after night, for I forget how many months, we trembled in our beds.

Douglas refused to have an air-raid shelter built and said if we had to die it would be in our beds. Our local aircraft guns were positioned on a slight rise above us and shrapnel fell day and night when they tried to shoot down the enemy planes. Our two large lawns were studded with jagged pieces of shrapnel – impossible to use the lawn mower. Oddly, none of the windows were ever broken but a few round little holes pierced the glass. One bomb fell in the lane fairly

Kathleen with 'Orlando' c. 1939.

near us, and Marguerite, our plump Austrian au pair, was lifted from her arm-chair and neatly set down in the same place. It left a small crater in the lane, which enthralled Peregrine and Nicholas. And all night a snow of ceiling plaster fell gently on us in bed.

The first V2 fell into ploughed land about a field away. It was about seven p.m. and suddenly we felt our house gently swaying like the gardens of Babylon and we stood at the open front door scouring the sky and landscape for the cause. Then came a breathtaking WHOOSH!! followed immediately by a huge explosion. The whoosh was the air torn aside by this new invention of Hitler's as it fell faster than sound. Miraculously the twenty Land Army girls who were lodged in a large house near the crater were having their supper in the basement. They were totally unharmed but their bedrooms were smashed, the bedding and their clothes, the rugs – everything they owned was destroyed by splinters of glass.

After the war, we were among the first to be visited by the repair brigade. We only needed two or three window-panes replaced. Since I knew that less well-off people had had roofs blown off, walls reduced to rubble, I was furious that we should be given priority.

Douglas's sister's husband Julek was borough engineer during the war and in charge of public safety, and from time to time he'd come to us for a night's rest. Once I noticed a strange metal object in a bucket of sand among our cabbages, and while Julek slept on, Douglas went out to look closer and realised it was a live bomb. Julek had brought it to show Peregrine and Nicholas, and then he took it back to London by Underground in a paper carrier bag to have it defused.

We were swamped during the blitz by friends coming for weekends for peace and quiet, but since we were on the return route to Germany over Hertfordshire and Kent, enemy planes often jettisoned their unused bombs. Our friends were terrified of our vulnerability, since we had no air-raid shelter. They also had to sleep on floors, sofas and armchairs, since all the beds were commandeered by the first-comers, and there was a thinning out of these unhappy visitors, for they preferred to stay in London.

Antonia White (who wrote *Frost in May*) came to live with us for about ten months, but we weren't up to her fine and original brain and she moved to a more intellectual milieu. When she came she was suffering acutely from writer's block and I was paralysed by a similar painter's block. So I decided instead of she moping in her bedroom, and myself twisting with guilt in my studio, we had better try and write and paint then meet for elevenses and tell each other what we had managed to produce. This did actually work, for Antonia wrote a film script, which alas was not used, but I sold some paintings.

A five-year-old niece came to live with us for shelter for a while. I found it fascinating but a little frightening to live with a little girl – she was so different from a boy, very gentle and feminine, while P and N were always rather macho. She called me 'Mother', as did my sons, and now, having reached retiring age from work, she still writes to me as Mother. It's just because she got into the habit, but I do like it.

On Douglas's twice-weekly visits to London for his meetings during the blitz he always arrived home in a hurry to reach the bathroom and get out the chloroform bottle and cotton wool. Then he would pull down his trousers and dab himself from thigh to toe, killing the fleas which he always caught travelling on the tube. Head lice and fleas were part of wartime conditions. Only when this ritual was completed did Douglas relax into an armchair with a glass of his favourite Glenlivet whiskey and the *New Statesman*.

Douglas bought two bee skeps and filled them with bees, beekeepers being allowed extra rations of sugar to feed bees. But we used the sugar to augment our meagre ration, and fed them some of their honey instead, so we were all pleased.

The bees hated me, and were positioned near the path to my studio, but they loved Douglas. He handled them without wearing gloves and was never stung, though he did look odd in a thick black veil draped over an old straw hat. Whereas I wore leather gloves lined with fur, and the bees clustered on them, trying to penetrate. I had to creep into my studio in secrecy and haste and shut the door against the alerted creatures.

There was an American hospital for wounded soldiers quite near to us and the British Council asked me if I would go and teach the ambulatory soldiers how to draw. I said, yes of course, how many will there be? There might be a dozen or so, they thought. I asked them would they supply drawing boards, rubbers, pencils, bulldog clips. No, they told me, I'd have to do that. Well, I wasn't very well off, and it would have been endless, what I had to buy and constantly replace. So I decided I would do drawings of the men, which they could fold up into an envelope and send to Mum. Of course they loved that. I think I really did the best drawings of my life.

I had a little case there open with my drawing materials and a bar of chocolate would appear, or a packet of fags or something. To begin with they were very suspicious of me; they said, 'What have we got to pay you?' I said, 'Nothing, it's the British Council, it's for free.' That was awkward for them. They couldn't understand that anybody would do anything for nothing.

There was a limit to the concentration I could manage. I would do about fifteen drawings in a long morning. Then, when the moment came and I couldn't do any more, I used to just go round and talk to some patients who were stuck in their beds. I got very involved with the whole set-up.

They were mostly wounded American soldiers from France. But when the prisoner-of-war camps were liberated by the Americans, we had a few English as well. Some were skeletons, literally. They couldn't even hold a newspaper up to read it, they hadn't the strength. Some of them couldn't bear the weight of the sheet on them. Within ten days or a fortnight – unrecognisable! They'd come up and say, 'You don't know me?' Then they'd tell me who they were and I'd realise, they had been these skeletons.

There was one man who couldn't move at all, and he asked me through the nurse, would I do a drawing of him? Do you know, I simply couldn't. I think it was very wrong of me, but he wanted to send it to his parents, and I thought, what are they going to feel? I didn't want to draw him. I was too upset. My tears were blinding me so I didn't do it. And he was not interested in having a drawing done a couple of weeks later when he was fatter and looking almost normal.

My drawing them was one of the ramifications of the war. There were all sorts of societies doing things for soldiers, and this, I suppose, was a 'how to keep convalescent soldiers happy' one. It was a good move, because it was very popular in the end, although none of them thought they looked like my drawings of them. Nobody does when they're really drawn. One time I'd been drawing some children – I made my living that way – and the parents were horrified. They saw their children as quite unlike what they really were. And there was a friend of mine who had a Siamese cat, one of the first Siamese to come to England, and he thought it was the most wonderful cat in the world. In fact it was one of those with a very long snout and a very strong squint. It was not a pretty cat. When I did it, of course, my friend just tore the drawing up.

However, when the war ended, I was rewarded by a letter from the British Council, which said that my work had been an 'unqualified success'.

Kathleen Hale's autobiography is *A Slender Reputation* (Frederick Warne, 1994).

WOMEN'S · ROYAL · NAVAL · SERVICE

join the
Wrens

AND · FREE · A · MAN · FOR · THE · FLEET

APPLY TO DIRECTOR W.R.N.S. ADMIRALTY S.W.I.
OR THE NEAREST EMPLOYMENT EXCHANGE

PEGGY HILL
Wartime Bride

The bravest part of Peggy Hill's war was facing the bombardment of the home front when she told her parents that she would have to leave her husband because she loved another man.

This was truly shocking news to them. How can we face our friends? … Do you know what you're doing to your father? … Have you no consideration for your mother?

In middle-class Britain in mid-century, breaking off a marriage still created shock waves which travelled far beyond the couple and their immediate family. You had to have lived through those times to appreciate the extent of the scandal it created.

This was doubly so during the war if the jilted partner was someone in the forces away fighting for his King and Country. And yet wartime was a breeding ground for hasty romantic marriages. Bride and groom hardly knew each other before he'd be posted away and they'd be parted for the duration of the war. Separately they'd grow up – often out of all recognition to each other.

It was a hot day and all the windows were open and someone had the radio on, and I remember standing still in the middle of a field behind some houses on my own and hearing the announcement that we were now at war with Germany. I didn't know what to think about it at all. It seemed an enormous thing to take in. I felt quite stunned.

I didn't at that moment cast my eye up in the sky in case the bombers were coming over. But everybody started doing that as soon as it had sunk in.

The LDV – the Local Defence Volunteers, which became the Home Guard – were very soon to be seen marching up the Mumbles Road on one of their practices in case there was an invasion. The warning – in Caswell Bay in South Wales where I lived anyway, I don't know whether they did it all over the country – was to bang your dustbin lid.

The officer in charge leading the Home Guard was a neighbour of ours. He was very short and very pompous with a little moustache, and it was just like *Dad's Army*, the way they used to march. It just tickled everybody in the Mumbles train as it passed by. But of course they didn't show they were laughing!

At this time I was still working as a shorthand typist in a shipping office in Swansea. I was bored. Not by being a shorthand typist – I actually enjoyed that and I think I was quite good at it – but the shipping office was being wound down, so it wasn't very interesting.

A friend working at the naval base was leaving because her husband was being sent to Ireland and she said to me, 'Why don't you try for my job?' She'd speak to the captain, which she did, and the following day he rang up. He said he'd like me to work for him but I'd have to join the WRNS. So I just said, OK and I went along a week later to the enrolment office.

I had a medical and a few days later I signed on. It was all very informal at the beginning because they were so pleased to see you. They weren't getting many people. I don't think the idea of joining up, or the war, had sunk in. It came on gradually.

I thought the WRNS was the smartest of the uniforms. Navy suit, jacket and skirt, black tie and a white shirt with very stiff collars which we used to take to the Chinese laundry in Swansea. After spitting on the iron to make sure it was hot enough, they used to get them so stiff that they cut your neck. There were standards to keep up, definitely. I don't remember seeing a scruffy Wren. It was a matter of pride.

Thick stockings at first. Lisle, which I refused to wear. Later on we got nylons from the Americans, and I think we eventually used to get our stockings from the stores. Then they were silk.

We earned about three pounds, with a small rise on becoming a leading Wren, which considering we had our uniform supplied and our shoes wasn't bad. And I lived at home of course. My mother and father were surprised I had joined up. I had no feeling of patriotism myself and I don't think they did at that time.

But it did give me my first taste of freedom. You were always on duty, so you were always away from home. You felt free in a different way from going to the office every day. You were in the Wrens and that sort of became an excuse for being out, half the night and the day. Before this I'd had to account for everything – where I was going, who with, and what time would I be home? You just didn't really think about it until you had a chance to be much freer.

My reason for going to church was not for any religious reason, I must admit. It was just to meet friends – and the boys. We'd go off somewhere afterwards, a lot of us together. Walks after church, out on to the pier. It was a good excuse. It was so respectable. I met R., my first husband, in this crowd – when I was about sixteen. We met so often but we were always with someone else. He was a year older than me and was called up when he was about twenty at the beginning of the war. And we married on 2 September 1940, when I was nineteen.

I was very naïve. Immature and inexperienced. The war must have added a more romantic feeling to everything. And probably pushed people, gave them a greater opportunity to get married. Normally people were engaged for years. But the war influenced everybody – there were a lot of rushed marriages in the war – and parents probably agreed whereas they wouldn't have done at any other time.

We got married in church and then went home to lunch with our families and one or two friends. And R. was sent abroad to North Africa shortly after that and soon became a captain in the Royal Signals. There was no thought that I could go with him.

We wrote to each other and just got on with our work. One thing I volunteered to do was rifle training. We used to go shooting in the rifle range on the docks one morning a week. I was quite a good shot. It was like playing darts, I thought! And I didn't give it a thought that there might be a person at the other end.

All of us – about fifty Wrens on the base – had to do drill every morning, just marching round the docks. My friend Sheila and I hated it and devised a way of getting out of it. We used to get ourselves at the back of the parade. At the naval gates, there were lorries between the naval base and our old office, and instead of turning left and marching correctly in to the docks, we used to do a right turn and scoot off, straight into the office. We were never missed.

On Saturdays we had to go on marches to the villages around Swansea and up the valleys, to raise money for the Benevolent Fund. We raised a lot, for the people in the villages were generous. They were very enthusiastic and used to turn out even when it was pouring with rain. Often we'd go back home on the train with water running off us. We weren't allowed to wear our overcoats on the parades for some reason. But the people made such a lot of us, we felt it was worth it. And you couldn't help feeling proud of being in the Wrens.

We had to attend the gas drills too. Our forces' gas masks were more complicated than the kind the civilians were issued with. I think we only tried the equipment on once or twice. They were a bit of a joke. We kept them in a proper forces' canvas bag but I do know that lots of the officers kept their pyjamas in it.

I was on a gas course at Portsmouth when Sheila rang up and told me that this smashing new officer had just arrived. And I thought she meant for her, you know, because she was so keen. But she said, 'He's just right for you, Peg,' which I could hardly believe she had said. I couldn't understand her saying it and with such force.

I was back in the office on the Monday and I was so bowled over. I really was. It was a totally different experience altogether. Something I had never experienced with R. With R. it was more like growing up together and then marrying because of the war.

I was still living at home, and one evening after working late at the base I was waiting with Geoff for the Mumbles train when I spotted a neighbour from Caswell. I knew then that I'd had it – she wouldn't waste any time letting my parents know.

So a few days later, when we were walking the dog across the cliffs, I broke the news to my father. At first he said nothing – but his look was enough and we walked back in stony silence to tell my mother. I expected them both to be very upset. Not that they were so fond of R. In fact when we got engaged they both told me afterwards that they'd always thought I would have 'done better'. But I was, after all, now in my early twenties, and was quite unprepared for the weeks of devastating rows that followed, and the feeling at home of complete isolation. What got to my parents most was what the next-door neighbours would say. What their friends were thinking.

The atmosphere at home was very bad. The only one talking to me was my brother, and of course Geoff wasn't allowed near the place. It nearly drove me into a nervous breakdown. I lost most of my self-confidence and was afraid to go into a restaurant or do anything like that on my own.

Shortly after all this R. came home on leave unexpectedly one night. By that time I hardly cared what happened, and I just told him. I remember feeling that maybe R. was relieved – or had also met someone else, or perhaps had also regretted marrying so early. His reaction was so quiet after all the previous upheaval. He left and went down to his parents, who lived locally, and I think his father said, 'What did I tell you?'

Once I got to work it was all right. All my friends were behind me. It was like going into another world. I would have known if there had been anyone who disapproved but absolutely no one did. And my friend Sheila's mother and father liked Geoff a lot, so we could go to their house and were completely accepted. That was a haven like the office.

Geoff worried about me very much. But once we were in the office we were safe. And I liked working for him. He was always very kind. And just considerate in every way to work for.

Wrens at the Swansea naval base, 1942 (Peggy 5th from right, front row).

The end of the war was a blow in lots of ways. I think everybody felt the same. Although it sounds an awful thing to say, anybody who was in the services said that they'd had such a good time, that the end was awful from that angle. It was like coming back to earth again. You missed the people on the naval base. You missed that kind of life where there was always someone around. It was the end of a completely different way of living. I think this missing went on for years. It took quite a long time to settle down and back to family life.

Geoff was moved to Liverpool and I had to stay on until the office was closed down and I was out of the WRNS. Then I joined him and stayed in his digs until he was moved to Egypt. When he left I moved back home for the winter, still to a cool reception from my parents, but they did come round when I said I was going out to Egypt. I think that was a relief, because I would be out of sight.

I was able to join Geoff in Egypt in 1946 for they only had one English-speaking secretary out there. I went out to be his and the commodore's secretary. And I had a whale of a time. In the commodore's office the social life was good. We went to parties and stuff like that. It was mostly men in the office. They knew Geoff and I were together and not married, but they didn't take any notice of that. And by now I was much stronger and more self-confident. I'd already

A new lease of war-life in Egypt.

gone out to Egypt on my own on a troop ship and sat at the captain's table. I was glad to leave it all behind – the country and everything else – and go to a complete change.

We lived with a Greek family and they completely accepted us. They did all the cooking so I didn't have to be the least bit domesticated. We were there for eighteen months and then we returned to England as Geoff had decided to leave the Navy; and we married that year and had to come down to earth.

The war was more an experience of life, of growing up. It gave you that freedom you'd never known, to be yourself. And I think that makes you what you are in the future, too. I suppose you thought for yourself for the first time in your life.

The confidence I gained in the war seemed to last when I went back to work after my two sons had gone to school. I was a librarian for a while; then a receptionist for two doctors with 2,000 patients. It wasn't organised like today. You had to do absolutely everything. I even did tests for diabetes. I only left there when I had to work for Geoff. His chiropody practice in our home was getting too busy and he couldn't manage the reception work as well.

So we were back again living and working together, which we did for forty-two years until he died in 1989.

I remember being surprised and pleased when we were selling a flat at one time, and the young estate agent who was taking down the details from us observed, 'God, you two are close, aren't you? You only just have to look at each other …'

After our divorce, R. married 'the girl next door', with whom he had kept in touch throughout the war. And in the end Geoff and my father became good friends. But I don't think my mother ever forgave him.

Molly Weir, fastest shorthand typist in the West!

MOLLY WEIR
Quick as a Flash

A month after war was declared Molly Weir married Sandy, her Glasgow childhood sweetheart. He had volunteered for the Royal Air Force, had been accepted in the photographic section, and was away. Molly was working in an office. In those days, if there hadn't been a war, a girl like Molly would automatically have given up her job (or been asked to give it up as a married woman) and she would have assumed her rightful place, as all good housewives did, at the kitchen sink.

Instead, the war enabled her to work full time in the typing pool of a munitions factory. Molly had demonstrated she was the fastest shorthand writer in Britain (maybe in the world, she added modestly!). In the lunch hours she startled the factory workers by mounting a 'Workers' Playtime' doing the entire bill with the help of a great friend, Mary.

And she learned German in case, as she put it, 'a German paratrooper landed in my garden. I wanted to know what he was saying. And I always kept a pepper pot so that I could throw pepper in his eyes if I had to.'

It was about this period, too, that her radio career – working with Gordon Jackson, Janet Brown and others in Glasgow – started to take off.

In Molly's case these activities did not stop with the war. She became a household voice with the long-running radio and television series Life with the Lyons; *a household face with equally long-running TV series like* Dr Finlay's Casebook, All Creatures Great and Small *and* Within These Walls, *and her advertisements for Flash; as well as a household name with her books. She's in the* Guinness Book of Records *as the person who has written the greatest number of autobiographical words.*

As an actress she has a fine sense of the drama of war, and as a comedian Molly Weir can recall some of its black humour.

I can still remember sitting on the floor listening to the wireless, and Chamberlain's voice telling us that war in Europe had begun because Hitler had not replied to the ultimatum. A terrible cold feeling came over me, and the next thing it seemed we were all getting measured for gas masks. Now I'm claustrophobic, and the very idea of putting a gas mask on was out of the question. I instructed my mother that if the Germans dropped gas, she was to put my head in the oven. I'd prefer a quick death by the ordinary gas we paid for than with that horrible mustard stuff.

I had a cold feeling of inevitability about the war. I've always been very aware of everything around about me, and I never trusted that man Hitler for one moment. We used to go to the pictures and see him doing his ranting and raving speeches – in front of all those thousands and thousands of young men raring to go.

We were always seeing him and Mussolini on the newsreels. Now for some reason we found Mussolini funny. My mother always called him Musseloni. My mother was the original Mrs Malaprop. I wasn't so frightened of him, but I was genuinely frightened of Hitler. More so perhaps because I had been to Germany the year before war was declared. My boyfriend Sandy and I had decided on a walking holiday there because I'd taken some German lessons and I found I had a good ear for the language.

I was eighteen in 1939 and working as a shorthand typist in an office. I was lucky to have this job. If my mother had had her way I'd have left school early and been in the Co-operative offices sitting behind a mahogany desk in a nice white blouse so she could get an extra dividend on our purchases, twopence in the shilling. But my teacher at school – she was a darling – said I could do better than that, and saw that I sat a test which got me a scholarship to college, which was great. I couldn't have gone otherwise as my mother was a very young widow with three fatherless children. She couldn't have afforded to buy the shoes and the dress and things like that which I needed for college.

To decide whether or not I was eligible for this scholarship, the board gave me a bit of what they considered really hard mental arithmetic. Well, I had always done the shopping for my granny, and I could add figures upside down, and it turned out I was the only child who was able to do this exercise. So I got the grant. At the age of fourteen!

I saw some great big girls of seventeen and eighteen when I arrived on the first morning at college and thought they were all schoolteachers. Anyway I left college at fifteen the next year with a bronze medal for shorthand and a gold medal as the best student. And I won twenty guineas in cash prizes for having over 90 per cent in all the subjects.

My mother just couldn't imagine that this changeling was so academically eager. You know, nowadays children are all encouraged. My mother didn't discourage me exactly, but she'd say, 'Away out and play, and don't be sitting at that table writing away all night. Go out and get some fresh air.'

I only knew two things: I wanted to write shorthand, and I wanted to be an actress. I'd always been performing. The very first thing I ever did when the organ broke down in the pictures, and they asked for volunteers, was to toddle up and recite a very vulgar – I'm not going to tell you what it is – a very vulgar wee poem somebody had told me. My brothers were absolutely furious, because, they said, 'Our Molly was up there on the stage and everybody was laughing at her.'

And then another time they asked for volunteers to get up and dance at the Rechabite [total abstainers] concert, and I did the Highland fling. It was like a striptease. I was about nine at the time, and I took off my granny's beads first of all. They were her amber beads down to my waist, and then I took off my cardigan, and then I took off my tammy, and the audience by this time were in hysterics, and then I launched into the Highland fling and nearly fell off the platform.

Meanwhile, the whole tenement life in Glasgow had a tremendous fascination for me. I saw all the young newly married girls coming to live in our tenements and putting their pots up on the shelves and we'd be sitting up on the windowsill looking in. And when they had babies, I'd ask to take their babies out – in shawls in those days, for there were no prams.

And yet I didn't want to be a wife and mother – even though I didn't even know there were careers at that time. What I wanted to do was write shorthand, and type – oh, when I was given a typewriter in college, to sit there and type was marvellous. I was second in typing and first in shorthand in all the championships. There was one girl, Lily Monroe, she was better than I was at typing. She always beat me by three or four words. But in shorthand I was way out in front, the Derby winner. I wanted that, but I also wanted to act.

Sandy and I had decided we would get married straight away when the war began. He was working in a shipping office, which was a reserved occupation, but he wanted to do something directly for the war. Being a good photographer, he got into the RAF photographic section. So he was away. And then I was directed to war work.

I might have joined ENSA but my mother said I was not going away with all those airmen and soldiers and sailors. She was dead against it. And I thought, well, actors are ten a penny, but I'm the only person in Britain who can write 300 words a minute, so perhaps I can beat Hitler with this. I was directed into this factory making what they called fragmentation bombs. I was proud to be there for I was very patriotic and never had any doubt that we'd win.

I visualised us as the good ones, and the Germans and the Italians and the Japs as the bad ones. It was as simple as that. I knew pals of my brothers who were being killed and wounded, and eventually a lot who ended up in prisoner-of-war camps. The funny thing is that I wasn't conscious of feeling terribly sad or worried about Sandy being in the war. There was a kind of inevitability about it. Everybody's husband or son or sweetheart was away. Apart from conscientious objectors, everybody who was of military age was called up at some time. It was a fact of life.

We kept in constant touch through letters. We used to laugh like anything, because the one thing I took with me when I left my first office was my typewriter. That was because I wanted to be a writer. I had to buy it, and I was very incensed because I had kept it in such immaculate condition that they wouldn't even give me a reduced price. They'd only sell it at the full market price, fifteen pounds. Anyway, on my two pounds a week I managed to save the money. It was my own lovely typewriter, and I had to have it.

I used to type all my letters to Sandy, on great big foolscap sheets, single spacing, telling him everything I had done. And when he got them, the boys would look over his shoulder and say, 'Are those our DROs?' (Daily Regulation Orders)!

Sandy didn't write as often to me, of course, because he was all over the place, in Cyprus and Palestine, and troop movements were very secret.

Thinking about it, I realise that the war sort of suited my temperament. Rationing didn't bother me too much. I was young enough and I didn't see any sense in hating things – except the fact that the Londoners took all our leeks and onions, because we could grow them better up in Scotland, and never sent any back to us. And I liked an onion to savour the food.

I had the advantage that my granny brought me up to be a good, plain cook. I used to lie in bed as a wee tot and watch what she was doing. Then she allowed me to put seasoning into the soup, then into the stews, then to mix the cornflour with cold water, and make the gravy, and chop up the vegetables. So, cooking was second nature to me and I was also very economical. According to my mother, granny was so thrifty she'd skin a flea. But you know, we wasted nothing, we couldn't afford to. I used to invite one of the girls from the factory up, every week, for lunch. And they'd say, 'How is it that you've only got one ration book, and you can always give us a meal?' But I managed because I'd been very disciplined all my life. I still am.

I loved butter and at the very most we only got two ounces a week, but I divided that out, to last the week. I would rather have, as my granny would call it, a wee scant of butter every day than eat a whole lot in two days and have dry bread or margarine for the rest.

Tiny Molly was always smartly turned out because she could be so 'easily covered'.

I managed even without the black market. The only extras I ever got was when Sandy was doing his training up in the north of Scotland. He was with this Australian airman who knew all the angles. He taught Sandy to go around the farms and say, 'I'm an Australian airman, ma'am. Can you spare anything for me? I've come 12,000 miles.' And of course they would give him an egg at one farm, and two eggs at another. And Sandy bought a lined box, which is up in our loft to this day, and put in twelve eggs and posted them to me. Do you know, not one was ever cracked. I loved eggs and if you're living by yourself, an egg can go an awful long way.

Do you remember dried eggs? My brother-in-law used to say I was the best person for transforming a dried egg into something quite resembling fresh eggs. I blended it carefully, and I beat it up with a fork, and I saved a little bit of proper good fat to do it in. Then I stood over it and got the heating just right. It was quite a good omelette. If you just mixed that powdered egg with water it smelt dreadful, and tasted worse.

Granny's tips came in handy for making soup with bones. You boiled up the bones – ham bones or shin of beef – and then you long, slow simmered them. And I could make wee moulds of potted hough, just with simmering the bones for a long long time, and adding the shin of beef towards the end, which formed a natural jelly. I do the same today.

I was very lucky about my clothes too. I taught a wee girl around the corner to write shorthand, because I felt that she had possibilities. Her mother was a widow, and she happened to be a very good dressmaker. I used to buy wee remnants of cloth, and she made them up into blouses and bits of skirts and dresses. And because I was very small I was easily covered. I remember somebody saying, when I was at college, 'Molly Weir must be very well-to-do, because my daughter says she's always very well dressed.'

The thing I really did hate about the war was the blackout. I felt that when the dim-out came and we would get a few lights, the war was over. When I went to bed at night I couldn't bear the blackout blind being down all night, and I used to put the light out and then let the blind up, and I used to do my little mantra before I went to sleep: 'When the sirens go off, don't put on a light. When the sirens go off, don't put on a light.' And I never did.

But in the blackout there was nothing like the lack of safety you feel today. There was only one time a man followed me, and I walked straight into a police station. 'Right, then, we'll come back with you,' they said. And by then the man had vanished. When things are reduced to a very tiny piece of security – when you don't know whether you're going to be alive the next morning – it gives you a wonderful sense of balance. One time during the Clydeside blitz, I had arranged to meet my mother in town for coffee but couldn't get there. I didn't know where she was or if she survived. I was in my brother's shelter all night long with flames all round us. And the worst part was not the sound of the bombs, it was the sound of the gunfire, the anti-aircraft firing. When we went indoors, the whole house shook and was lifted up.

When I stayed at my mother-in-law's she and I crouched under the table for I wouldn't go in the cupboard under the stairs. She was a wee fat soul, my mother-in-law, and she'd get cramp. I'd tell her to straighten her leg, between giggles. She'd say, 'Dinna laugh, dinna laugh' and we'd end up in hysterics. And sometimes the raids would go on all night and in the morning there were great big craters in the road. There was no transport, so they sent the soldiers in lorries to pick us up.

My mother loved contributing to the war effort. She liked being part of it and she looked the part in her turban and wee suit of dungarees. She loved, above all things, listening to Churchill – and even though she was pretty deaf his voice got through to her: 'Here he comes. The British bulldog. By God he puts new life into you.' I absolutely adored Churchill too. He was the only one who had got the measure of Hitler. I never met anyone with a word of criticism for him. We loved his deliberate mispronunciations like *Nar-zees* for Nazis. He could touch the soul and heart of a nation. I don't think we'd have won with anyone else.

The only certainty you had in the war was this moment. And consequently, petty personal enmities didn't come into it. You could have left your doors open, for nobody would have stolen from you. Mind you, we were very hot at making sure we got our just deserts. When women were buying potatoes they demanded that the greengrocer knocked off all the clay before he weighed them, because it all mattered.

There was not a lot of money around. The highest wage I got was three pounds seven and sixpence a week, and ten bob from the government for my husband. The funny thing was that you calmly accepted that the country was spending thousands on munitions, but just as long as you were safe you were not expecting to pile up your own cash. Women were now working in the factory since most men had been called up. And since they'd never earned money in their lives, they were delighted to get any sort of wages. And I can truthfully say, during those war years it was a very much more contented society.

A lot of women provided what they called 'dilutee labour'. There was a sort of foreman in charge, and all these married women were on a kind of conveyor belt. Not quite that, but each was taught to perform certain very basic movements with the machinery, then they'd move the work on to the next stage. Young women were anxious to get this work, but they were always refused once it was known that they had young children. The welfare officer wouldn't take them on, because what would happen if one of their children was ill? They'd stay home and break the factory line and then down would go production. It was like being in a chorus line. Nobody could be out of step.

It's a terrible thing to say, but the war came at the right time for me. Because as well as my job, I was doing amateur concerts and getting noticed and then I was asked to do some broadcasting. Gordon Jackson, Janet Brown and I, we all started together, and when London was being bombed, the BBC would ring us up, either at home or where we worked, and say come straight up to the Broadcasting House as soon as you can. When we finished work at half-past five we'd queue up for the tram car – there was no such thing as taxis – and get up to the BBC. Gordon Jackson used to say, 'Molly, you have a fantastic ability to act straight from the script.' I was used to this from my shorthand demonstration days. Sometimes the script was really coming hot off the duplicator, and we were doing it live into the microphone.

Gordon and I were the young lovers in many a play, and he was always getting into trouble because he couldn't look at me without laughing. The producer would say, 'Gordon Jackson, if you can't look at Miss Weir without laughing, stand behind her where you can't see her.'

Then London came up with a play, *It Depends What You Mean*, with a part for me in it. I was the right age, right size, and the right cheeky thing for this comedy part. I went home, packed my trunk, and was all ready to go to London. Then next morning, as I was walking through the factory, taking the dirty teacups back to be washed, Eisenhower's voice came over the Tannoy: 'This morning at 8a.m., the second front in Europe was opened.' A telegram awaited me at home: HOLD EVERYTHING. NO TRANSPORT. STAY TILL YOU HEAR FROM US. And that was the end of my big chance in London. Did you ever know that for a piece of timing? Had I been older and more experienced, I would probably just have gone, and said I never got the telegram. But I was far too innocent and inexperienced, and wasn't used to dissembling. I just accepted it – rather as I accepted everything in the war. I said well, it wasn't meant to be. I went back and unpacked my trunk, got my typewriter out again, and stayed where I was.

But I did lots of amateur concerts during that time. I did all my impersonations – Gracie Fields, Dietrich and her 'Falling in Love Again'. All the sailors would say to me afterwards, 'You were just looking at me when you sang that, weren't you?' And I'd say, 'Oh yes!' I couldn't hurt their feelings and I was immensely flattered.

I was also smart enough to dress up for the part, for they hadn't seen any females for goodness knows how long. I was in black lace and velvet, my hair all piled up. I mean I was a cheeky little monkey. But only in a professional way. I don't know whether many girls were more free and easy. For the first time nice respectable girls were going to dances by themselves, and it wasn't unknown for them to occasionally pick up somebody on the dance floor. But I was far too interested in rehearsing, and acting in shows, and going up to the BBC, and doing my factory job. Gordon and I worked together many times as sweethearts on the radio, but I don't believe we even thought of a chaste peck on the cheek! The Scots aren't a free and easy kissing race. Not until we were going up to London did we see people greet each other with a civilised kiss on the cheek.

And then, of course, there were the Americans. They had a reputation with some of the younger unmarried girls, it is true. But as far as I was concerned, they came to see our shows and I got bars of chocolate and I gave them to my mother. Some of them would be quite pleased to come home with other members of the cast and see a Scottish home, and have a cup of tea and bring us a packet of fags!

I started to smoke in the war. My mother used to say, 'I'm quite glad to see you smoke, because it makes you sit down for fifteen minutes.' I had to sit and smoke as if it was something terribly important. It was like a Japanese tea ceremony. A combination of things made me take up smoking. I have a very sweet tooth and there weren't enough coupons to get enough sweeties. I think a lot of us women took up smoking because we were always a wee bit hungry.

I remember going to a house one night to meet a woman with whom I was doing a number in a concert. She was there with her sister, and I'd been asked to have some tea. Of course I was looking at the pancakes, the jam and the butter, but when the woman I was to sing with passed me the butter, her sister snatched the little dish away: 'That's my butter. Give her yours. She's your guest!' I was shocked.

My husband's mother just never got used to rationing. As soon as her rations came she ate them. By the middle of the week she was putting sweeties in her tea, acid drops, anything, just to sweeten it. I never knew anybody, though, like her for making a jar of paste go so far. One of those wee jars, about four spoonfuls of paste in it, and she'd make about twelve big doorstep sandwiches with it. Since then, I always have more filling than I have bread. I think it's a hangover from all that hunger.

I had to leave my job because the factory closed down before the end of the war. Three of us were chosen to take an inventory of every single nut, bolt, screw, sheet of paper in the place. I did that for about two months, and we had a very nice letter back from the government saying it was the finest inventory they'd seen in the course of the entire war.

Now, I thought to myself, after all these good shows I've done in Glasgow, the revues and musical comedies, why don't I try for paid work in the theatre. So I wrote to Sandy, 'Can I have a shot at London before I settle down? Because you're not going to be back for ages.' And he said, 'Yes, get it out of your system before I come back.' He was very good. So off I went to London.

I had done a wee film in Glasgow just before I left. It was called *Birthday*, and was about a young girl – my part – whose husband was at war and who has to bring up their first baby in dirty old digs in Glasgow. The film producer was asked by a West End theatre producer if she knew of an actress who could play a funny part. She said, 'Well we've just done a film up in Glasgow, with a splendid wee comedienne. She was acting quite against type for us, but she had us all in tucks coming home in the bus.' The result was I got a telegram … PLEASE BE AT THE GLOBE THEATRE AT TEN O'CLOCK TOMORROW MORNING. And so I got the part in *A Play for Ronnie* – A.E. Matthews was in it – which was going on a fourteen-week tour. And after this they were casting *The Happiest Days of Your Life* and looking for an actress to play a schoolgirl of thirteen – one of those terrible cartoon characters with gym tunic and wild hair. Somebody asked A.E. Matthews about me: 'Molly Weir looks about eleven. And she's got a thick head of hair bobbing up and down,' he said. So thanks to that, I auditioned and got the part, which lasted two years.

Margaret Rutherford in the leading part was lovely, and we became absolutely close, close friends. When I was taken ill with flu, she brought eggs to my digs in Clapham, climbing a circular spiral staircase, three flights up, in her cape and with this little basket of three eggs which were still on rations. I always felt that she had the soul of a fairy, of a beautiful person. But she had very sad eyes, for when she looked in the mirror she couldn't believe in the reality. I think it was a physical surprise because the inner woman was so different. You know, delicate and angelic.

When Sandy came home, I was on tour with *A Play for Ronnie*, and he joined me in Liverpool. He hadn't seen me for three or four years, and of course the whole cast was so excited. Perhaps they were more excited than I was, because it all seemed terribly romantic to this older crowd. They lent me lovely crêpe de Chine things, undies, which I didn't want to take because I was frightened I'd spoil them when I ironed them. I just wore my utility horrors!

I was on the stage, in fact, when Sandy arrived, and he was standing in the wings when I came off. He said, 'You're awful wee.' And I said, 'You're not very big yourself.' And those were our first words to each other. And then Sandy came on the rest of the tour. It was terribly funny because, being so disciplined and organised, I had written in advance to the digs in the Equity address list to book for the whole fourteen weeks. Well Sandy joined me in the fourth or fifth week, so I had nine landladies to write to and tell them to make it a double room. And then I began to hope they wouldn't think I'd picked up an Air Force chap on the road, as they were all coming home at that time. Sometimes the landladies replied, and sometimes they didn't, so anyway we used to stand on the doorstep, ring the bell, and then jump indoors with our arms stretched out announcing, 'We are the Flying Scots', as if we were an acrobatic act. Sandy found it so funny. He said, 'It's the most peculiar contrast – like Priestley's *The Good Companions* – to come back from the war and to be launched into a theatrical atmosphere.'

After all, for years Sandy had been living with Air Force chaps, and they'd been doing all the photography for the D-Day landings and that bouncing bomb, and being out there when the Palestine thing was blowing up. And then suddenly here he was with a theatrical company. It was like an unexpected honeymoon going from place to place, and we had the most lovely weeks at Penrith and Cambridge. It was beautiful because we never could take for granted that both of us would survive. And this is what gave everything an added edge.

I've always believed today is the first day of the rest of your life, so don't waste it. And I think the war deepened that philosophy, yes I'm sure it did. Do you remember that Dennis Potter interview before he died? He was saying the same thing. 'I live in the present now. A child lives in the present. Gets up in the morning and observes everything, every minute thing. We can't bring back yesterday and we don't know what's going to happen tomorrow.'

Diana Hutchison, VAD, left.

DIANA HUTCHISON
A Lowly VAD!

Ask Diana Hutchison where she was born and she says in St Thomas's Hospital. Most people name the town. Is it because she was a nurse that she gives her mother's confinement its accurate medical base?

Her first memory is singing 'God Be In My Head' in babies' class and by coincidence this was the hymn she was practising, at the time of this interview, in her village choir.

Her choir is deep in the heart of the beautiful border countryside of Shropshire and Wales. She has achieved part of her young dream to live in a remote stone house; the other part has so far evaded her – to become an air pilot.

I went to Croydon High School, a girls' public day school. There were only about six people in the sixth form, and they were all what I would then have called bluestockings. They all wanted to go to university. I had no aspirations like that, so I chose something unconventional. Women didn't become pilots in those days.

That idea flew out of the window. For the first thing my father did after I had taken Matric, and before I could take a breath, was to get me a job in the Legal & General insurance company. I wasn't asked. But I was there for only a few months.

My cousin was training as a doctor at Westminster Hospital. I told him I'd really like to go and nurse in the Army, and he discovered that I could join the Red Cross, and be a mobile VAD. So he took me to Grosvenor Square, and told them I wanted to join. I had to fill out a lot of forms and they vetted me and eventually said yes, we'll take you.

I had to do three months' training in a hospital, Sutton and Cheam Hospital, near where I lived. And then I waited to be called up. Just as I loathed my short time in the insurance office, I loved my nursing straight away.

They called me up at the beginning of 1942. I went straight into the Army but as a VAD, I had to buy my own uniform. We went up to Garrould's and bought all these dresses, and aprons, and a navy blue suit, a navy blue coat, and a proper hat. I loved it. I'm great on uniform.

I don't think it's subservient, I think it looks nice. A uniform identifies you, and ours was reasonably prestigious, because it said you had volunteered. You were the Voluntary Aid Detachment, the VADs. You could be a VAD who was not going to be sent away from home, or you could be a mobile VAD, which meant that you could be sent anywhere.

I went anywhere in England, but I didn't go abroad. The first army hospital I was called to – with Queen Alexandra's nursing sisters lording it over us – was the No. 2 Company RAMC at the Connaught Hospital, Woking, which was actually Brookwood Mental Hospital. An enormous, bleak mental hospital, as they used to be. Even so, I loved every moment of it. It was wonderful.

We were an army skin hospital. There was a VD ward, all male. And all sorts of ghastly skin things that people get, impetigo, dreadful boils. You don't see this now so much. The trained staff were conscious that we VADs were not properly trained and that only certain types could afford to go into voluntary nursing. So they were quite rich girls. And it took a while for the others to realise that nevertheless we were willing to work, and that we could learn, and that we would do what they asked us to do. Some were all right but some of them were down on us. The sisters always were. It's only in the last twenty years that sisters haven't been hard even on trained nurses.

We were worse off financially. We had, at that time, thirty-nine shillings a week. But we had to buy all our own clothes. We paid a pound a week for mess, so we had only nineteen shillings a week to spend.

We ate alone, except for the pharmacists who ate with us. They were always in a difficult position, too. They had joined the Red Cross and were neither accepted by one lot or the other. A terrible lot of class distinction went on. But I must say I was so blissfully happy about it all I didn't notice it then!

I was posted to East Grinstead, to what was known as a camp reception station, which was a lovely big house owned by the Snelgroves, part of Marshall & Snelgroves. It was just ordinary ill, not very badly wounded. That's what camp reception stations were for; they were the intermediate treatment.

It was quite near the famous plastic surgery place for the RAF. We saw quite a lot of them walking about the town. My sister reminded me last year, how I had told her, 'You've got to dance with these people with their terrible scarred faces. You've got to look at them as if they were just the same as anybody else.'

I lived out in another large house, which had two maids still, and one old lady whom I never saw again after the day I arrived. They had rooms for people who were on night duty, and there was a gas fire in my room. As it was very cold, I lit it just while I undressed for bed. Next morning, the elements had been taken out – they probably didn't think I should have lit the fire. This was practically pre-war behaviour, though it was 1942. Things were still like that.

I got up at five or six o'clock in the evening, went to have a meal, and then I was on duty from eight o'clock until eight the next morning. It was very hard staying awake all night, even if you had slept in the day. Four o'clock in the morning was the worst time, and if Sister came round and found you asleep she rapped your knuckles. We had very little time off. I think it was three months on, one night off per week, and then three days off at the end of the three months. Otherwise we were on duty all the time.

My home was in Surrey. I probably went home, but I can't remember how often. The trains were terribly cold. There was no loo paper, or soap or anything, no refreshments, no heating in the trains. But I enjoyed it all. I know I wasn't homesick. When you're young, you're not worried about anything much in this world. There was never a question of being too tired. After being on duty, if there was a dance you went without sleep.

Next I was posted to the head injuries hospital in Oxford, which was St Hugh's College, the women's college. It was a marvellous place to be because I worked in the operating theatre. Brigadier Cairns was working there, later to become Professor Cairns and a very famous surgeon. Soldiers were flown to the hospital direct from D-Day in Normandy. Here we used penicillin, which saved so many lives. It was stored in a wooden refrigerator lined with zinc and kept in the corridor.

Working in the theatre was terrifying, because they looked at you, and you were expected to know what they wanted. You had to go away and get it, post haste, and no words were spoken. But I was always able to stay cool in the theatre. I was never squeamish. I thought operations like sawing through skulls were absolutely wonderful. I have no recollection of being the least bit frightened.

Nor do I remember seeing anybody faint. You'd jolly well better not faint, you know. It was disgraceful to faint, like when you were on parade.

The work was marvellously interesting. Of course, in those days you had to take swabs, and you had to get things ready to put into the autoclave, a sterilising unit. You prepared all the boxes of sterile things. You rolled bandages. You'd do that on night duty. And all the dressing and things were boiled up in the autoclave. I don't think they do anything like that now, because everything's in little packets. I once saw some trained nurses using towels to clean their shoes. They just wiped them and put them in the bin for laundry. But it struck me as not quite right.

I thought the surgeons at the time were rather terrifying. You did, as quickly as possible, what was required of you, and then made yourself invisible.

When we became privates, we always had to call the women doctors 'ma'am', the men doctors 'sir'. I thought, well, they've spent a lot of time getting themselves to where they are. They're quite important. As long as they behave properly, why shouldn't I call them ma'am and sir? I didn't mind all that. I was far more afraid of making a mistake, because I wanted to do well.

Next thing, I was posted to a camp reception station in Oxfordshire at a place called Ambrosden. It was an enormous ordnance camp, with what seemed like thousands of men plonked in the middle of the countryside. Ambrosden was a village of three or four cottages and a pub with hens walking in and out of the door. There was a lot of flat land, so the RAF put up ever so many aerodromes there, and Bicester, five or six miles away, was the nearest town. The camp reception station was really a miniature hospital; I think it had three wards. And there was the most marvellous RAOC chef who cooked just for us, the ten or twelve VADs. We slept in a dormitory, and we had five blankets each.

On St Patrick's Day 1945, that was before VE Day, the corporals had a dance and invited the VADs. And I won the jitterbugging competition with a corporal. To do it with a corporal was no great thing by now. We were getting much more emancipated.

The CO of the battalion, who was a half-colonel, came and presented the prizes and said to me, 'Will you come and have a noggin at the King's Head?' The King's Head was in Bicester. That was Hugh, whom I eventually married. He had just come back all the way through Italy.

And then unfortunately, my whole career was cut in half because my mother got cancer of the liver. My mother, who was forty-seven, was given three months to live, though in fact she lived for another four years. I wouldn't have wanted her to go into a nursing home. I was able to give her injections, and look after her. I wanted to do it for my mother, so I did. I was on permanent compassionate leave but I went back and forward a bit between home and the hospital until the end of 1946 when I was eventually demobbed. I remember I was there for VE Day with everybody falling about and drinking too much.

We had all volunteered to go to India, and my group went off to Poona. But I wouldn't have dreamed of going, I couldn't bear to think of my mother with no one to look after her. My father was going up and down and travelling all over England, my sister was in the BBC, and she wasn't at all inclined to do it. She didn't say so, but she wasn't.

In the mean time, I did get married to Hugh in 1946. But I stayed on at home for three months until Hugh said to my father that he'd like me to go and live with him. My father said, 'Well, we had a gentleman's agreement you know.' And Hugh said, 'Oh, blow that!'

I didn't want to leave my mother, but just at this time she was a lot better, so I went to Hugh's posting at the Military College of Science in Shrivenham. But I still went backwards and forwards looking after my mother until her death. That was in 1949, the year my elder daughter was born. In those days you stayed in a nursing home for a fortnight with your legs up, but my father was ringing up and saying, will you come? So when my daughter was ten days old I left her in the nursing home, which everybody thought was quite scandalous, and went to my mother. I stayed with her when she died, and after the funeral went back and collected my daughter.

I always thought my mother was a bit trodden under by my father. She did exactly what he wanted her to do, because she thought that was the right thing. Perhaps she really didn't mind. I have these constant conversations with my younger daughter, who's a tremendous feminist, and can't understand why women do anything for men at all! And I say, you've got to be fair: if somebody keeps you, you've got to do something for them, and after all he is supposed to be your best friend!

Diana had married Hugh despite the fact that at thirty-one he'd been diagnosed as having Parkinson's Disease. A second, and rather more encouraging, Harley Street opinion was that he might be in a wheelchair in twenty years' time. But a combination of his own specialised talents and the Army's sympathetic support allowed him to remain in the War Office until the normal retirement age of fifty-five. And he lived until 1981. Diana increasingly had to act as his nurse: 'It must be difficult to look after people who are difficult, but he was always so easy, and nice, and pleasant.'

SISTER HUSSEY
The Second Best-kept Secret of the War

Pamela Hussey has dual nationality, British and Argentine. Her mother was born in London, her father in Mexico, his mother in the old Danish West Indies which had been bought by the United States. But when war was declared she was in no doubt as to which country she owed her allegiance.

In 1942, as soon as she was twenty and entitled to decide for herself, she left Buenos Aires, her birthplace, to join up in Britain.

At the end of the war she left the WRNS and worked in Argentina for the next five years, 'and then the Lord called me to come back to England and join a religious order'. Sister Pamela has never returned to Argentina.

I felt strongly about what was happening in Britain in the war. My family was very politically conscious, my father especially. We used to listen to the BBC – the Overseas Programme; they didn't call it the World Service in those days. People like J.B. Priestley and Vernon Bartlett were talking on *Britain Speaks*, and I felt very patriotic. There was a huge British colony in Argentina in those days, about a quarter of a million, and loads of young people were going over to Britain to join up.

So I volunteered. The only thing I stipulated was that the British government must assure volunteers that we would be given a place in the forces if we went. They were saying at the time, you can come if you want, but we're not going to guarantee that you'll get into the forces.

I didn't feel Argentine in the same way, even though I had dual nationality and therefore two passports. I felt I had to contribute to the war effort, not only for Britain, but to stop what was happening in Germany, and the whole horrendous business. Now my ideas about military involvement and military intervention have changed, but in those days, I certainly wouldn't have felt the way I feel now.

The Falklands war was terrible for me. I knew what the Argentine government was like. I knew about the disappearances and the torture, and I thought this would put an end to it. So when Britain sent troops out to the Falklands, I thought it was a good thing, and in the end it did result in the overthrow of that repressive government. My ideas have changed. But in those days, in the 1940s, I was pretty conservative really.

I was living at home. Most girls of my age coming from my kind of background did. I only knew one of all my circle who had a flat on her own. I didn't toe the line all the time, but I loved my parents and I respected them, and I understood how they felt. When they said to me, Pam, we don't want you to go until you're twenty, I thought OK. I had to consider what it meant to have their one and only daughter leave. But when I was twenty I had to go.

It was very dangerous. I mean, ships were getting sunk all the time. My friend Mary came down to the docks to see me off, and a long time afterwards she told me she had never seen anybody cry the way my mother had when my ship went out. My very balanced mother, who never showed her emotions to anyone.

We were five weeks on a voyage that would have taken two in peacetime. We had to zigzag across the Atlantic to Freetown. The ship that left before us was sunk. The ship coming after us was sunk. There were U-boats, there were Japanese submarines and there were German dive-bombers operating from an African airstrip. Everything was going down; that was June '42. So no one did it lightly.

I need not have decided to do this. What gave me the courage? Well, listening to what was going on in Europe when you were in exile – and you could think of it as being in exile, since you were out of your heart country – it was just impossible for me to do the social rounds as if nothing was happening.

We were all knitting and running Red Cross bazaars and putting on shows for the Navy. There were very patriotic sentiments around. We would call it jingoism today, I suppose, although I didn't in those days. Some girls wanted to go because the men were going. One friend of mine told me, I'm going because unless I go Charles will marry somebody else. But I felt that I had to get where the action was. I've always had that feeling really. I suppose that's what impelled me later to go to work in Central America. I respond to a challenge.

I didn't cry as I was leaving, either. It's the people who are left behind who suffer. My memories were not of sadness – nor of fear. But we did hear when we'd crossed over the River Plate and docked in Montevideo that the ship's officers were very apprehensive. They knew what we were going into.

In uniform at last, Wren Pamela Hussey in 1943.

We had to have our suitcases always packed to take to the boats. We used to laugh about it and somebody said we ought to wear black stockings. Sharks don't go for black.

We docked at a port in Sierra Leone, Freetown, which was packed with shipping. So we thought, good, we would be going out in convoy. But we left alone, and after Freetown we sometimes passed bits of wreckage but were told that even if we saw a lifeboat we wouldn't be able to stop because it was sometimes a decoy.

When we got near Britain we slept in our clothes. We knew that now was a very dangerous time. It was June and the sea was as calm as a millpond. And that was quite scary. If you went on deck you couldn't light a cigarette; its glow would be seen for miles, from one horizon to the other. I think this was probably the worst part.

We docked in Scotland and left for London in a packed train. I can remember stretching out on the floor because there wasn't any room to sleep anywhere else. There was a sense of real excitement, of now we're here. Now we're in a country at war. This is the real thing. I'm not hearing about it from 7,000 miles away, and unable to do anything. I'm here.

I had with me a letter of introduction from the naval attaché in Buenos Aires, and that helped me get into the WRNS. My father had been in the Royal Flying Corps, but my choice was the Navy. My father had also come to Britain from

Argentina to serve in the First World War. That must have influenced me.

I went to stay with an aunt in London, who lived in Prince of Wales Drive, Battersea, and I joined the WRNS in Finchley Road. There was a big training college there, which had been turned over to the Navy. It was a great time, because London was full of Argentines who had joined the forces, Anglo-Argentines like myself. The Overseas Club off Piccadilly was our meeting point. There was also a restaurant called Pepe's in Dean Street, Soho. They used to serve *dulce de leche* there, a light-brown, milky, creamy stuff.

I ended up stationed most of the time in Scarborough. First they sent me to Surbiton Towers in Hampshire, where I was to learn Morse code. But when they realised that I already knew Morse – I had prepared myself in Argentina by learning it – they sent me straight off to train for 'interceptor work'.

This was very hush-hush in those days, and for a very long time afterwards. We were told we would be picking up German naval signals from U-boats and other ships, listening all the time. And so, after training, I ended up in Scarborough at a wireless station right up on the moors behind the town.

The station was underground and well defended with guard dogs. Identity cards had to be shown every time we went to work. We picked up signals from German ships and shouted out the frequency, 500 KCs or whatever; if B-bar, it would mean it was a U-Boat. The charge hand would take away your message as soon as it was finished. Then it went off to Station X, which we later learnt was Bletchley, and it got decoded there.

The Poles had managed to get hold of the German coding machine called Enigma, and they'd handed it over to us. So we were able to break the German naval code all through the war, except for one point when they changed it. The Germans were very slow to change things, you know. You could tell when one of their U-boats was transmitting a message, because they always used exactly this same B-bar code thing at the beginning. It was B with a bar on the end, da-di-di-di-da, twice. So you knew that was a U-boat.

Radar stations all over the British Isles took bearings, which gave them the actual location of the German ship or U-boat and they alerted our ships in the area, who went and dealt with it: if it was a U-boat, presumably by dropping a depth charge.

I remember seeing a play not long ago, called *Breaking the Code*, about the man who broke the German code, and as a homosexual broke a social code too.

We didn't think in terms of killing people then. If we hadn't got the U-boats, the U-boats would have got our ships. That was the kind of world we were in. Now, I might think differently, but in those days it was black and white as far as we were concerned. We had to stop this war.

We worked long hours. The longest shift was from one in the afternoon till eleven at night, which was absolutely bonkers. We had the earphones on all the time, and you might have atmospherics crackling away in them. And we maybe got two ten-minute breaks. We ate at the set. Somebody would take over while you went out to the loo. It was really killing. Then there was an eleven to eight watch, a night watch; the morning watch was from eight to one.

I couldn't have worked those hours if the cause hadn't been close to my heart. It's come out since that winning the U-boat war was vital. This country would not have survived had the U-boat menace not been beaten. We knew this at the time, really, even if we didn't quite appreciate its significance. So that took precedence. There were all kinds of small things that we kicked against in the WRNS, the food for one thing, but the big thing was, we were doing our bit in the war.

Even so, the long hours were deadly. Especially if you thought of the work as taking down messages without knowing whether they were important or not, or whether targets were hit or not. Absolutely deadly. People used to go off their nut.

When we weren't working, we got round Yorkshire, a beautiful part of the country, lovely air. We worked underground, in shocking airless conditions. So when we got out we hired bicycles and cycled over Yorkshire. We knew a lovely pub where we used to go and have lunch. There was a very good crowd of people with us, and plenty of men, because there was an RAF training wing in Scarborough as well. There were army people there, too, so there was quite a lot of night life. But social life was not as lax as it would be today!

At the end of the war I felt great relief. You see, by this time I'd been three and a half years away from home. Then in December '45, I was suddenly called by the WRNS, at a moment's notice, to report to Portsmouth, as there was a ship going out to Buenos Aires. I was staying with my aunt in Battersea, and I'd arranged to go to the theatre, so I didn't pay much attention to this. I said, well, I'll go down later, when I'm free. But there was another frantic phone call, get on the train and come, so I did. All kinds of rumours were going round Portsmouth. One was that we were going out to Port Said, another that we were going round the Caribbean. We did both.

On board there was a whole crowd of us from Argentina, and from other Latin American countries as well. We went up to Port Said and took on about 1,500 black Caribbean troops, who were put in the hold. Then we sailed down the Mediterranean and across the Atlantic. Two weeks cruising around the Caribbean, dropping these servicemen off at their various islands, and then another two weeks down to South America and Argentina. So that was quite an experience.

I can't remember mixing with the black troops at all; with some of the white officers, we did. Unbelievable when I think of it now. It was segregation. And we had all fought in the same war. I can't remember seeing them on the boat deck, which was where we played all the games and sat around. But in those days, I don't think I questioned it. Little boats used to come out to us as a lot of the islands weren't big enough for us to dock. The boats would come and take them off, with much rejoicing from their families.

At last I arrived home, and there was great jubilation. By this time my brother had joined the Navy, and he was still in England, so I was the first one home. My parents, of course, were delighted.

I very soon got a job at Henry Martin & Co., chartered accountants, where I stayed for a few years. It was interesting to work for a financial wizard, the man who put the Biro ballpoint pen on the market. My boss financed it, and I was with him at the time he was getting it patented, and keeping Sheaffers and Parkers out, so it was a thrilling job.

But once back in the social round, and having a newspaper ring up to ask me what kind of dress I was going to wear at so-and-so's party, I thought I've got to do something more than this. So one Lent I took seriously to my prayers to ask the Lord to guide me.

I don't know what happened, but suddenly in the middle of an Easter service, the thought came into my head, 'I'm going to be a nun.' I walked out, and that was it. Neither I nor any of my friends would ever have expected it. And my parents were upset for it meant I was leaving them again, but they supported me in my decision.

But I believe, I'm absolutely certain, that it was a direct call from the Lord, because I never looked back – never had any doubts, although it's been a very difficult thing for me. I'm not an easy person to live with in a community. My mother has sometimes said to me, have you ever wanted to leave? And I have said no, never.

May with friends climbing in the Pyrenees, 1939.

MAY LAWTON
What the Teacher Learned

In 1994 – the ninetieth year of her life – May Lawton happened to admit to her nephew Keith that she'd like to go up in a helicopter. He arranged a flight for her as a birthday present, and asked a neighbour if they could land in his field, next to her pink-washed cottage on Sweeney Mountain in Shropshire. The pick-up was at around eleven on a Sunday morning in May.

Robert would pilot her and then land her at Keith's farm for some bread and cheese at lunchtime. In she got and up she rose in her ear muffs, with her walking stick.

What she did not know was that her nephew had asked all her family and friends to be in the field, a stone's throw from the mill where Aunty May (as she's known by everyone) was born.

She arrived in a bubble a bit like the Pope. Well, she was waving her arms like him, as soon as she recognised the little figures waving to her as the helicopter whirred closer to the ground.

None of us will ever forget it – nor will she, but then she has a head for remembering history, and that day is history, already, along with the war.

I'd been camping and climbing in the Pyrenees and when we got to Paris it was obvious war was imminent. We'd gone through all this trusting Hitler, had some false alarms, peace in our time and all the rest of it. There had been so many moves backwards and forwards that it wasn't relief exactly when we heard there was going to be war. But there was some satisfaction perhaps that at least now we knew.

And from the doldrums of the thirties suddenly everything woke up. Even in farming, people became important. People who had been of no importance in the depression became key figures. Perhaps the British are at their best under stress with their backs to the wall. People find something in themselves that they didn't know was there. The trivial seems to go. Everybody dug like mad. One year, I grew 72 lb. of shallots and sold them for the Red Cross. People, you know, were healthy on rations.

When war was actually declared on Sunday, September the third, there were the usual reactions. Everybody got a fright and they put up air-raid shelters in the streets. And in a couple of months they were flat on the ground. They had got the wrong cement mix. It was said the cement was Belgian. That might be slander. But anyway they collapsed. It looked as if they had been hit by a bomb.

Soon after the declaration, the alarms went off. Everybody had to carry a gas mask and go to a shelter. All-clear went and you went back to work. I had been in a school at Ellesmere Port, but then I moved across the Wirral to Ness and taught there. I was very happy in Ness, and then we started to have to take in evacuees. Everybody had to. Mine were a very odd teacher from Liverpool and her aged mother. They were highly nervous. When I took them a cup of tea to bed in the morning I heard a great shuffling of the chest of drawers as they pulled it away from the door.

The two of them were devoted to the local vicar, which I wasn't, and they went to church every Sunday morning, which I didn't. And they would come back to my kitchen which was full of the local Home Guard. (*Dad's Army* on the telly got the Home Guard exactly right!) They were scared of them. I don't suppose they had ever seen so many men in one kitchen in their lives. They stayed with me until they got homesick and then went back to Liverpool, preferring to risk it. Most of the children went back. They were all too homesick.

At the same time as the mother and daughter, I had an airman and his wife. That was four. Then my cousins came from Seaforth police station near Liverpool when they were bombed out. They came to me still covered in soot after spending the night in the cells there. Shocking time. I can always remember one particularly bad night in winter. Bootle was on the waterfront. They were not quick enough to realise that Jerry would drop bombs on the waterfront. The whole place was up in flames.

I also had a captain of a Belgian vessel and his wife staying with me. He had a crew of fifty and I was invited on after one of the fires. As we wound our way through Bootle to the docks, I saw the notice: LOOTERS WILL BE SHOT. Fifty-six ships that night all along the waterfront and every one damaged. They weren't ready for it.

I had a little dining room for the Belgian wife, and she stripped the walls and put up the Belgian royal family. I had the Belgian royal family for months. She was very impatient with the British: 'The English lion, he sleeps.' My dear cousin who was bombed out couldn't stand her. Still, they were with me – all six of them – for a very long time.

We were full house. I would sleep anywhere there was space. But in the midst of all this there was quite a lot of humour. There were many casualties but there was a lot of fun. You couldn't take things too seriously.

I was paid a pound for each evacuee. I cooked for some of them because they couldn't cook. It all had to be accepted.

I happened to be in London when the first doodlebug was dropped, though at the time we didn't know what it was. They tipped out the children from London, and I was left with two lads to look after. One was a right tough, but the other one was gentler. They were about twelve or thirteen. I had a lot of trouble with the one – pinching apples, running round the garden at teatime in his socks. So I made him wash his own socks once and he told his mother. I had quite a row with her about it, for she even came up to see me. I reckon women had a pretty bad time in the war – separated from their children. And some-times it wasn't easy filling your house with evacuees, either.

One Saturday night about seven years after the war, there was a knock on my door and, 'You won't remember me.' But I did. Mark was nineteen or twenty by now and in the Army. It was the gentler one. He had come back. He was like a faithful dog.

Every Saturday night and often on Thursdays I couldn't get home because I was driving an ambulance. I used to go to the old police station in Ness and sleep in the cells.

Our business was to be responsible for Liverpool pregnant women who were near their time. They were all in one place while they waited and then we had to whisk them to the maternity home. If it was a bad night they would go off one after the other. It was hilarious: one would set the other off. Occasionally we had to take a case over to the hospital in Liverpool. And it was no use telling us that we must wear our gas masks. I refused. I could not drive in the half-light with my gas mask on. We had these tiresome gas masks and we never had any need for them.

I don't think anyone realised at first what it was like driving in the dark with poor lights, even though there was hardly any civilian traffic on the roads. I had to have a police certificate to drive an ambulance. That's the only thing I've ever had to show that I can drive. I have never passed a test, except this police test.

On Sunday mornings we had to deliver one load of VAD nurses for eight o'clock to the hospital at Clatterbridge where they had brought the wounded. And then we had to bring back the night staff from there. They were glad to see us. Sometimes after a busy night, instead of going home I would take myself by bicycle down to the marsh. It was peace with the birds and the all-clear. It was sanity for a while down on those Dee marshes.

Of course in the war you did other extras – only too glad to. We had to give out orange juice and cod-liver oil in schools. A good thing, too. I have happy memories – it's a funny thing to say – about the war. I laughed more in the war. There was nothing else you could do if you had a house full of people often squabbling. But then when you met the people who were bombed out and who had lost everything – they had such courage. They were so marvellous you couldn't complain about anything, could you?

In my holiday I'd go home by train to Welshpool and replenish the food stocks. I always returned on the last train at night. Everything was blacked out, you could hardly find the station. I came back one time with 52 lb. of damsons. Everybody wanted damsons. I nearly killed myself carrying them!

Another time I got eggs, some butter and we killed a pig while I was down so I got a lot of pork. I had filled my rucksack with this food for my return home on the mail train. I arrived at half-past twelve at night. All the lights were out and a bicycle followed me. A fellow asked, 'Can I help you?' and he took my rucksack. 'Do you mind telling me where you live?' he said, 'and I'll ride on ahead with the bag.' And off he disappeared. That's it, you silly twerp, I thought – and you can't go to the police and report the theft for you aren't supposed to have off the rations food. When I got to the end of the lane there he was, waiting for me.

I don't remember a single nasty incident about the blackout. There was friendliness, kindness in the war. People forgot their pettinesses. They shared. If you had a car (I'd got rid of mine) you could pick up anyone and safely give them a lift. Somehow the war brought out the good in us. I suppose war also brings out the bad. There's a stratum of people who are violent. Now, when life is more comfortable, there's less neighbourliness. What's left of the last war for me is a memory of people's kindness. Most of the people I knew came through, but I knew quite a lot who didn't.

I knew one neighbour's lad. He was eighteen or nineteen when he was taken prisoner in 1939 for the whole of the war. A country lad. They brought him back and put him in one of our army camps. They dared not let prisoners have too much good food at the start or else they would have been ill.

When at last he was demobbed he used to visit me and pull a few weeds up and come into a quiet home. He was twenty-four then, and a different person. He said he couldn't mix with the boys like he used to. He'd got more thoughtful. There was a big gap. His one ambition was to go back to where he had been prisoner, to see the mountains. I can't imagine why.

I remember coming back from London with a young soldier – he was eighteen and he slept on my shoulder until Wolverhampton, in the total dark. I was terrified he'd wake up and realise I was not a young girl (I was thirty-five) and be disappointed.

I could never take war life that seriously. On parade one Sunday in our uniforms our gas-mask cases were inspected. No gas mask in mind – out came my knitting.

Some people grumbled in the war about food shortage. But some people grumble at anything. The cities were the worst off. We did quite well on the farms. There was the odd leg of lamb, a bit of butter and anything that was going. People lived by exchange. I had my fair share of everything. And at the butcher's – well I taught his two boys! We had eight pennyworth of meat a week. We used our wits. It was harder on older people who couldn't garden. I grew no end of stuff and so did our headmaster. We grew veg and brought them in to sell cheaply to the children. Having no other table, we put them on top of the grand piano.

Humans, being what they are, lived a lot by exchange. I can't remember ever going short. Sugar was the thing desired by the country people. With it they could have bottled fruit, and made jam.

We never bothered about clothes, for which you needed coupons. But I had my ambulance uniform for a long time after the war for the garden. It was tough. The stuff they put in uniforms was good. And straight after the war I bought a pair of sheets for fifteen shillings. One of them split just last night. That's what, forty years? Some wear! That is good quality, nothing shoddy.

'When the war is over,' I used to say, 'I am going to have a full day in bed.' I didn't. Instead I went off to Bangor, on the first train to my friends and Snowdonia.

Oh! I can't tell you what it was like. It was May. Was it the fifth? I sat in the loggia on this evening. And the music, it was *Swan Lake*. Good light music, just right to put you in a happy mood. Rejoicings didn't interest me. We had gone through so much. People had suffered so much, I did not want to celebrate. *Swan Lake* on that beautiful May evening, and the war was coming to an end, that was enough.

Taking the King's Shilling: Patricia was proud of her ATS uniform.

PATRICIA PITMAN
Private Hatred

The war altered Patricia Pitman's politics from red as the blood of a martyr to blue as the supposed blood of an aristrocrat!

She then set out deliberately to change her way of speaking – to exchange her broad northern accent for the careful vowel sounds of the would-be posh. Pat willingly admits to this act of genteelism while always remaining a rebel ...

All education went awry when the war happened. I was evacuated, and I hated that, so I ran away.

Home was Bradford, and by some act of lunacy somebody decided that a good place to send us would be Burnley. So from one industrial town I was evacuated, with my fourth-form peers, to another nearby industrial town, which for various reasons I loathed.

We got on a chara on the Friday morning, that was the first of September 1939, and we were waved goodbye by our tearful parents. We settled down for the drive to ... we didn't know where we were going. Nor did our parents.

And we didn't have any stamped addressed postcards, as all evacuees are said to have had. Perhaps because we were older and all together, we simply wrote little notes when we got there. We had our names printed on cardboard, and all the way to boring old Burnley we sang, 'Run Rabbit Run' and 'South of the Border' and 'The Isle of Capri'. When we arrived we went to a church hall, and it was like a slave market. We were all there, the ugly, elderly ones like me, and the pretty, younger curly-haired tots. And of course the latter all went first, and the ones like me were left. It wasn't very good for our morale. But eventually we – me and my friend, a fellow fourth-former – were billeted with a family, who were not very appealing, and who were in it for the loot, or what they imagined was the loot. I think they got fourteen shillings for each evacuee, and they soon got fed up with us.

They lived in a big, stone, terraced house right in the middle of Nelson. The daughters were all mill-girls and very nice, but the old girl was a bit of a horror. My friend and I were extremely left-wing, and this was a Tory working-class family, so we got off on the wrong foot right from the start.

We got back one day from school to find a note on the table. Both of us to be re-billeted with some poor wretched spinster who didn't want any evacuees. If people had rooms, they were simply commandeered to take us. Our stay there lasted one night. She told us, 'I never wanted you, you know. As far as I'm concerned you can pack your hook and go home,' which is what we did. We started to walk back home to Bradford the following day.

Thirty miles to go but we got a lift on a lorry, fortunately. My dad gave a guffaw. My mother was a bit cross, but then very angry once our old headmistress came and said it was disgracefully bad behaviour. My mother, who was always a little bit of a moral coward, turned traitor.

Our runaway was reported in the *Burnley Express* under the headline TWO LITTLE GIRLS FROM SCHOOL.

By this time I was fed up with school and I got myself a job. This was in 1940, just before the fall of France, and just before my fifteenth birthday. My mother had to pay twenty pounds to have me taken away because I should have stayed at that school until I was sixteen. It was a grammar-type school. In the other schools you had to leave at fourteen.

I got a job at the Post Office as a probationer, which meant you cleaned phones and did menial tasks like that, before you eventually became either a telephonist or a telegraphist. I soon got fed up with that too, and from then on I was marking time until I was seventeen and a half: magic date, because at that age, with my parents' permission, I could do what I wanted to do. Join the Army and kill Germans, because that was really what the war was all about. It wasn't for freedom or anything like that.

I was extremely patriotic. I still am. I was brought up in a very political household, so I was also extremely politically conscious. Until a couple of years ago, until I lost it, I actually kept a political notebook from the age of twelve. It could be valuable now. It was mainly about Hitler and the rise of Nazism.

The morning of 24 August 1939 stands out. My dad had already gone off to the bakery, and, when I woke, I used to like to get the *Daily Herald* before my mother did. I pattered down, and saw the paper on the floor in the tiny little hall. I was in my nightie, and I can still feel the cold oilcloth under my feet. I couldn't believe what I read. Ribbentrop in Moscow, non-aggression pact signed between Russia and Germany. And it was like a blow, I thought, this is it, and went into my mother's bedroom: 'Mother, Mother, we're going to be at war soon. Look!' It was a terrible shock. I sat down at the end of my parents' double bed, I couldn't believe what I was reading.

It shook my mother, who had always looked upon Russia as Paradise. And, of course, I was brought up to believe that it was the most marvellous place on earth. She had no idea, as most people hadn't, of the killings that were going on in this Soviet heaven.

Anyway, back to Hitler. I'd actually read all of *Mein Kampf* when I was thirteen, and it didn't need a little political genius like Pat Tennant (my maiden name) to see what was going to happen. I thought he was a maniac. My great argument was that Chamberlain was prepared to barter peace with a man who actually knew about the German concentration camps in '38, and my youthful soul was genuinely outraged. So it came really as a relief when war was declared. Oh I really wanted to fight the Germans. And I regret to say, part of me still does. My daughter Alice lives with a man who won't even drink German wine. Well, I won't go as far as that, but it amazes me that a young man of his generation can feel like that.

The people who were very, very much against my joining up, of course, were my parents, and I had to get their permission. And, of course, the Post Office, since I was in a reserved occupation. They were very nice about it. But my parents were refusing to sanction my leaving home. I said look, I shall have to bow down to you now at seventeen and a half, but as soon as I'm eighteen, I shall go. So they knew they were defeated, and shortly after I was seventeen and a half, in 1943, I went along and had my medical.

The medical rather shocked me, with, 'Make water in a pot.' I didn't know what was meant by this. I was extremely naïve. I was a child – I literally hadn't stopped growing. At the end of this very long medical, lasting about two and half hours, at the Mechanics' Institute in Bradford, I was ushered into a room where a woman in khaki, a junior commander, which is the female equivalent of a captain, told me I'd passed the medical and I was now in the Army. 'There you are,' she said and handed me a shilling. I'd got the King's shilling. This is true, they actually give you a shilling, when you're a volunteer.

I've never been interested in clothes, but I took quite a pride in my uniform. We had a curious Bakelite thing that you slid down your brass buttons in order to protect the fabric from the Bluebell polish you shone them with.

They issued us with three pairs of white woollen knickers, and three of khaki rayon, a pink suspender belt, which was more of a corset actually with hooks and eyes. Bras, pink bras. I'd never worn a bra in my life and I didn't have any bosoms to put in it, but I put on my army bra! Six vests, three shirts, three pairs of khaki woollen stockings, brown shoes, the undersoles of which you had to keep polished – not the bit you walked on, but the arch. Khaki gloves, and of course your khaki cap.

Oh yes, and a greatcoat. If you joined up very early on, your greatcoats had a belt at the back, but if you joined up later on, they were just shaped at the back. I longed to have a greatcoat with a belt.

I adored the initial training at Harrogate – the drill, the saluting, the senseless marching along. I'd had the most awful time in the Post Office; this to me was freedom. A couple of Sundays we went on church parade with a band. 'Colonel Bogey'! Bliss! Absolute bliss!

I had a few moments of dismay. It was my first night, and I continued to feel elated in this room with thirty-nine other girls. But all I could hear was sobbing, girls crying for their mothers. I thought they were mad. I thought, why the hell did they join up, if they're going to blub like this? Of course what I didn't realise until the following day was that they were all conscripts. I was the only one in the barrack room that had volunteered.

These were the first real cockneys I'd come across, and when they learned that I'd volunteered – and not only volunteered but I'd been in a reserved occupation – one of them said, 'Cor, you must have rocks in your 'ead.' They couldn't understand why somebody should want to leave home.

The only time I thought that I might have made a mistake was when we had games. And games were compulsory. I thought to myself, I didn't join up to play bloody rounders. I hated games. But it was the only time the wretched Cockney girls cheered up.

And then at the end of six weeks, with all my immunisations and vaccinations over, my little hour of glory had arrived. I went back home in my uniform. I walked into the lounge and my mother approached me. Then she recoiled. I wondered what was wrong. She said it was the smell of my uniform, it brought back the Somme. 'Fred,' she called out to my father, 'it brings it all back.'

I'd known my mother had a sweetheart called Frank – I'd come across some of his postcards from somewhere in France. And I knew he had been killed in the Somme. In my part of Yorkshire there were very few men of my mother's age, because they'd all been killed off. You've heard of the Pals Regiments? Whole regiments were taken from streets, and they were called the Leeds Pals, and the Bradford Pals. Sixty thousand men were killed on that same day, 3 July 1916. It was a curious smell, the smell of the khaki.

After my few days' leave I went back to barracks, where I was getting on well with everyone, after they'd got over thinking I had rocks in my 'ead. I'm inclined to like my own company, but in a barrack room you could be very alone, which is just how I liked it.

We'd had aptitude tests during our initial training, and I had taken them for wireless telegraphy. It was found I had – don't laugh – a high aptitude for

Morse code, which is the most useless thing.

I was sent up to a place called Strathpeffer to do my training as a wireless operator, which I loved, and passed out at the end of six months. I became entitled to wear the jimmy thing, what's it called? We called it the jimmy. It's Ariel or Mercury, or something like that. It was one of my proudest moments. By that time all the girls who'd passed their exams had to go to Edinburgh, where we were marched through the city, and I thought all the people were looking at us and thinking how clever we were. I should think they couldn't have cared a damn, but I felt tremendous pride.

Then we awaited our final posting. I longed to be sent to London. I'd only been in London once before, on a school trip in May 1939, and I'd loved it so much. I used to go to bed in the Army saying, 'Please God, make my posting be London.' I was posted to Aldershot, which to me was London. Some poor buggers went further north, up to Scotland.

The official name for my job was OWL – operator, wireless and line – so I not only received and sent Morse on a wireless, but I also used something called a fullerphone.

On the wireless, it was very little plain language. It was all code, which I could do incredibly quickly. Thirty groups a minute both sending and receiving. Plain language on the fullerphone, a little slower, about twenty-five words a minute. I couldn't do that speed now, of course. That was all to do with the Second Front supplies; tanks and guns, things like that. It was incredibly dramatic.

And when the V1s started, that was dramatic, too. Quite a few came within range of Aldershot. But I really experienced them in London. I shouldn't have done this, because by that time London was out of bounds to us for some reason. But I used to hitch-hike with Canadians down to a station called Ash Vale, and catch the London train from there. I loved the atmosphere of London during the V1s. I absolutely adored it.

I don't know why. Because I was a stupid little girl, I suppose. I loved going down into the tube, and they used to give us a blanket – the ladies serving tea – and I used to make up my unit number, saying I'd come from Ash Vale, not Aldershot in case I got found out. And I just used to roam the streets.

But the most important thing happened to me at Aldershot. I met my husband, and that changed my life. He worked on television a lot and wrote for the *Express* – Robert Pitman. I met him in February 1944, at the St George's Institute in Aldershot at a play-reading. He was then waiting to go to Bletchley, you know the code-breaking place, and meanwhile he was doing a typing course at Aldershot. At this play-reading, he was Macbeth, I was one of the three witches, and he became my first boyfriend. I thought he was absolutely marvellous, and fortunately he thought I was.

I felt in lust with him immediately. And loved his accent. I hoped that he would turn up to the next play-reading, which he did. It was, I remember it well, *French without Tears* by Terence Rattigan.

I sounded him out politically. I had an idea he would be left-wing like me. Well, most young people with any sense were. I changed as the years went on. He asked me if I would meet him at W.H. Smith's bookshop in Farnham, and that was our first date. We went on from there, and shortly afterwards he was posted to Bletchley. He did military Japanese, because he'd got an exhibition to Oxford. He did Greats, I think it was called. Latin and Greek. They wanted Greats scholars for the military Japanese, don't ask me why, but they did. I often went absent without leave in order to see him. I was caught a good many times. You were confined to barracks for about three or four days, and you were put on a charge. You had to face a little sort of tribunal, always having to remove your cap, in case you threw it at the junior commander! But I didn't mind; as long as I had my weekends free, it didn't bother me at all. I don't remember them being particularly stern or strict. I wonder if that was because I was good at my job.

Then Bob got sent out to Australia for a year with his military Japanese. I wish I'd kept all our letters. I've got very, very few. I think I've got one air letter upstairs in a desk. It's from me to Bob – my writing was so small I can hardly read it now.

I was narked he'd been sent away, but I enjoyed writing letters so it didn't bother me overmuch. And we'd already decided to get married, which we did as soon as he got back from Australia. We both had to get parents' permission again, because in those days you had to be twenty-one and over to get married without permission; we were both about nineteen. We were married on 6 January 1946, both in uniform. I didn't have any civilian clothes at all.

But before then, when Bob was in Australia, I was posted to Ireland, to bandit country, Armagh. I used to love it there, taking long walks – something I wouldn't do now in the British uniform. A lot of people in Eire, in fact, crossed the border and joined up. I longed to see Eire but we weren't allowed to go over the border to southern Ireland. If I had gone in uniform, I'd have been interned. I hadn't joined the war to be interned. I'd joined to kill Germans. And very soon in my army career I realised that I was going to help kill them through my Morse, but that I was never going to actually kill any. The nearest I could have got was on an ack-ack unit, shooting them down, but alas and alack, you needed maths for that.

God only knows why we were doing Morse in Ireland. The ways of the Army are mysterious. I can understand Aldershot, because we were in the thick of it. Aldershot, before D-Day, was full of Canadians. I was on night duty that night and I was aware of many, many planes and gliders going over. The following day, it was a city of the dead. All the Canadians were gone – all these lads of eighteen, nineteen. There was something so incredibly sad about it.

These same lads used to run dances every night before that June the 6th. We danced the foxtrot, the quickstep and that terribly popular one, the hokey-cokey. And the conga. To tunes like that one of Frank Sinatra's: 'I Didn't Sleep a Wink Last Night' – he was just becoming terribly popular then. And it was always, 'I'll see you again whenever spring breaks through again', and 'Deep Purple', and ending with, 'Who's taking you home tonight, After the dance is through? Who's longing to hold you tight, And whisper I love you, I do.' And all of us in khaki. It was incongruous – all these khaki-clad boys and girls dancing together.

And then suddenly the boys had gone. The camp was just like a ghost town. It was weird.

Robert Kee, in one of his books, puts it very well. He said that there's a tremendous boundary between those who lived through the war properly and those who were out of it. If you actually lived through the war, it never leaves you. Never. Ever. And that's the only way I can put it.

Clemency Greatorex, too delicate to join the forces, was a pillar of strength in the WVS.

CLEMENCY GREATOREX
Invalided into the War

Clemency Greatorex has suffered from severe asthma since she was three. At that time, 1918, there was not the effective medication there is now. She was so ill that her parents decided she had to be educated at home by Swiss 'mam'selles' until she outgrew their educational capacity, and then by governesses.

She was in her mid-twenties when war started. All her friends went off and did active things but she couldn't, and it depressed her. Until a rather outspoken friend of her mother's said, 'Go and join the WVS [Women's Voluntary Services] – they'll take any old crock.'

That's just what I did. I went along to the WVS office. They wanted a secretary, so I dug out an old typewriter from home and walked in with it. Then I couldn't open the blooming thing, because I'd never used it.

I couldn't type! But I soon learned – with two fingers, you know. And then the organiser for Lymington retired quite suddenly and left two of us in charge. The other person was the same sort of age as me. She was looking after an invalid father, which was why she hadn't joined up. There we were, very inexperienced, and we had to take on the running of this centre. We weren't being paid, you understand. I was living free with these friends. I don't know how I'd have managed otherwise.

They put us in a Sunday paper shop, so we had to put all our stuff away on Saturdays ready for the weekend sales. And then take it all out again on Monday morning.

Life was full of challenges, and I was a very lucky woman to get the job. It meant I could work as much as I was able, and when I had an attack of asthma

I could go home and get over it. Well, not back to my real home. The Army commandeered our family house during Christmas week 1940. That was a bit of a schemozzle. They just marched in, more or less, and took it over. Only my mother and I were living there at the time. It was not particularly big – about seven bedrooms, something like that. Anyway, the Army wanted it, and we didn't want it by then: it was too big for just the two of us.

My mum went off to live with an aunt of hers, some friends took me in, and that's how we spent the war. I didn't feel bleak about that. Not a bit. So much worse things were happening. One was just thankful, in a way, that one could stay in the same place, and be able to do something.

When we got going on it, the first thing we were asked to do was the house-wife service. Have you heard of it? It was fascinating.

We divided up the town into different areas, in case there were air raids, and people needed help. The first thing that the housewives had to learn was 'immediate aid'. Not first aid, mark you, not as far advanced as that, but immediate aid. At the first lecture, one of the more stalwart ones fainted away at the mere thought of blood. So we didn't think we were going to be very useful. But we did our best, and we were very lucky. We never got bombed in Lymington, except in the river, which didn't really matter much. It made a nasty noise and a splash, but that was all.

What did our organised localities actually do? When the Army was camping round us and wanted hot baths, we'd tell the key housewives that the soldiers were coming on such a such day, and they would tell all those nearby to expect them. So they'd turn on the hot water – we were so short of fuel that there wasn't hot water available as a matter of course.

The soldiers were absolutely sweet. This was towards the end of the war when they were camping in the New Forest, where they wouldn't be visible from the air. We had a lot of Army, a lot of Yanks too, all camped round us.

We also took meals over from the British Restaurant, which we started, to the people building the Mulberry harbour. We had to swear all our members to absolute secrecy, because of course nobody was to know where the Mulberry harbour was being built. And we had one of our chattiest members on this job. I had to impress her with the need for absolute silence. I was very firm with her – and she was old enough to be my mother.

Another thing we had to deal with was some Southampton evacuees. And rather a lot of schoolboys from Portsmouth, too. We had to billet them, and that was fascinating. One got to know people really rather well.

We had compulsory powers to insist that households took these children. The first time we used them was on our doctor and his wife, because they hadn't got any evacuees and we thought they could set an example. We put in three schoolboys, and of course they were very nice to them.

But we had some funny times. Not all the children settled down in the billets we'd chosen for them. There were two women who came into my office hopping mad with each other – one was an evacuee mum billeted on the other. I could see they were going to say something shocking and awful, and I was trying to calm them down, because I had an elderly member working in the files. I didn't want her shocked. And one of them stood up, arms akimbo, and said, 'You don't know what she called me!'

I said 'No, but I don't think I need to know.'

'Oh yes you do, she called me a cow!' Well, I thought she might have called her something much worse. And dear Hodgy, who was working on the files, collapsed in a heap in the middle of them. She thought it was so frightfully funny.

We had some pathetic children, but I think that evacuation did a power of good. The country learned how the townspeople lived, and vice versa.

One of our householders came in to me one day and said, 'You know that child?' – I think the little boy was from London, though we didn't have many from there – 'he doesn't know how to sit at a table for a meal. He sits on the doorstep and expects just a bit of something. But we're teaching him.'

It was a panicky time, but I don't really think evacuation was a panic measure. I mean, we fully expected to be invaded, and we did have a lot of bombing in the towns. I think we did save the lives of a lot of town children.

They were often homesick and that was difficult. Isn't it awful, I can only remember the funny stories. One mum came storming into my office with her son aged seven or eight, and said, 'I'm taking him home unless you can find a billet for him where they have Viyella sheets.'

I said, 'But we've never heard of people offering Viyella sheets, have you?'

She said, 'No, but I'm not going to leave him here,' and she took him back to Portsmouth. Well, too bad, I couldn't go round the householders saying, 'Have you got flannelette sheets?' Extraordinary.

The children were wonderful. There was one who was dumped in my office because his householder had to go away to look after a sick relation. She couldn't take him with her, so she had to leave him with us to find a temporary billet.

I started ringing round, but I couldn't find a place for him for that night. Our own house was bursting. I thought he must be getting worried, so I put down the telephone and turned to him to make a reassuring noise. But he got in first. He said, 'Don't worry, Miss, you're doing your best.' I practically burst into tears. I long to know what's happened to him now.

A very elderly lady walked into my office one day, when we were told the Portsmouth schoolboys were arriving, and she said, 'Clemency, I'll take five.' 'Five?' I gasped. She said, 'Yes, but I must have one that is a prefect.'

So we jolly well got five with one prefect, and sent them. She had them all out on the lawn in the morning doing PT before they went to school. She was marvellous, the widow of a naval officer. She had them with her for years.

There was a bombed-out family who arrived one day – Mum, three children and a baby. We were already very full with evacuees, and I couldn't get them all into one house. So I decided to put the eldest boy, aged seven, and the next one, in a neighbour's house. The eldest boy rounded on me, really very angrily: 'You can't do that, Miss.'

'Now look, you're a big boy. You can manage perfectly well with your brother,' I told him.

'Oh, it ain't that, Miss. Mum can't manage the baby without me. Look, he needs changing now.' And he was right.

I certainly didn't come across the bad side of evacuation. The few difficulties got much too much publicity. There were so many households who made it easy for the parents of the evacuees to stay, even though it meant putting them up on the floor. The houses were very, very full. You see we'd not only got the children, we'd also got war workers, and this was what caused the problems.

Some people who wanted to join up found that the Army, the Navy and the Air Force were full. So they were compulsorily sent to a factory that needed them, and we had a lot of those. I was very sorry for them, because they were longing to do something else in the war, and they didn't get a very good reception at their billets.

We were working at this stage for the Ministry of Labour, who decided that the war workers would be sent round in busloads of thirty at a time, and dumped one by one in their billets all over our area. I objected to this but they insisted. Well, they were the boss, so I went off with the first lot.

I wanted to take them individually, so that if one got a bad reception nobody else would see. I'd informed all the billets beforehand, and I knew one was particularly sticky and didn't want anybody. When I got this young man to the door, I rang the bell, took his suitcase and as the door opened, I pushed it in. The door slammed in my face. There was no question of being able to get it open again. And now his luggage was on one side of the door and he was on the other. The busload behind us were taking all this in.

I said firmly, 'All right, we'll come back later.' And I walked back on to the bus, terrified of what the people on it would say. They might have been very angry. One man at the back called out, 'I say, Miss, are you 'appy in your work?' I could have kissed him, because everybody roared with laughter. Afterwards I went to the chief person in the local authority, and he took this chap round himself to the billet and insisted that he should be allowed to stay there.

I think it was all right. The householder realised he'd really overstepped the mark. Of course these billets were paid for, but the owners had only to provide a bed and access to sanitation. No food. The workers were fed at the factory canteen.

Some of the workers were women. Two were compulsorily billeted on an admiral and his wife, and the wife wasn't a very easy lady! She came storming into the office, standing very straight: 'Do you know what they've done, Clemency? They've hidden all their sanitary towels under the mattress!' I had to move them after that, and I gave them a piece of my mind. But they hadn't known what to do. They were shy. They didn't like to say to an admiral's wife, 'What do I do with my sanitary towel?'

All the time, whatever was happening, one was nervous about invasion. One night we thought we heard the bells. The church bells were meant to ring in the event of an invasion, and that's what it sounded like. We were right on the coast at Milford and sleeping downstairs. I was on the sofa and my friend was behind it. I thought, I can't run anyway, and I told her she'd better get on with it. My friend said, I don't think I'm going to run either. What's the good?

In the morning we found out what the church bells were. There'd been an almighty gale, and they'd got these metal invasion repellers all the way down the coast. It was a coastline of pebbles, and the pebbles had been washed against the repellers, and that's what sounded like church bells. We felt so stupid.

Never having been to school, I'd never picked up measles or German measles or chickenpox or anything. Now I caught them all off the evacuees. I was a perfect pest. We had our own evacuee, called Roy, in the house, and he and I had measles together. We were sitting one in each bed, and we heard rockets going off, whoosh! He didn't like them much, so every time I thought one was going I'd say whoosh, and he'd suddenly start saying whoosh, and that was better.

I think one of the things we learned in the war was that women worked happily together. So often people have said that women fight when they work together, and it's quite untrue. I don't think, either, that 'old busybodies' was ever a suitable remark to make about the WVS. I mean, there were the few bossy-pants, but you get them in anything, don't you?

DENISE HATCHARD
War Widow

Denise Parr met Edward Hatchard, an engineer, in 1929 when she was nineteen. They fell head over heels in love with each other at their first meeting. She was a student training to be an architect and her mother tried to persuade her to carry on and finish her course. But after she married she had four babies in rapid succession.

If war hadn't intervened she reckoned she would have had six. She had been an only child and had longed for brothers and sisters.

In 1939 they were all living in Leigh-on-Sea – close to the coast, for they liked sailing. 'We had very little money. Doctors' fees in those days used to be one month's salary every twelve months.' But life was good. She loved her children: 'Not other people's. I found it difficult even to touch other people's.' She enjoyed her role as a mother. Her own upbringing had been a matriarchal one. She doesn't remember her father, and her grandfather had died before she knew him. She wasn't hankering after a career. She had already discovered her lifelong love of gardening. (Her present garden, which she built up from nothing, is delightful and open to the public.) Yes, life was good – especially when she and her husband were able to snatch the occasional horse ride at dawn before he went to work. Then war put an end to this contented life.

He joined up and they waited for him to get a permanent posting where the family could join him and be together again. It was a shock to find instead that he was posted overseas. He was there for two years and was OC his unit before he was killed.

Shortly after war was declared my husband said at breakfast, 'Do you know, I think I ought to go and fight for my wife and family. I don't feel happy letting other people do it. What do you think?' And I said, surprisingly, that I thought he should.

It was odd because we had started off being conchies, and I was ashamed – when Czechoslovakia was left in the state it was – I was ashamed of being British. We should have done something then.

Since my husband was an engineer as well as being in the civil air guard, he could have said he was in a reserved occupation, but he didn't. And within ten days he had gone into the Air Force.

Up to now I hadn't thought much about the war. I was more concerned with bringing up my four small children. The youngest was only eighteen months and there was six years between the oldest and the youngest. It's a very good thing we did have a family in a rush, as it turned out.

While I was waiting for my husband to be posted, we had the most ghastly time. We were on the Thames estuary. There was an enormous gun on the golf course, and our garden ran into it. When that let fly, I couldn't hear the children yelling. I had to be solely responsible for four little tots, because really that's all they were. And getting them used to gas masks! I was frightened of the darn things myself.

Then the government evacuated the family. Not Gillian – she was too small. She went over to my mother, who was living with my grandmother. The day they went, I had to have the three children, with labels, down at a school on the arterial road at six a.m. It was a beautiful summer morning. And they were going to – I didn't know where – with their labels. And I said, 'I'll be with you within six weeks. Wherever you are, I will come.' And I went back to that empty house. It's something that anyone who's suffered will never forget, ever. You couldn't.

When children were evacuated, parents gave them a stamped addressed postcard to send back, telling you where they were staying. They had been sent to Derbyshire. David, my son, was with some people who kept a sweet and paper shop. The house had no bathroom or anything – only an earth closet. David was exceedingly naughty but he liked things right and was particularly fussy about washing. The couple did not mean to be unkind to him, but it was such a different life for David and he couldn't cope with it at all.

The girls were happy with their mining family. They took to it so that when we met they told me, 'Mum, you do talk funny.' And when it was time for the miner to come home, we all went out to meet him, this black man walking home from the pit. My two girls said, 'Ee, 'ere comes our dad.' It didn't bother me in the slightest because they were happy.

David ended up suffering from malnutrition. The people he was with were not at fault. He wasn't eating because he wasn't happy. So we sent him to a very proper aunt of mine, but that was another huge contrast which wasn't any good for him either.

About this time another aunt of mine living in a big house in the middle of Essex had a whole East End school billeted on her, and she also took Gillian, my youngest, because I wasn't the least bit happy having her with me with all the bombing going on.

In 1940, I think it was, my husband was posted near Chippenham. I went down there for about six weeks, and it was delightful. But then he got his final posting to North Africa, a terrible shock. He had to go up to North Wales for extra training, so I decided to go and stay with my mother and grandmother. With my two heavy suitcases I took a train up to London – the day after the first fire raid, so there was chaos. I got a taxi a bit of the way, then I got out and was aiming for Fenchurch Street station. A man in morning dress was marching along to his office, and there was a door burning. So he just picked up a fire bucket, chucked it at the door and went on walking. It's a wonderful vision, that.

When I got to Fenchurch Street, the station was out of action. There was a sailor there with his ditty-bag, and we decided we would try and get to Liverpool Street. So he carried my two cases and I carried his bag. We got there, took a train, and although it had to stop because of an air-raid warning, I eventually got to my grandmother's at West Cliffe.

That night, they dropped a bomb at the end of the road, and five very large windows caved in on me. And the most disgusting stench a bomb makes! I could hear my mother singing out, 'It's all right, Gran, it's all right, Gran.' She was ninety-two. Every door that was open was blown shut, and vice versa. There wasn't a window left – all the glass was out of the house, and all the tiles were off the roof. And there was snow on the ground.

I couldn't get to sleep for the blazes. The gas main had been fractured. There was the awful noise of workmen working, and then next day we got up to find that the chimneys had been swept clean right across the rooms, all mixed up with the glass. I phoned my husband and they gave him leave to come down and help.

I wasn't frightened, I was cross. I never took shelter, ever, not even when I lived in London. I used to sleep through the noise of the raids, even when the house would be bouncing about. Yet if my next-door neighbours were talking on their doorstep, I would have to ask them please would they not, because it woke me up.

I was determined to go comfortably. But during that time I did have three

The war forced Denise to be self-sufficient.

horrific dreams, when I thought I was in the middle of an air raid. And those were nights when there was nothing, so I had to shut up about that.

By now the other two girls were with Gillian at my aunt's with the evacuated school, and soon they all talked with a wonderful East End accent. Because his father had been killed, David went a term early to his father's school, Brentwood, and I went to do my war work in London at the Ministry of Works – which was going back, in a way, to my wanting to be an architect. We were designing underground factories and I concentrated on the plumbing side. I'd

All four of Denise's children were evacuated from Leigh-on-Sea.

always found plumbing very interesting. I became known as the lavatory queen.

I had found myself a little house in Chelsea with a controlled rent. When I'd asked for the keys to go and look at it the estate agent said, 'But madam you can't live there' – I must have gone in looking elegant – 'it's a cottage.' I said, 'I can and I want to. May I have the key, please?' I kept the key and used to give scrubbing parties because it was so filthy. Friends from the Ministry would come and scrub, and I had half a bottle of whisky once a month on rations, so that I could offer them an inducement. I went there in May, and my husband was killed in December. Thank God it was that way round, because otherwise I would never have had the courage.

In December '42, two days after my birthday, eleven days before Christmas, a telegram came at half-past eight in the morning. I had three pages of it. I got down the first page: THE WAR MINISTRY REGRETS THAT ... and I had to turn the page to read KILLED. In January our Christmas presents from him kept arriving. And I kept dreaming, and in the dream he kept saying 'I'm not really dead.'

I don't know quite what happened. In his last letter he had written to say he was so tired he didn't know what to do, and that he had this last trip to do with the Americans.

The two elder children, Jane and David, suffered terribly from their father's death, for they could remember him. David had been his father's shadow when he'd been at home.

At one time I might have thought a breakdown was a sort of romantic thing to have. It isn't. It is horrible. I used to be travelling on the underground to work and tears would stream, they'd just stream down my face. I eventually went to the doctor and she said, 'You're having a breakdown, dear, you'd better knock off work for a bit.'

This breakdown – I suppose it went on and off for two or three years – would stop me in my tracks. I would feel as if I were going to fall over backwards. I wanted to hold on to something all the time. They wanted me to go into hospital but I said no. I just didn't want to go. I always had a passion to be in the sunlight in the garden of my little house.

By now the children were in boarding-school and I did mind when they were sent home for half-term with no coupons for anything. I wrote to the housemistress and she said, well don't tell anyone else but I will send them home with emergency ration cards. I didn't mind the shortages for myself. I drank weak tea and used little sugar and I used to mix the silly little bit of butter with some marg.

But there was one funny incident over food. I used to pushbike to work (and home for lunch) so I was cycling seventy-eight miles a week. One morning I got a puncture. I was desperate, as I was going to the dentist and a cyclist passing by at the time said to take his bike for now. 'I'll bring yours back repaired this evening,' he promised.

Now, not only did he return my bike – his was a better one than mine – but from then on I was the recipient of gifts. Eggs were left by the garden gate. And butter was put through the post-box. And this went on for some time. The supply just ended. I don't know what happened to him. Prison? He was, I gathered, embroiled with black-marketeering. I never discovered his name.

I wasn't particularly aware of a community spirit in the war, perhaps because I was just given to getting on with my own immediate problems, which were various. I do remember in one of the severe winters mine was the only house left with water so I'd leave my door unlocked for neighbours to come and help themselves. I believed in lagging all pipes.

When the war ended I thought it was boring. I mean, VE day itself was exciting. Everybody was celebrating in Trafalgar Square. It was a wonderful thing. VJ day was horrible. The same place both times. The feeling was dreadful, it was frightening. And they were throwing firecrackers into the crowd, so entirely different. I don't know why.

For me there was nothing happening. I was used to bangs and bumps. There was no husband to come back.

One never had much to do with people. People were all right, but I used to upset the other architects at the Ministry when I would say: 'Good night; one day nearer the grave.' They didn't like that.

I was all intent on my struggle to keep the children at boarding-school. I wanted them to have the same education that we had. I didn't see why that should be denied them. Why should they suffer? I had no assistance, and it was a huge struggle really.

I had been making all our clothes, including our winter coats. I managed to get my dinner cleared by seven-thirty and then I started dressmaking. I remember making handkerchiefs out of tracing linen for the three girls. They needed two dozen each. The school didn't temper their demands because of the war. I gave my daughter Judith a rocket because she sent too many clothes to the school laundry, and consequently the next term she didn't send anything.

Yes it was a hard slog. Especially when they were home for holidays after my mother died. I would ring up and see how they were. It's terrible having children under those circumstances, you're looking over your shoulder all the time. What's the time? I must get back.

Luckily they were all great readers. They would go down to the little Kensington branch library, and come back with seventeen books, which they weren't allowed to have. They'd take a large shopping basket with a scarf to put over it to hide the extra books, and they'd have finished them by the end of the day. They would sit on the couch, each with a pile of books, and fight because somebody had finished their book and wanted somebody else's. 'No you can't have that, I haven't read it.'

There was a nice small bookshop just around the corner from us, where they would let the children borrow books and then post them back through their letterbox. Yes, for those sort of things, people were nice.

Children on their own! I had a collapsible canoe, a long rubber thing, and they used to take that down to the Thames. And I created a thing with wheels, pram wheels, for them to push it on, for the river was only just down the road. I went and watched them one day. Thank God for the river police. The Thames runs at a shocking rate down there. If I'd been around I would never have let them do it. The children were always talking about the river police and how kind they were. I don't know how many times the river police rescued them.

I was definitely bored with my life by now, and decided to sell my house in Chelsea. I had been able to buy it for eighteen hundred with some money I inherited when my mother died, and I sold it for eight thousand. I wanted to move from London. I'd meant to go to Wiltshire. Then I saw this place between Welshpool and Newtown. Oh! yes, madness. I had to have this place, and paid five thousand for it in 1959.

When I came here I thought I'd probably live on my war widow's pension.

You can't. Really, the war widow's pension was a farce. My friends in France got far better pensions. Our pensions were adjusted at last after the Falklands War, but at that time things were so difficult. I had the choice of keeping warm or eating. I couldn't do both. But people who came here were astounded at what I'd done to this house.

And that is how I went back to architecting. I used to have a queue, which I hated. And I'd say no, I don't want the work, go to somebody else. But they wouldn't. And I'd do a little bit. And do a little bit. And do a little bit.

The Ministry of Works in the war had given me a more thorough training than I would have had if I had finished my college course. By the end of the war you really knew what was what. We used to dread qualified young things coming to us having just passed their exams. They'd take on private work and get themselves into a devil of a mess. You'd have to rescue them.

I went on working on this house, of course. I am good on the actual construction. I just like it. It's what comes naturally. My husband, my father were engineers. My son is an engineer. I love tools; I hate tools being abused.

I built all the garden. The ground was awful. It was two foot up against the house. I used to do twenty-four barrowloads a morning, twenty-four an afternoon, to get it away. I laid all the tiles, which were in the old kitchen. It's surprising what I have done, when I think back. I can't now, which I find infuriating.

Although, I suppose, I was always tough and strong physically, I couldn't say boo to a goose at one time. But I learned to. You had to, to survive. You were determined that you weren't going to let your family down.

DOREEN TAGHOLM
Engineered by War

When eleven-year-old Doreen Fairclough passed the scholarship exam her parents had to sign a bit of paper to say they'd keep her in education for five years. But after that she had to leave the grammar school – which she loved – as money was so desperately tight.

She got a job in the library in Hull and happily imagined that's where she'd stay, working her way up through the system. Her mother prophesied she'd never marry because she was too particular!

That September, when she was sweet sixteen, war broke out. In 1941 she was required to register under the National Service Act.

In 1944 she was called up, as were all girls of her age, and directed to work for the BBC as an engineer, a job which before the war had not been open to women.

First, I'd better explain about my family. I was the eldest. After I was born, Mother went five years before she had my sister, Margaret, then another five years before my sister Mary – and then within the next five years, had three more children, which seriously affected my teenage years. I was eighteen when my last brother, Michael, was born and people thought he was mine.

I loved my mother and father and hated them at the same time. I used to wish they'd get their act together. The house was always full of kids, and babies, and no money. I had this strong feeling that it would all fall apart without me. Indeed, my mother said, in her later years, 'I'd never have brought the family up without you.'

Certainly I made a financial contribution. That's what worried me about going away when women were being conscripted in 1942. Anyway, I went on working in the library.

Hull was being badly bombed. It was one of the north-east cities which was never mentioned by name on the news bulletins. My mother's cousin and family were killed in a direct hit on a communal air-raid shelter. Our family, I'm glad to say, was never bombed out but there was destruction all round us.

My mother was absolutely terrified. Remember, she had small children and because of the raids and sleeping in air-raid shelters, she didn't have her clothes off, in a manner of speaking, for several years.

You might be frightened, but you didn't panic. You got up the next morning, you went to work, kids went to school. If the all-clear had sounded before one o'clock in the night the children didn't have to go to school until the afternoon. If it was after 3 a.m., they didn't have to go to school at all next day.

I had to do my air-raid welfare service, which amounted to a very hasty get-together the morning after air raids in a church hall, a school, or any available building, with services such as the WVS, the local housing authority, representatives of the Chamber of Commerce, local chemists, hardware stores, that sort of thing, to provide some sort of relief.

The libraries were used to disseminate information. We had a certain amount of training about what sort of notices might be required, what sort of psychology to use to help people who were suddenly in grave distress. Our notices went up: 'Rest and Information Centre', with arrows pointing to wherever. We simply helped people to sort their way through finding lost relatives, issuing them with extra coupons for food, or sometimes just food itself, and blankets.

Often people were totally bombed out. We had lists which were fed in continuously as the day went on, from other organisations such as the police. Sometimes there were American servicemen round and they also used to help. We had lists of bombed-out streets, bomb-damaged streets. There were always local ministers at hand, Roman Catholic and Anglican, because people were often in extreme grief. I was all of twenty when I was coping with this.

Somebody might come in and say, 'I hear Morpeth Street's been hit. My sister lives there, do you know anything about it? It's all barricaded off at the moment, I can't get in.' We would refer to a list and have to inform them, 'Numbers 1 to 39, direct hit. As far as we know, no survivors.' I'm simplifying now. 'And 2 to 40 are damaged but habitable. Two are believed killed. Three people have been taken to Beverley Road Hospital.'

People would ask, 'Can we get down Anlaby Road yet? We couldn't this morning, there's a crater' – that sort of thing. Throughout the day, information would be coming in. Some of it was arbitrary. It had to be. We were in a situation that had never been coped with before in England.

At this time I was against the war. When you're young, you're certain about everything. You're definitely a socialist, an agnostic, red's your favourite colour, or whatever it may be. And I believed in pacifism. I thought everything could be sorted out without killing. I didn't think all Germans were bad. I wasn't at all imbued with patriotic fervour. My senior history master at school used an expression: 'the bombastic, nationalistic, flag-wagging attitude of the British government'. Those words stuck in my mind, though his reference was to nineteenth-century politics.

I was a socialist, my father was a socialist, my grandmother was a socialist, and we had the Co-op written up almost in letters of flame above the door!

Obviously I had to register when I was eighteen, but I didn't want to go and join any of the services, partly because of these feelings, and partly because I had a great commitment at home.

I didn't have time to mind – it's only in retrospect that I think I might have lost something. I'd felt middle-aged since I was about fifteen. I remember working out that my mother was pregnant with me when, aged eighteen, she married my father. That shook me rather at the time. It's very difficult nowadays to realise just what an impact conception outside marriage still had.

I went on working (and taking exams) for the library because my boss had asked for, and got, my deferment. Then in 1944, the government decided that all females born in 1923 were to be called up – things were tight. A lot of men had been called up, so manpower was severely depleted. The only debarment you could plead was that you were looking after a sick relative. And if you were married, you were deemed immobile. You could be sent to a factory in your own area, but you weren't sent miles away.

When I went for my interview, they told me they were putting me on a thing called the Technical Service Register. One of the organisations on it was the BBC, and I chose it. The BBC carried an aura of glamour, and because my initial interview was in Leeds, I thought this would give me a break from the bombing in Hull. But afterwards they sent me straight down to London, and a V2 hit Selfridges the night I arrived. The BBC hostel was very near there.

I was anxious about leaving home. But as luck would have it, I earned a great deal more money than if I'd been in the forces – and more, too, than I'd been paid in the library. So I was able to send money home to the seven of them.

The nature of my work at the BBC was highly technical yet I was termed 'Woman Operator'. After a while this became rather laughable, and we became known as Technical Assistants, either Class 1 or Class 2, depending on whether you took the Class 1 examination.

This is from a BBC manual which covers the war years and shows what the climate was like just before I got there. It's so patronising:

We have every reason to be satisfied with the performance of these girls to date, and, provided their interest in the job is maintained, there seems to be no reason why the experiment should not prove a success. My own impression, based on what I have seen of these girls, both during their B course and subsequently, is that provided we keep them strictly to operational work, there is no reason whatever why they should not fulfil an extremely useful job.

But the manual admits that women also met a certain amount of outright antagonism:

The BBC, like any big organisation, had its share of reactionaries, who did not favour the idea of women invading what had always been a man's preserve. An Engineer In Charge sought to limit their activities as much as possible, because their clothes got caught up in the components. In the next breath, he was complaining about women wearing trousers on his station. He had forbidden them to do so, except on the night shift, in contravention of the official line that there was no objection to trousers, provided that they were of a reasonably quiet colour.

Back to my work. Did I meet male resistance? Obviously there were old diehards amongst the engineers, but they wouldn't just be engineering diehards, they'd be male diehards who would say women are just not cut out for this sort of thing. But no, on the whole, you could go as far as you wanted to go.

I went first through the BBC Engineering Training School, then I was posted up to a comparatively new and enormous short-wave transmitter at a place called Skelton in the wilds of the Lake District. It was one of the most powerful short-wave transmitting stations in the world. The American Forces Network went out from there and broadcast to South America, to France. You know the programme *'Allo, 'allo* – some of those messages are not really so funny as they sound. They actually did happen. 'There will be no chickens hatched tonight', for example, was sent to the underground forces in France, Norway, and eventually Russia.

It was a twenty-four-hour operation. We worked evenings, day and night duties. It was interesting, and completely new to me, this technical work. I had only done elementary physics and chemistry at school. But within what was set down and taught to us, if you applied yourself and were reasonably intelligent – and if you could apply what you'd learned to what was in front of you – then it was OK.

As well as sending to the American forces, there was a lot of foreign-language stuff, much of which we couldn't understand. The same with codes; and these enigmatic phrases to the Resistance forces. We were not meant to interpret but

Doreen with Grover, her husband to be, outside the BBC overseas station in Cumberland.

to transmit.

It was here I met my husband. Sometimes I required his signature to clear something that I had to operate. He used to scribble 'G.E.T.' and I wondered if his name might be George Edward. Who could have guessed it was Grover Emanuel Tagholm?

Grover and I were both interested in music, which was one of the reasons we first got to know each other. I used to go through the *Radio Times* and mark programmes that I wanted to listen to, and looking over my shoulder one day he said, 'Oh, I do that too.' (I think he probably had more of an eye on me than I had on him.)

We were married in Penrith register office in 1946. It was a Wednesday. One of the girls on the station made me a blue woollen frock, using some of my coupons to buy the material, and my mother and father came over from Hull.

Did they approve? I think it was just the next thing that was happening in their lives. They lived a bemused sort of life really. They were pleased with Grover, I'm sure.

Anyway, the wedding was no great shakes. It was just quiet. We went back to the digs afterwards, and my mother and father and Grover's father and step-sister had lunch with us. Then they went home, and we went to Edinburgh till Sunday. Then back to our digs and we were back on duty again.

But we couldn't work on the same shift any longer. Husbands and wives weren't allowed to. We didn't see each other much. We'd leave notes! It's absolutely true. Was the BBC thinking of safety, attention to detail? It could also have been something to do with working night duties. When you had your hour's rest period, you might have gone off and had it together. But there was no reason why you couldn't do that with any of the existing MEs or technical assistants on the station.

I gave up work about the end of that year. By then, there was a tremendous emphasis on women going back into the home. I can see now that it was largely political. The men were coming back from the war, and the government needed jobs for them. The great thing was, get the women back home. And I accepted this without resentment.

Having a family was the next natural progression, though I'd never ever thought, oh! I want a baby. I had four eventually. My mother used to say they'd bring their love with them, and I think that's absolutely true. You don't know this thing before it's born, and then suddenly there it is, and you'd kill for it, wouldn't you?

Because of the war, I think my generation gained a seriousness over and above what was required. We seemed to be *sensible* somehow, but we did go through the mill at a time of our lives when it really affected us. I used to think of us as over-serious, over-earnest, over-justifying, summed up in the phrase, 'Well, during the war, you know ...' to the point of boring people silly.

Doris, one of the gorgeous Windmill girls, shown here on a Black Cat cigarette card.

DORIS BARRY
A Song and Dance Girl

*The Windmill Theatre is famous for never having closed in the war.
Famous, too, for its tasteful nudes who never moved, unlike the soubrettes
who wore fetching costumes to suit the dances they danced, the songs they
sang, the acts they performed.*

*One such appealing soubrette was Doris Barry who, because of the war,
had to leave the theatre. She went to live in Blackpool with her mother and
became a civil servant.*

*After the war she applied her new-found organising ability to represent-
ing her now internationally famous sister, the Prima Ballerina Assoluta,
Dame Alicia Markova.*

*It didn't stop there. She joined Hughie Green as programme associate on
the TV show* Opportunity Knocks, *and helps to run the London Studio
Centre, a leading theatre school, which was founded by the late Bridget
Espinosa.*

In the summer of 1939 the theatre management at the Windmill told us to be
ready no matter what happened. Everyone was apprehensive about the possibility of war, but since the announcement was to be made on the Sunday I
wasn't at the theatre. My boyfriend came to our flat just before eleven o'clock.
There we all were waiting: Jimmy, my mother, my sisters Vivienne, Alicia and
Bunny – Alicia was in London because she was due to open with the Ballets
Russes at Drury Lane Theatre.

We heard the news. War. A few minutes later the sirens went and we all put
our gas masks on. To this day we laugh about it. We didn't know what to do, so
we sat there in our gas masks – waiting for what? Then the all-clear sounded.

We were living at Number 11 Marble Arch, W1, a wonderful flat with big
windows all along the side facing the park. We could see a barrage balloon right

opposite us where Speakers' Corner is.

We got to know it very well, and when we had raids, we knew as soon as we saw them get ready to put the balloon up that we had twenty minutes before the siren went. They used to get the message as soon as the enemy planes were sighted leaving their base.

That gave us time to collect our little bits and pieces which we kept in a case. Our passports – where we were going, I don't know! Some money, a bit of make-up, of course, and the door keys. Oh, a torch. We never went anywhere without a torch.

Just round the corner was the Cumberland Hotel where we had friends staying. It had a very deep restaurant, the Grill, which was the shelter. If you were in there before the siren went, you were allowed to stay. So we had twenty minutes to put Tinker, our lovely cat, in a comfortable place, grab our little bag and rush out.

From the day war was declared, all theatres closed – except for the Windmill. So we were there, ready and made-up and waiting for our calls. There was a call-board by the stage door with the timing of each number. Some people, like the comic, were only in one number, whereas a soubrette might be in four. A lot of people don't know the word soubrette any more. It means young leading lady: you had to sing, you had to dance, you had to act in the dramatic sketches and be a feed for the comics.

I was so naïve, I hardly got any of the risqué jokes, but everyone thought we were worldly. We had a reputation – 'Oh, Windmill girls,' they used to say. It was because some of the show girls took their clothes off. In fact, we were very sheltered. Vivian van Damm was very strict with us. No Stage-Door Johnnies got past Ben, our doorman.

A lot of men turned up, but most we never got to see. Not unless they wrote. Or we'd met them properly at our anniversary show and party, when we'd get invited out for lunch to the Trocadero, across the road from the theatre. In the war the lunches stopped. Our licence to open was for performances between midday and six o'clock in the evening. That was because of the blackout.

We had absolutely packed houses every time, because we were the only entertainment in London. All the Forces came. Our clothes at that time were regarded as scanty but nowadays you wouldn't call them that, except for the nudes in the tableaux, of course.

When van Damm first told us he was introducing nudes, we were all going to leave. Nobody wanted to be associated. But he was a most persuasive man, a marvellous character. He argued: what was the difference between people coming into the theatre and looking at a naked woman and people going to a picture gallery? The human body was beautiful.

The very first tableau he put on was September Morn, and it was just like the painting. We had to agree it was beautiful, with all the wonderful lighting. And the nudes did not move, that was the thing.

He had also said, it's much better that these men come here than go into brothels and places. Well, we were not at all sure that we agreed. For young girls – and most of us were not only young but younger than our age, too – it wasn't very good to be up there on the stage with an audience full of men with raincoats across their knees, half of them playing with themselves. This is what was going on while you had to sing and dance. You couldn't help but be aware of it. And this opened my eyes, certainly, and gave me a rather bad opinion of males in general.

At that time, when I went to cocktail parties I'd meet a lot of people who would say, eyebrows raised, 'Oh, you work at the Windmill.' And I could have turned to some of the men and said, 'Yes, *you* know. The Windmill where I've seen you sitting in the front row.' They never realised how far we could see.

We used to get lovely presents. On an anniversary once, there was this beautiful great big basket of flowers for the three soubrettes. When we started sharing the flowers out we found three boxes, each with a precious stone in it. I had a beautiful star sapphire. I still have it, and we never ever knew who they came from.

I remember a rather romantic episode. I used to meet a very naïve young man – not much more experienced than me – for supper at the Trocadero. After supper he'd booked the hansom cab that was a landmark outside the Criterion Restaurant at Piccadilly Circus, and he took me home in it all the way to Ladbroke Grove, where we had a flat, before the war. We were two babes out together. We had a nice cuddle along the way.

A friend who used to come down from Manchester also took me home in this cab. First he bought me an armful of violets from the flower woman under Eros. They're very romantic memories.

It was strange; it wasn't a matter of 'your place or mine?' That was unheard of. A kiss was really quite a big event, and yet here we were on the stage, dancing around. One or two girls liked going out, and liked whatever came after. But the rest of us used to think, oh, how could they? One girl used to stand on the stage (it was so tiny, you were almost on top of the audience), and ogle the men. I don't think she did it for the money. I think she did it just to go out and enjoy herself.

When mother and I were bombed for the second time in our flat, my sister Alicia sent a telegram from New York where she was performing, saying that she couldn't dance knowing we were in London. We must go up to my other sister Vivienne, a pucker civil servant, who had been evacuated to Blackpool with the Ministry of Health. (Bunny was on tour in *Black Velvet*, repeatedly being bombed out of blitz cities.)

Alicia had to return to the United States as she had an American contract which they would not release her from, and the powers that be in this country said she would be much more use over there. Which she was – paving the way for ballet in America and also sending back dollars which we needed desperately.

It must have been agonising for her. We were a very close family. Lots of times letters didn't get there or she'd send us packages which we never received. It was eight years before I saw her again, because she went in 1939 and I didn't go over until 1947.

The bombing was pretty horrific. We'd converted our box room into a sort of air-raid shelter, put the bed in there, and the torch, and some water, and we took Tinker in with us. I just couldn't take being underground in the Cumberland Hotel. And Mother said, 'Well come on, we'll take a chance.'

We were the only ones in the building when the bomb dropped outside in the road and shattered all the windows, even though they were done with tape. The bombs came in fives, and each one got nearer. I was saying my prayers, which I do every night. I kept on saying my prayers through one, two, three, four bombs. After the fourth bomb had dropped, Tinker leapt underneath the bed. He had a sixth sense. There is a noise, a strange noise, that a bomb makes. You never forget it. With that it came. We had all the blasts and the flashes, and we both lay there and wondered, are we all right? Mother said, 'Don't move.'

I still went into the Windmill the next day without any sleep. But by now Mother really was quite badly shocked; and our doctor said we ought to go up to Blackpool where Vivienne had been evacuated with the Civil Service and they were wanting temps, so I applied and got a job. Later I was sort of conscripted into it, because this counted as war work.

At the same time I was organising the entertainment unit for ENSA up there. Blackpool was the place for entertainment. Max Wall was there, for instance and many other famous names, all in the RAF. The act I did was a medley of Wishing songs, and some dancing – high kicks in a very short pretty pale blue dress. They liked me, I was told, because I was ladylike. The other act I did was, 'Oh Johnny, oh Johnny.' I sang it to a soldier with that name. There was always one! I did a lot of hospital shows but that eventually got me down because you'd have your audience in stretchers etc. They said I was so sweet that I wouldn't send the temperatures up too much.

And I used to do 'Christopher Robin saying his Prayers'. One night I went out to an American camp and for the only time in my life, I got the bird, as you might say.

It was all going beautifully, and then there's the line, 'and wasn't it fun in the bath tonight …' I'd sung it hundreds of times, but this time I got wolf whistles. I couldn't go on: all my years at the Windmill, coping with everything, and this was the first time I was ever speechless. I *made* myself go on but it just got worse: 'the cold so cold, the hot so hot.' How I ever got to the end! Of course, I was a riot. But I could never do it again. And if I hear it, I'm back at that army camp called Wheeton.

I never thought I was really Civil Servant material. To me I was playing a part, but by the end they made me an established civil servant with a grade. Our father had been a wonderful organiser, and I found that I was. I'd think, why are you doing it that way, why don't you do it this way? But I didn't stay in the Civil Service very long after the war, it got me down. I went to the States to visit Alicia.

If it hadn't been for that job I would never have done what I did later, when I worked with my sister internationally. I looked after all her business contracts. And when we did concerts all over the world I arranged the travel, the programmes, stage-managed everything. On tour there were only four of us. Alicia, her partner, musician and myself. I found a file the other day, and I thought, did I do all this?

Oh! One last thing about the war. I was the first to introduce 'Boomps a Daisy' and perform it as a Can-Can!

Women were needed in the factories, and Jean had no choice but to go and make shells.

JEAN WYNNE
...And Pass the Ammunition

Jean Wynne, like lots of girls of her time, wanted to be a nurse. Her mum had been one. But her father, like so many dads of her time, ruled the roost. And he said no.

When the government started conscripting girls, Jean badly wanted to join the WAAF, but even after she had wept and pleaded with him, her father still said no. He resolutely refused to let her join up. She had to stay at home. There was no choice left: she had to go into one of the Sheffield ammunition works. It was the last thing she'd ever expected to do.

When you're a child you have visions. I was going to be all sorts of things. In reality, I went straight from school to work in a cabinet case factory. I was in the cutting room, which meant I cut out the satin linings for the inside of cutlery boxes. I enjoyed it, but it didn't last long. The war began and I was sent to work in an ammunition factory, in what they called the shell shop.

I used to do everything with shells – cutting them into shape, turning them, boring shells out, putting the end on the shells. It was very heavy work: I've got some scars on my hand to prove it. I nearly had my finger off a couple of times.

When we went in, it was horrible, because the young chaps who worked there knew very well that any moment they would have to go off to war. They had to stay on just long enough to show us how to handle the machines. You can imagine what it was like between the women and the men.

They were mad because they'd been called up. They were mad at us for taking over their jobs, even though we had no choice. They didn't want to show us what to do and they made things really awkward. Never clearly explaining anything. The machines were difficult and dangerous, and it didn't help, either, that I didn't want to be in this work anyway.

I dreaded going in each day. Gradually the men came round when they realised that they'd got to leave, and we had to be shown how to do their jobs. Finally there were just a couple of chaps left whom they called setters-up, and if anything went wrong we had to go to them. Sometimes they could be very difficult, too. They used to make us wait. And since we were on piece work, if we didn't get our machines working properly we were down on our earnings. Delays lost you money.

We were on three shifts: mornings, six to two; afternoons, two to ten; and then the night shift. It was very awkward later, when I was married, because my husband, who was in a reserved occupation, was on different times from me.

He was in the factory at the Admiralty. It was a bit hush-hush, his work – blueprints and what not. When the war got going properly, we hardly saw each other. I could be going to work in the morning for the six o'clock shift, and meet my husband coming up the road. And when I was coming home off my shift, my husband might have already gone to work.

We first met two years before the war at a dancing school, when I was sixteen and he was twenty-six. Then we started going out to dance at weekends to get some practice in. And after that we danced together whenever we could. We used to go twice, sometimes three times a week. Modern dancing we liked – to Glenn Miller and music like that.

It used to be long dresses – oh! it was lovely. Chiffon dresses that floated out when you were doing your double spins round – it was great.

We got married in 1943, when I was twenty-one. It was a problem getting married during the war. We were swapping our rations to try and get the right things to make a wedding cake. I wouldn't say it was a very nice cake, really, with dried egg in it! You couldn't make it any other way. We all had to go down to Tookwoods in Sheffield, a very high-class cake shop, and queue for some cakes and bread. And this was me on my wedding morning.

I had a long dress in oyster satin, lovely, with a very long veil. It wasn't made. My mum and dad bought it for me at Ann Leonard's. It was supposed to be *the* nice shop in Sheffield. I had to have the veil tinted to match the dress, because veils were white and my dress was oyster.

We got married in church and we had to have the reception in the house. It was just the food we could all rake up together from our rations. And do you know where we went after? We went to the Empire, the big show-place in Sheffield. We booked in. We had two seats in the stalls. It was just what I call a straight variety show, when they used to come on, do their turn and go off. It poured with rain, and we got a taxi there, and nobody knew where we were going. Afterwards a taxi took us up to our new home.

During our engagement, we had managed to get a house – and furnish it. Instead of going on a holiday, we used to buy something for the house, saving up

Jean in her oyster satin wedding dress from Ann Leonard's in Sheffield.

bit by bit. The youngsters don't seem to do this now. They just want everything at once and done. I thought it was fun to work and save money and then buy a carpet or something like that.

The shop kept all the bits and pieces for us until the wedding. The day after they'd brought our furniture to the house, the furniture shop was bombed to the ground. We were only just in time or we'd have lost all our home.

We very nearly did anyway. Just a walk away, a bomb dropped and left a great big crater. At the time of this raid, we were sitting on the cellar steps, and my sister-in-law was with us, visiting my mum. She was an insurance lady, and she'd got this bag of money, and what with the crashes and the big bangs and vibrations, the money went all over the cellar. It rolled down the steps, and was all over the place. But I'll tell you this much, we said our prayers, as we sat on the steps that night. Gosh we did.

The next morning, nobody knew what to do. Everything was in a shocking state. Naturally we thought we had to go to work. But there was no transport anywhere. The lines were all up and everybody was walking. The sights we saw were unbelievable, oh, terrible. We saw bodies all over. In the centre of town, the big stores got direct hits. And they had to put down lime because they couldn't do anything else with so many dead bodies.

My brother had gone to work on a night shift, and he didn't come home for two days. He was just digging bodies out. They could hear people under the debris all the time.

Nobody knew what to do. People went to their work, and their work wasn't there. We'd no water or anything, we couldn't get washed. The water cart used to come round and you could just have a jugful at a time. No gas, electricity, or anything for I don't remember how long.

My husband and I were worried about each other all the time. Well, we were so much in love, you know, we just lived for each other. And yet we hardly saw each other to be reassured. But he could see what it was doing to me. When you've been brought up in a sheltered way, and you're a quiet sort of person anyway, it is a shock to go into a munitions works. However much I tried to hold my own, it was much rougher than I'd ever expected it to be.

In the shell shop, you couldn't hear anything because it was next to what we called the stamp shop, where the big hammers went boom boom boom all the time. You certainly couldn't hear music while you worked. Well I couldn't. I'm a little bit deaf now. I'm sure it's from that.

I was actually lonely when I was in the works. I felt isolated because although there were so many people about, you couldn't talk to anyone. You couldn't take your mind off things by chatting to another woman. You were simply getting on and doing what you needed to do or else you didn't earn enough money.

Oh, it was a big strain. They praised the chaps for going to the forces, but nobody ever bothered to think what the women were going through. We really had it rough, you know.

Then of course, the sirens kept going, but we didn't stop until we got what was called the red alert. Then we had to close the machines down and all go into the shelters, where they taught us first aid. We'd got to do something all the time! You couldn't just sit. We had to practise on each other.

It was all getting me down. When I was on nightshift I couldn't sleep during the day. I was getting desperate. I was so tired. Then you make mistakes, don't

Happy and relaxed on a day out from the ammunition factory.

you? And you're using great big machines nearly the length of a room.

There was no time for yourself. It was just all bed and work. And my husband was in the Home Guard as well. He used to work twelve-hour shifts, and at the weekend he had to go to a shooting place on the outskirts of Sheffield and stay overnight in tents. So we were separated then, too.

The only way that we could see something of each other, we realised, was for me not to work. And I couldn't leave my job unless I was expecting a baby. So I went in for my son, even though the world didn't seem a safe place for a baby. I left work and we moved house quite near to my mum and dad.

I fed my baby myself, which was a good thing when everything was so uncertain. My husband got cod-liver oil capsules at work, which he'd bring home for us. The baby had his orange juice and vitamins from the Welfare Clinic. And once a month my husband got one bar of soap.

It was an all-morning job doing nappies. I'd put them in a bucket and soak them overnight, and then I put another big bucket on the gas ring to boil it up – there was hardly any soap to wash nappies in. It makes me wonder, how did we manage? Everything was scarce. If you happened to be out shopping and you saw a queue, you'd join the end of it and then ask what you were queuing for.

All through the war I was always frightened. In the bottom of my stomach. I felt as though something was about to happen. I was full of trepidation all the time. The war really made me nervous. I'll never know, but I wonder, would it have been different if my father had let me go to the forces?

Then after the war at least I achieved the nursing job I wanted to do. The looking after people part of nursing, anyway. Because I was a home help for fifteen years and I loved it. I had so many on my list and they were just like an extension of my family.

PHYLLIS PEARSALL
Artist on the Shop Floor

All that thirty-year-old Phyllis Pearsall wanted to do was to paint for her-self. She got into map-making by chance – to help out her father in America who wanted to make a street map of London. So she started walking. The outcome was the familiar, invaluable A–Z of London. And nearly sixty years later she still heads her prestigious map company when she isn't painting landscapes such as those recently commissioned to hang in the Governor's House in Hong Kong. Which leads us neatly into the start of Phyllis' wartime tale.

In September 1939 I was in Golders Green where I shared a house with a friend who would later have a daughter, Lavender, now wife of the governor of Hong Kong, Chris Patten. Lavender's MP grandfather had come back from London on that afternoon of the third and said, 'Most extraordinary. I always walk around Westminster on a Sunday, and as I came out of the tube today there was nobody about at all. I couldn't believe it. I went to the House, and realised we had declared war. Well, I'm wondering, what to do this evening. Shall we play tiddlywinks?' Which we did most evenings throughout the war when I wasn't fire-watching. It was more or less like Drake with his bowls.

Immediately, I thought I could help in the war with maps. I already had a map of Europe drawn, showing strategic railroads and so on. And as a student without a penny, I had read the German High Command apologia for losing the First World War. In it they said that the Schlieffen plan for encircling France should have started further north. So I had my draughtsman draw Scandinavia and Finland; and separate war maps of Holland and Belgium. So all these maps were ready when, sadly, these countries were attacked. I'd started the business in 1936, you see.

As soon as the war began, the sale of all large-scale maps was stopped by defence regulations. So I thought, well, just bring out war maps, I can do that. The Western Front with the Siegfried and Maginot Lines, showing all the gun emplacements – everything there. It sold enormously. I was able to pay off all my debts from the other maps I could no longer sell.

I brought them out at sixpence in Woolworth's while everybody else was bringing them out at three and sixpence or something. We must have sold about a million. Then I got a letter from Woolworth's asking for another million. And just as I was about to give an order for that million to my printer, a phone call came through from their buyer, Mr Prentice, who was fond of me. He told me, 'Pay no attention to that. This is how we break firms, because we don't want to be kept waiting for anything which is a good seller. Don't give me away.' He's died now, so I can say that. He saved me from a disaster, because I would have printed too many. Meanwhile, W.H. Smith and everybody else took them.

I'd got time between maps to draw women at war. It was a new subject for me and I was always drawing something or other. I knew I would need passes for this so I went to the Ministry of Information and the person in charge was Graham Greene, the novelist, who gave me the permits. He wrote out a thing which allowed me to go anywhere, including into the munitions factories.

The women in the Ordnance factory I went to in Blackburn were absolutely superb. The morale was high even though they were working under unbelievable pressure. And they carried on their own charming little conversations about their boyfriends and this and that, while they were working happily to *Music While You Work*.

They made fuses, and the people who were checking the gauges realised that everything they did had to be perfect. The lives of their own brothers and fathers and friends and husbands were in danger. After El Alamein, when we were chasing the Germans across the desert, there came a rumour that our shells weren't piercing the German tanks. This was Lord Haw Haw in action, and it was very upsetting for the Ordnance workers. So a plane was sent out that very day and came back with a photograph of tanks pierced by their shells. It was put up in the factory the next day to show them that the work they were doing was bang on!

Just before the conscription of women came in, the Ministry of Labour were shown some of my drawings. They said, marvellous, we'd like to commission you and use them to help recruit women. But first we've got to go to the ATS and the others to make sure they're happy with them. But the head of the ATS didn't like the one I'd done of them having foot inspection [p.210]. Owing to its comic realism, I imagine. So the Ministry had to say no.

Anyway, about this time I was conscripted. We had to go to special points according to our surname initial, and I arrived with a friend, Arnot Robertson.

Women working at the Ordnance fuse factory, drawn by Phyllis Pearsall.

As we stood in the long queue of mixed ages (mostly eighteen-year-olds) we saw how old our contemporaries looked, and realised that was what we, being both in our thirties, must look like too.

The Ministry of Labour person asked Arnot, 'What can you do?' She said, 'I write.' The response was, 'Well, I'll put you aside, I don't know what to do with writers.'

Then it was my turn. 'I'm a map publisher,' I told her. She said, 'I didn't ask you what you are, I asked you what can you do. Can you type?' I said I could. 'How many words to the minute?' So – I said 'Oh! I'm not any good like that.' I tried to tell her mapping was quite important, but she wasn't interested. Then she asked, 'Have you any languages?' I said, 'Yes, I've got a lot of languages.' 'That's easy, then … you're for the censorship.'

Censorship was in the Prudential buildings off Holborn, which was quite nice for me because my own office was there, too. We were supposed to be censoring all letters that came through, but the person in charge of our table thought some of them sent to or from neutral countries needn't be. I disagreed after I read one or two. Information was getting through to Germany about the

Resistance movement and people's lives were being lost.

I reported it to the head of my department but he didn't think there was anything wrong. I asked if I could put my objection through to somebody higher up. No, he forbade it. So I ignored him and wrote a careful report and sent it in. As a result I was called to see the head of censorship. 'Mrs Pearsall, you're guilty of a breach of the Official Secrets Act.' I said I thought that even in wartime England, surely no one was guilty until it was proved. I had friends in France and Belgium and Holland, and lives were being lost simply because letters weren't being properly understood.

Did they heed the warning? I don't know. I moved shortly after to the Ministry of Information on what was called 'Home Intelligence'. We had to report every week for Churchill on what people were thinking, and about the troubles they were confronting. We had intelligence officers in thirteen regions who would send us reports every week.

Some of them just gave their own opinions, but in Newcastle upon Tyne, for instance, I found they had several thousand people writing in. It was the only place, by the way, where there was anti-Russian feeling after the Russians came in.

Then there were complaints about the treatment of young girls who left home for the first time to join up. I know the WRNS were always well treated, but sometimes in the other services there was no camp for them to go to. They just arrived and there was nothing. Well, that kind of thing we picked up immediately from the mothers.

The evacuation of children was the saddest thing that I saw in the war. These little creatures with the label on them. Food kept them happy for a while, but when they were put to bed it was, mummy, mummy, mummy. It was very

ATS foot inspection, by Phyllis Pearsall.

Phyllis Pearsall, artist on the shop floor.

difficult for me because I was drawing them, and when you're drawing an animal or a person, they know that your full attention is on them. So these little creatures would come up to me, and I thought no, I've not got to let them feel too much affection. They've already been torn away from somebody, they mustn't be torn away from me as well. But you just wanted to put your arms around the whole lot of them.

It was also terrible later when they went back. Those very poor ones who had been billeted in middle-class houses returned with posh accents and so on, and their parents wouldn't have anything to do with them. They became misfits.

I knew Anna Freud at the time, and she wanted the parents to be allowed to go and visit. The government didn't want them to, because there were always tears when the parents left. But it alienated families through not meeting.

Certain pictures remain. I was in Coventry after the bombing and in Plymouth when it was hit. When bombs had fallen and people were buried under the rubble, we would all try to get them out, alive or dead. And the worst sight was, of course, a child's hand sticking up out of the rubble. There was such sadness.

I think that people who experienced the last war probably do have more universal sympsthy. When other parts of the world are experiencing wars and disasters you understand what they are suffering. You have seen what killing is, and you know what losing people you love is like. Because of my faith, I pray for them.

I would say that women found their feet in the war. They found that they could do things which they thought they couldn't do. Some realised they were better than men at very careful concentration on detail. And that was appreciated by the men as well.

MYRA ROBERTS & EDNA MORRIS
Flight of the Nightingale

Myra Roberts (Jones), Edna Birkbeck (Morris) and Lydia Alford, who has died, were the three women chosen to make the first experimental flight of the Normandy air evacuation ambulance service. It was carried out as a very secret operation, which was entirely understandable at the time.

But dangerous, heroic work carried out by women in the last war was invariably given the hush-hush treatment long after there was any need for secrecy. Apparently, it was simply not 'on' for women to be seen risking their lives.

Somehow this attitude stuck even after the war. It was left to the good old Imperial War Museum to give the 'Nightingales' a fiftieth birthday party in May 1994 and so bring their story to light.

Myra's story

No sooner had Myra Roberts started to train as a nurse at the Angel Hospital in Birmingham than she had to give it up. Her father had been taken ill with duodenal ulcers and her mother needed her help. They were a large family, eight children altogether, and the six youngest were still at home. Myra was naturally disappointed at the time but, happily, she took up her vocation again – unhappily, because of the war.

I was a naturally very pale person who always looked undernourished. Everyone assumed I was ill. After Dad had recovered from his stomach troubles, a cousin who lived by the sea suggested I go and stay with her. She believed that the air would be good for me. My mother suggested that I stay on there when a job turned up for me in a big house in Aberdovey – keeping an eye on a very old lady during the day.

It was here, nearby in Tywyn, that I met my future husband.

He was working in the garage, and this chappie used to be standing outside as I got off my train on my days off from work. He knew jolly well which day I was coming. And it was wonderful. The only thing was, at weekends he'd say he had to go back home, to go to chapel. He seemed to have to attend chapel an awful lot of times. I could never understand this.

He came back to Tywyn after one of his home-chapel visits and asked if I would clear off to Birmingham with him. I asked him why, and eventually got him to admit he'd been going around with a girl he'd known at school. He'd got her into trouble, his parents were pushing him to marry her, and he didn't want to. He thought if we were to clear off to Birmingham they wouldn't know where we were. I said, no. You go and eat the stew you've been making for yourself.

I joined the Air Force, the WAAF, to get away. I was sent first to Bridgnorth in Shropshire, and did all the rigmaroles, the square-bashing. Right foot forward, left, right, left, right, about turn, salute, and all of that. I broke a bit of my ankle in the middle of all of this. I bunged myself up with bandages because I didn't want to split up from the girls, the pals I'd made there. Got through it with a black and blue leg.

I wasn't all that enamoured with that marching past and saluting stuff so I was very glad when I was directed into the medical section for we never had to do a lot of saluting again – even for our pay!

From here I was sent to further my nursing experience at a school in Sidmouth in Devon. Oh, that was beautiful. We were billeted in a small hotel called the Little Glen. It was wonderful. I've been there since. I think it's called the Royal Glen now – a lovely place in its own grounds. After that I was in Sawbridgeworth in Hertfordshire for a couple of years.

I'll tell you something funny that happened to me there when I was in charge of the girls' FFI inspections. Free from infection. Nits, and crawly things in your hair. And routine strip-checks for scabies. I'll always remember this girl. She was really good-looking and acted as though she thought she was it! I was told she'd missed two or three inspections, and when she came to see me she still tried to get out of it. 'Have you got to do it?' she asked me. 'Please, I've tried, and I can't help what you'll find.'

Now this was the girl who always made us green with envy, for she was always being seen on the arm of one of the lovely officers. She had marvellous hair which she used to roll round a ribbon. It was the style then – we all used to wear our hair like that.

My God, I ran for a mask, and some rubber gloves, quick. I've never had

Air ambulance Nightingales, left to right *Lydia Alford, Myra Roberts and Edna Morris.*

such a shock in all my life, ever. Each strand of her hair was white with nits. They were everywhere. She was alive with head lice. And she looked perfect, beautifully made-up.

I thought, carbolic and scissors. But she begged and begged me not to cut her hair off, prayed for me not to. The usual procedure was to crop it off straight away, and burn it. And I thought, oh dear, what can I do? I had her sitting for hours using this carbolic mixture. I nearly burnt her head off. I was visualising her, as I'd often seen her, with her head on some guy's shoulder!

Just when this hospital patch was becoming a bit humdrum, and I was wishing for a change, the medical officer had a talk with me: 'We've been asked to find people for flying duties, air ambulance duties. But you've got to volunteer before we can recommend you.' He warned me I'd have to do some extra, hard training. I volunteered immediately.

They did put us through the mill in our training. It was up in that Jewish part of London, Golders Green. We really had to grind down the grindstone there!

In the main cookhouse they had great big cauldrons full of boiling custard. And someone had put one of them on the floor out of the way. One of the cooks turned around, stepped backwards, and put her foot straight into the boiling mixture. And she had these lisle stockings, you know the service stockings on. Oh dear, I'll never forget that, ever, it was terrible.

A Polish doctor came to the sick bay with me. He cleaned it up as much as he

Returning with the wounded from Normandy: above *Myra; and* below *Edna on the first evacuation flight on 13th June 1944 (the aircrew were later killed at Arnhem).*

could, and told me to make a poultice to put on it. And then he told me to make it with cod-liver oil. I said, 'You mean cod-liver oil and malt!' and I showed him the jar. I'd never heard of this. Yes, he was sure. But I was worried, so I rang the senior medical officer of the station, and I said I'm sorry to do this but the doctor has told me to make a poultice of cod-liver oil and malt. The officer said, 'What do you mean, cod-liver oil and malt?' I told him I had even shown him the jar to make sure there was no communication trouble. Well then, said the MO, you've got to do it.

The same Polish doctor had instructed me that the poultice was to be left untouched. My God, by now we couldn't go into the room. The smell was dreadful. In the end he said, 'All right then, take it off. You may have to reapply one, get one ready.' I took it off, and do you know, the skin on that leg had mostly healed.

Not long after, I had orders to go to a place called Blake Hill farm. I was to pack all my stuff and get on a train to this place near Cricklade in Wiltshire. When I got there, good gracious. It looked like a place that had been torn out of fields. There were buildings going up, and roads being made. An aerodrome was being built, but it was grim. You had to wear boots or wellingtons everywhere because you were knee-deep in mud.

I was told that I was going to become part of the air crew of a Dakota. Ten of us there from different parts of the country were billeted in Hut 5. There was Minnie from Trinidad, she was a great big tall girl. We shared a double bunk. Minnie was the daughter of the Reverend Hakabe, who'd gone out as a missionary. She had plenty to say for herself. Very assured, and she used to recite lovely rhymes from the Trinidad schools. Another girl, Wynn, was from Yorkshire. Then Edna Morris from Gloucester, and Ethel Lloyd, a lovely blonde from Prestatyn. Eventually there were about twenty of us at the station.

This training of ours was for D-Day but nobody knew that. We just did as we were told, but we realised that there was something big happening. We had to have flying experience. So we went up in the plane whenever the crew of our plane went up. Sometimes they'd do glider towing; and they'd practise circuits and bumps, they called it; sometimes they'd be taking six of the airborne troops up and letting them jump out. And day or night, whenever you were allotted you had to go with it, you were part of the crew.

The pilot of the Dakota in which I did my training flights was Scottish, W.O. Jock McCannell. After the first few trips I had the feeling he didn't want me aboard the way he was banking the plane about. On one particularly bad trip when I turned green I asked why was he making it so difficult? He said it was nothing personal. He'd come from a fishing family and fishermen would never put out to sea with a woman in the boat. It was considered bad luck.

We girls were grounded that first week of June, while all the planes took part in the landings. Jock's was one of the few that didn't return on 6 June 1944. And I thought about the woman in the boat.

On 12 June the air ambulance pool were summoned to the CAEC headquarters and given a pep talk by Sir Harold Whittingham, director-general of RAF medical services. He chose three of us: Lydia Alford, Edna Birbeck (Morris now) and me. We were taken to collect our gear and be fitted with parachutes, told that we were operational the next day, and spent the night in sick bay headquarters. We were awakened before dawn on the thirteenth, given our 'flying meal', then taken to an aircraft each with our medical panniers of equipment and large flasks of hot tea. My panniers went aboard the plane, which was already loaded with supplies – mostly ammunition, so there was no Red Cross insignia on it. But we were given fighter air cover for the first few weeks of the operations.

My first flight to France began with a handshake and 'bon voyage' from the Air Chief Marshal, and he gave me a newspaper to read on the outward journey. I remember thinking, silly chap, does he really think that I shall be reading a paper? I'd be too busy wondering what the next few hours had in store for me.

We flew in over the coast, which was an indescribable scene with boats and ships of every size and shape, barrage balloons, and all the debris of the landings. Our three planes landed in Normandy on an airstrip which was a cornfield with a metal strip laid down the middle as a runway, about two kilometres from the shore where the boys had just got in and the Germans had just vacated their trenches.

Our planes were quickly unloaded of supplies and then loaded with the wounded. Lydia's plane took off almost immediately but the weather closed in and Edna and I were told there would be a delay until the weather improved.

We were taken by a newspaper correspondent on a short tour of the area towards Caen where the action was fierce. We could hear the bombing and see the shelling and sense the snipers in the trees! As we made our way back to a farm where there were some refreshments, we passed convoys of soldiers who, when they saw us in the jeep, yelled 'Blimey! Women!'

I was given a bouquet of flowers by a very pretty girl called Giselle. Then back to the aircraft and Edna's plane took off. Just as we were closing our doors, an ambulance came tearing up. 'Sorry to do this to you,' said this young MO. 'I have a badly wounded soldier and no place to keep him. He probably won't make it, but for God's sake don't let him die on the plane – do your best.' These first flights of air ambulance evacuation were very much an experiment, but the military were keen that they should succeed. They did – and became a regular service right up until the end of hostilities in May 1945.

Why me? was my first thought, while I was fixing this dying soldier up with oxygen. Slowly to begin with, gradually increasing it. And as I did, he started to use the most frightful words in Welsh. He was badly injured internally – he was minus a leg, and an arm had gone. I thought, he'll not last ten minutes, let alone make it back to the base. I got hold of his hand, and told him I was sorry that I couldn't speak Welsh but I could understand it! I read his label and he was from Tywyn. I told him I knew his home-place very well and not to worry, he'd be back there. And then I got the wireless operator to ask for a medical officer on the base as soon as we landed. The soldier had to be seen immediately. I was glad to hand him over still alive, and I wondered if he'd make it.

Do you know what? Six years later, when I was married by then and living near Tywyn, my husband Jack came home one day and said: 'Guess what? I met this chap on a kind of trolley wheelchair who asked me who was the girl he saw me with the other day. I told him it was you, my wife. And he told me you were the girl who'd fetched him back from France.' In the hospital they'd shown him a picture of me, which had been in the papers. And he'd remembered the face. So next day we went down to the pub and had a drink with him. And he lived for a good twenty years, you know.

Anyway, to go back to that first successful ambulance lift that he'd been on. After all the casualties had been removed and all the equipment had been put into the ambulances, just as I was coming out of the Dakota I was asked to pose for a picture with my bunch of flowers from Giselle in my arms. There was a sea of cameras and all the army big bugs and the air force hierarchy were there. For this trip was a feather in their caps. It was a boost for everyone to know that if any of our troops were wounded they could be brought back swiftly and safely.

After that, we followed the fighting. They'd make an airstrip near the latest fighting, we'd take in supplies and bring the wounded out. We went right into where the action was going on. Near Arnhem was unforgettably dreadful. We knew the boys. We'd played around with these Six Airborne in socials and dances. We knew these dead bodies in ditches and hanging on the hedges; no one got to Arnhem for a long time.

The last D-Day celebrations in '94 brought it all back and I had terrible nightmares. The Bosnia war really affected me. I had to go back on my sleeping tablets that I had got myself off – having been taking them for years from the pain of my osteoporosis.

One trip I'll never forget. I prayed more earnestly than I have ever prayed in my life. The weather was grim, one of the casualties started being sick and more followed. I was trying to wedge sick-bags under them. One soldier had a tracheotomy tube in. I had to undo this and clear the inner tube so he could breathe and fix it back. And I began to feel so sick myself. Please, please God,

Myra with the bouquet given to her by a grateful girl in Normandy.

don't let me start vomiting now, I begged – for once you start you can't stop. So I kept my head back and prayed.

Another time for prayer was when we had to crash-land. We'd taken some casualties to Oxford and were returning to Wiltshire. And I couldn't understand why the pilot was circling, and circling, and circling the drome. In the end I said, 'Hey, what's the idea?' The answer was, 'Well, we're using up as much petrol as we can, and we're deciding what to do with you. You'd better get your parachute on, we're deciding whether you're going to jump or not.' I asked what they were going to do, crash-land?

'Yes, that's why we're burning up the petrol.' I said, well, then, so am I, and I opened my chute. It's no good then, once it's opened. No, I definitely didn't want to jump. I'd seen so much ... oh no, I couldn't. I'd rather go down with the plane. And I put myself with my hands behind my head and curled up into a ball. This way you could roll and take the impact. I ended up at the foot of the plane, but it wasn't too bad a crash-land. We skidded along.

The other time was going over the Channel. We had lots of armaments on, there were barrage balloons up and quite a lot of shelling going on, and we were getting lower and lower. I thought if I put my hand out of the window, I could touch the sea. We tried three or four times, then we turned and had to go back. We couldn't get over into France that day.

We flew to Le Bourget in Paris the day the city was liberated. I had part of General de Gaulle's entourage, his staff, with me. I didn't have him, but some of my friends did, and we had to wait ages until they repaired the runway and we could land. Everybody was trying to land there, and we were carrying all kinds of supplies for the people there. That day, it was just a quick down, and back out again; there was no such thing as celebrating.

We were overworked, really. You could be on duty that afternoon, come back at night and find you had to stay put for the next flight back. We had very little leave at all. And it was dangerous work, though none of us seemed to suffer from nerves. We were carrying ammunition. We had bombs at our feet, and once I had to sit on the edge of one, because there was nowhere else, and you couldn't stand.

At the time you didn't think anything of it. You became acclimatised to it. I don't know why, your brain realised – you were helping, you were doing your duty, kind of thing, and if it was your duty, you did it. There was an urgency. You didn't have time to think, really. Once or twice it was a bit harrowing. Like the time of the V2 bombs. They were frightening. You could hear them, but if they stopped, you knew they were going to drop. We were near Antwerp, there was a strip on the centre like a field where the lads in their lunch hour started kicking a ball about. I'll never forget the scene. A bomb landed in the middle of them, and there was nothing but bodies.

Eventually the lads out in Europe got to know that we were coming straight back to this country, and they'd bring letters for us to post. And we'd raid the cookhouse and ask for any spare bread to take back to them, as food was even scarcer out there. Many a time I've taken the parachute out of its bag and shoved rolls and bits and pieces in it, and there'd be a crowd – they came from everywhere – when they saw this plane coming down to land. They'd run like blazes to get to the field and we'd hand the food out to them.

The local inhabitants in France or Belgium, they'd run down to this airfield, and they'd have bunches and bunches of grapes for us. Oh my goodness me, I couldn't look a grape in the face for a long time after that. There'd be grapes on the floor in the plane, and you'd skid on them, and soldiers on stretchers would start pushing them down and choking.

We really were exhausted most of the time. If you weren't tired you had a day off and went out larking around. Down to Swindon to the pictures and back again, and perhaps you'd go to a dance, only a local thing but you'd go jigging around.

Yet we were not regarded as important, you know. We were women. Leaving out the pilot, we weren't even thought of as part of the air crew. The male dominance was there. I realised it at the time, and I thought, well, why don't we have the same recognition as the men? We didn't get it. We were classed as dogsbodies, in a way.

They sent ten of us women to a squadron in Lyneham. The men in charge did not inform us as soon as they knew the flight was going, but we needed the same notice as the pilot did. We had to get our fresh stuff together. Make sure we'd got all our splints, bandages, morphine capsules, make sure the oxygen was working. The communication wasn't there, somehow or other. It dawned on me slowly that it was because we were not considered important enough.

I remember this chappie in charge of flying control shouting at Rosemary – an Indian army brigadier's daughter, whom you could never ruffle – 'Catch that plane, girl!' The plane was taking off. 'Come on, girl,' he shouted. She turned around ever so quietly: 'I'm so sorry, sir, I was never any good at hurdles at school.' You know, we had a giggle over that.

The importance of women was played down, I'm sure. Yet, how would they have managed the anti-aircraft batteries? It was all women on these. The barrage balloons? Women kept those going up. There was a tremendous number of women in communications. Nurses on ships … Everybody taking part in the war effort was important.

And how did we all keep going? Oh, songs helped. They definitely did. I can hear one, it's in my ears now. A nice hunk of a Canadian boy – we were just friends, nothing more – often saw me home after the dance was through, or after the flicks, and he'd sing into my ear, 'I'll be seeing you …' And when I hear it again, it does bring it back.

Churchill encouraged us. He had that way with him that commanded attention, and because Churchill had said it, it was supposed to be right. He was a little god, in a way. It wasn't until after the war that we became aware that there was more to life than listening to somebody telling you what you should do for your country all the time. You started questioning and asking why things were not more equal.

The war taught me to stand on my own two feet, I suppose, and keep an eye on other people at the same time. It made me feel capable of taking things in my stride – I'm not talking about anything too outlandish. I didn't shirk from anything.

And I tell you also what it taught us – to be able to do without cash, that there's a way around everything without having to put your hand in your pocket all the time.

War also brought Jack and me together again. The boy I was courting before the war, and split up with when I joined the forces. I was walking back one night from the railway station to my billet at Lyneham, and I could hear this whistle coming down the road, and I thought I know that whistle. Who was coming down the road but Jack Jones. He said, 'You see, with all the people in this world, we'd never have met like this if it wasn't that we were supposed to be together.' It took him four years to get a divorce and for us to get married. During that time I nursed in London. But eventually I returned to Wales, where we brought up our daughter.

But I still maintain that somehow or other the truth about the last war should be put over to the children. Now, before it's allowed to get forgotten and become just entertainment value. To convince them that it wasn't just films and glory, that it was true life, and that it should never, ever happen like that again. I don't know how, but I think this coming generation should be made aware of what our generation went through.

Edna's story

In the early 1940s Edna Morris felt a bit grounded by her job as a civilian nurse. She was not at all bored with nursing, only its routine. She had itchy feet. The war gave her an escape route – the bird flew the nest and joined the Women's Auxiliary Air Force. 'At that stage, I never thought of any danger, I never thought of anything happening to me. I suppose we all believed we were invincible. I never felt any fear at all, even when I crash-landed …

The engine of our plane caught fire, so we couldn't keep the altitude up. We were flying over occupied Germany and got permission to land at a drome where the RAF were. Whether the pilot came in too quickly I don't know, but anyway we crash-landed, and the propellers all churned up into the earth, the undercarriage went. Our cargo was a load of jerry-cans, tied together, full of petrol. But when we hit the ground they all broke loose. We scrambled out and I caught my foot in one of the handles, I can remember that. Not funny.

But what was the funny part, about half an hour afterwards, Glyn, my husband, flew over. We'd only been married about a month. He saw the plane, knew it was one of ours and wondered who was on it. When he got back to the station he found out I had been on it. I did have a headache! But no injuries.

I had, like Myra, volunteered to become an air ambulance nurse. And we met with the other Nightingales at Blake Hill farm, before we went into action.

Let me tell you my version alongside Myra's … we landed on D-Day plus 7, 13 May. We were the first WAAFs to land, and it was an experimental flight, and the one and only occasion when we ever had any escort at all. It was a test flight to see whether we could get successfully in and out of enemy territory with casualties. We did, so we carried on all through the war.

About a week before, we had to go to Wroughton hospital, that's the RAF hospital, for a refresher course. When we got back we found that the camp was all under curfew – no one could get in or out without passes – so we knew something was going to happen. And then D-Day came, when the planes all took off, and a few days afterwards we were called up to a marquee, a field hospital ready to take the wounded.

A senior medical official gave us a pep talk, and said that we would soon have to be – well, doing the work we'd trained for, and then pointed to Myra, myself and Lydia. He said, 'You three stay here. All the rest can go.' Then he told us he wanted us to go and pick up a Mae West – a life-jacket – and a parachute, and take it up to the crew room. In the crew room, of course, there were one or two of the air crew, and one of them, sounding a bit miffed, remarked that it looked like the girls were going over before them. They'd flown over, but they hadn't landed, you see.

Edna Morris, one of the 'unsung Nightingales'.

From now until we left, we were not allowed to go back to our own WAAF quarters at all. They sent someone to get our night clothes, and our instructions were not to go out, not to speak to anyone. The WAAF sergeant came along: she gave us best hospital blankets to sleep on, not the old grey ones, and a tray with cocoa on it. Lambs to the slaughter!

Someone came in and said my boyfriend was outside and wanted to speak to me. I'd only been going out with Glyn a short time then. Well, of course, I wasn't supposed to, but I popped out and had a few words with him. I could see he was worried about me, and wanted to make sure I was all right before I went.

The airstrip we landed on was only a cornfield that had been flattened down, and it still had poppies round the edge, but all the rest was barren. And there was a concrete dugout, a German dugout, so I went investigating there.

It was strange to think that only a few days before, Germans had been walking round in the dugout. I picked up a German helmet, a gas mask and a bayonet. I've still got the bayonet, and also a hand grenade – I was very naïve about hand grenades in those days. I'd never seen one before. Anyway, back in barracks it went up on the shelf above my bed, and there it stayed for twelve months, until I got married. When Glyn my husband saw it. Good God, he said, it's live, and he promptly took it off to the armoury. It could have gone off at any minute if it had fallen and the pin had come out. I had no idea.

You know, throughout the war, Glyn and I never had a single quarrel. I suppose there were more serious things to think about. Either one of us was flying off, or the other was. Sometimes you might not see each other for a couple of days. It meant that any time we had together was very precious to us.

We seemed to take these comings and goings in our stride, somehow. But when he was on the bigger ops, on D-Day of course, that was worrying. Then he was on all the follow-ups, dropping supplies. And on the Walcheren Island one, the crossing of the Rhine, Arnhem – he went through all those. That seemed enough but no, we learned, he was going to be sent to Burma, even though he had really done all the flying he should have done.

Then the announcement came that war with Japan had ceased, and Glyn said, 'Oh, good, we won't be going now, no way. I'll pop down to the drome and see what's happening.'

But the next thing I knew, I heard all the planes take off, and I didn't see him for a year. Yes, just like that. It was very worrying even though he wrote. For although the war against Japan was over, planes were still getting shot down out there.

Not one of the Nightingales was ever commended after the war. There were all sorts of rumours that we might get a half-brevi. The half-wing, which the men alongside us – the wireless ops, navigators and observers – all received.

All right, fine that they did, but it would have been very nice if we had been given the same. I mean we were flying all the time like the air crew. But nothing ever came of it.

After the war I was sent (so was my husband) the France and Germany Star, the 1939–45 Star, the Defence Medal, the Victory medal. Glyn also got a bar for his service on coastal command. But it was as if I had never flown!

I did miss the flying and the work after the war. I missed the casual way of life. You'd go up and see if your name was on the list for flying and if it was, off you'd go. And you didn't know when you'd come back. Sometimes you had to stay the night. You might take cargo over and drop it somewhere in France, take on another load up and carry it off into Belgium or Holland or somewhere. Then on your last trip you'd pick up your casualties.

When all the casualties had been brought home, we carried ex-prisoners of war. One of them recognised me before I recognised him in the state he was in. He lived next door to my uncle and aunt in the next road.

By the end of the war I had done about seventy, yes, seventy flights with 233 Squadron. All this changed me certainly, because I was a really shy person when I joined up and before I started flying, but that gave me a lot of confidence.

After the war Glyn came home and we settled down to married life, because in those days women didn't go out to work, once they were married. Our three daughters started to come along, and it was family first, which I never regretted.

Glyn went back to the job he was in before the war, working on the railway. Eventually he got to be a foreman but when diesels came, he said, that's it. Steam engines were his love. He finished when they did.

I decided not to go back to nursing. I can't really say why I didn't go back. I think it wouldn't have been exciting enough. Nursing in a hospital would have been tame after the flying.

The flying, and the extra bits to the work we did, were very satisfactory. In the early days, we used to try and find any newspapers around the camp and take them out, because the troops didn't get any. Oh! they went mad for them. And also any spare loaves of bread that the cookhouse had left over from the previous day. At the beginning, it was that horrible ersatz bread they had. Dark, very, very dark brown horrible stuff. When we had to stay the night, especially in the early days, there was no food provided for us. We just had to scrounge anything we could. They sometimes put us up in hotels, but they didn't have any food. We had the bed and that was all. We often went hungry. I think most people were.

When I was up at the War Museum (for our bit of recognition at last!) one or two of the present-day air force girls were there, and I said to one, 'If I was younger I'd love to join the Air Force again.' And she said, 'No you wouldn't, it's changed beyond all recognition.'

I quite think it has, because in wartime things were bound to be different. We probably didn't suffer the protocol there is now. When we weren't flying, and we knew we weren't booked out to fly that day, we just did as we pleased. It was, oddly, a free and easy life.

There is one other thing I'd like to mention about the work we did. We never thought of ourselves as being brave or anything like that. I mean, it was our job, and we just did it. None of us ever thought of ourselves as heroines – but surely it was a bit unfair that we were quite so unsung, we Nightingales?

HELEN BAMBER
Anthem for Doomed Youth

Helen Bamber was the youngest member of one of the first relief units to enter Belsen concentration camp shortly after it had been liberated, as part of Unrra, the United Nations Relief and Rehabilitation Administration. At nineteen, she had never before even travelled abroad on her own, and now here she was 'outside the gates, about to go in, and my fear was palpable'.

Was it because of this experience that she eventually founded the Medical Foundation Centre in London which deals with victims of torture? And was it her own disconcerting childhood that equipped her to do this work?

I was born in London on the first of May 1925, the only child of a very unhappy couple. It was an arranged marriage, and quite a tragic relationship with deep silences, little communication and later separate rooms and angry quarrels. This was coupled with my father's loneliness and isolation in the knowledge of what was happening in Nazi Germany.

Even before war was declared I was a very frightened child. My father spent much time in monitoring and lobbying decision-makers about the existence of concentration camps. It wasn't difficult to know about them – the world just didn't *want* to know. My early years leading to the war were dominated by my father's efforts to help refugees, not only Jews, by the way, who frequently stayed in my house. These were the years 1936, '37, '38, when the increasing persecution of Jews and others caused great anguish to my father. I was not spared from the knowledge of what was happening. My father would listen to the German radio every night, and he would translate it, giving me every detail.

I had been very ill as a young child with chest infections, later thought to have been tuberculosis. I used to get recurrent episodes of fever and delirium in which I seemed to be in a twilight existence. Refugees were often given my room and I slept under a card table in the front room. I didn't like that.

I remember one particular man, whom I didn't like, coming to read to me. I'd given myself up to the illness, I'm afraid. I didn't fight the illness very much. He said, 'If you want to get better, you will get up and you will walk. You will force yourself to walk around the room three times, and you will increase the number of times that you walk around the room each day. You will touch things and you will say, "I am getting better. I am going to be strong." '

I felt he was critical of me. I have the feeling that I'd been doing it most of my life. It was a turning point for me, gaining the insight that this was my way of escaping. Refugees were people who couldn't get away from the reality of their lives – they had to find a way to survive. This is what he was saying to me. Later he described how he had survived, and I began to like and admire him more.

There was an event which I remember well, and which indicates the mood of the household in which I grew up. I had a dog which I loved. He became ill and needed to be put down. It coincided with a visit from my mother's cousin, who had arrived from Palestine *en route* for Germany. He was also involved in helping people to leave Nazi Germany. I took my dog on the bus to be put down, and returned to the house in floods of tears. My mother's cousin remonstrated with me: 'Look, you're weeping over a dog. I'm here to find ways to get my brother out of Germany where he will be killed. And there are thousands of people in Germany today in danger of being killed.'

This was the message I often got from my father and his companions. It was difficult to be a child in this world of adults intent on very serious business. It wasn't that I wasn't loved. It was that I was never treated as a child with my own needs.

But I wasn't all neurosis and fear. When I was about eleven or twelve I joined a gang of Jewish kids – we used to follow the Mosley Fascists to their meetings and do our best to break them up, particularly in Finsbury Park, which was a famous place for the meetings. We could climb trees there and cause a commotion, and were often chased away by the police.

There was an occasion at the Nag's Head, Holloway Road, when we were mercilessly chased by the police and hit around the head. And another at what was then the Regent Cinema at Stamford Hill, where there was a meeting, and we were literally thrown down the steps by the police.

As the war drew nearer, my fears increased. The British on the whole never seemed to feel that they were going to be defeated. I don't think they faced that reality, but my family did, my father did. He felt, being a keen strategist, that the Germans were likely to invade this country. And indeed they could have done. I think it was probably a series of mistakes and misjudgements, especially on the

Russian front, that prevented a German invasion. As Jews, we would certainly have been destroyed, and for some time during the war I found myself isolated from my contemporaries who did not share these frightening preoccupations.

Nevertheless, I was quite popular. I had learned to negotiate within relationships. You couldn't survive my family without it. And I think that's where some of my skills came from – negotiating in a somewhat mad household. And it was mad.

I had been a fearful child, but interestingly I was quite unafraid during the bombing in London. We had a shelter in the garden like everybody else. But my parents would argue, and so I stayed in the house. If it got very close, one of them would shout, but I often didn't go in even then. I realise now that I wasn't afraid because I didn't feel picked upon as an individual. I was one of many facing the bombing in London.

However, my life was deeply affected by the bombing. My aunt, my mother's sister, to whom I was very attached, was killed in an air raid. She was very different from both my mother and my father, and she had quite an influence on my life. She was left-wing, a teacher, a vigorous person. She had a number of boyfriends. I always remember her advice to me about life and sex: 'Your shoes come off last.'

She worked a lot in the East End of London with left wing activists, and was involved in the famous battle of Cable Street. I don't mean that she was actively involved. It was the people who lived in the East End who took their furniture, their beds and anything they could find out into the streets to stop Mosley marching through. But she had been very much involved in the planning, and I admired her a great deal.

She was killed, with her fiancé, who was a soldier and had survived Dunkirk,when the Café de Paris received a direct hit. Their bodies were never found. There was little attention to my feelings about her death. I don't think either my mother or my father really understood my relationship with this incredible woman who smoked, drank wine – which in those days was quite adventurous – had bobbed, peroxide blonde hair, wore very short shorts and was fun. She made me laugh, and she took me to the theatre, and we used to go to have huge ice-cream sundaes afterwards at Lyons Corner House, and Welsh rarebit. She was an immense joy to me.

Later I was in a bombing incident when I had been fire-watching in Holborn. The building I was in did not receive a direct hit, but many people in the square were killed that night. I'd been standing on some steps going down to the basement of a solicitor's office, and the steps collapsed under me. I was underneath the rubble for some time but not hurt. I've not been very good about going down steps since then. What I remember most was the smell and choking sensation of the dust. I can smell it now in old buildings that are being demolished. I still get the sense of dust entering my whole being.

By the time the war was well on its way, my parents separated. I went with my mother, and my father continued to lead a rather lonely life. As I got older I began to understand him better, and while I recognised my anger at what he had taken and not given me, I also recognised he was a good man. There was genocide throughout Europe, and he cared most deeply about this, in anguish that nothing could be done at the time to stop it.

As the war developed I began to feel that we might win, that we might get through this, and if we did, I had to do something for the people who might have survived the concentration camps. Now, this wasn't a lofty aspiration. I think a lot of it was to do with guilt – the guilt of the survivor. I'd survived while relatives of my father, and my mother's Belgian cousins, I was sure had not.

Some of the boyfriends I had known had been killed, in particular a Polish airman of whom I was very fond; many of his friends, too. Young, vigorous men, good-looking in their uniforms – people I'd spent evenings with, been to concerts with, danced with, had fun with, and talked with, were no more.

I began to feel that I couldn't go on to higher education, or do the things that either of my parents wanted of me. I felt I had to go to work for the people who had survived the concentration camps. The feeling was very strong.

By then I'd already met my husband-to-be, a German-Jewish refugee. Every member of his family had been destroyed and his father beaten to death in front of him. He didn't really want me to go, nobody really wanted me to go. My mother refused to speak to me about it.

I trained for a year with the Jewish Relief Unit, a unit under Unrra, whose members were to work in the concentration camps once they had been liberated. The unit was made up primarily of Jewish people, although there were also Quakers and others who were equally committed.

The first time I went into Belsen I was with three other people. The truck waited outside the camp gates. My fear was palpable. Certain things remain for ever in one's mind. What I remember most about the distressed, emaciated survivors is their hands, very thin, unrecognisable hands, as if there was no flesh on them. They would hold on to your hand, digging their fingers into it, and talk. But you couldn't always understand what they were saying. It was a thin rasping sound. It was like a vomit, a constant expulsion of something terrible.

At first I thought, my God, there's nothing we can do. We had established a hospital at Belsen, and our trained nurses could do something, as could our Search Bureau, which was helping to reunite remaining members of families, who were desperately trying to find out if anyone was left alive. But you were still left with the voices, the hands, the nails, and I suppose the smell of emaci-

Helen, with UNRRA at Belsen, 1945.

ated sick bodies, a strong acid smell.

I then realised – and I don't know at what point I realised – that it didn't matter that I couldn't do anything, I couldn't take away the horror. What did matter was to listen, to hold them as they rocked backwards and forwards, to receive the horror so that they did not hold it alone, to hold it with them. And it is the same today in the Medical Foundation. Despite all our training, it sometimes comes down to something as simple as listening and holding. There is nothing more you can do, or should do, in that moment.

I think it did take a toll on me, yes. I remember once when I wanted everyone to die, myself included. I wanted the heavens to open up and engulf all those involved in the drama which I could not bear.

When Belsen was first liberated by the British Army, there was an atmosphere first of horror and disbelief, turning into compassion and anger. But as time went on compassion turned to irritation as the survivors of the camps recovered and found their capacity to protest at their fate in not having a country to go to and having to remain in the former camps. They were seen as a nuisance, as is so often the case with present survivors of man-made catastrophes.

I noticed it particularly when I was sent to accompany a young man who had been unable to negotiate with the Army for food for a group of Polish-Jewish refugees who had broken camp in order to find their relatives. They had gone, as it were, illegally into Poland, walking many miles, only to be met by angry villagers who turned on them, killing some. The villagers had, of course, taken their homes and their possessions. One young boy told me how he'd buried his father's watch, in the garden of his home. He didn't want the house, he just wanted that watch, and even that was denied him.

The survivors were forced to flee and there was no alternative but to return to Germany. They were in a dreadful condition, starving, and many couldn't walk. The British officer was at pains to tell me that they were 'illegal', and as far as he was concerned did not exist. I found the situation unbearable: people were weeping, moaning, some looked as if they might die, and it was then that I wanted the heavens to swallow us up. Eventually we were able to negotiate for food and the travel passes to enable them to return to Belsen. To await what? Nobody wanted them. They had to face life as Displaced Persons.

I worked in other former concentration camps and later became a co-ordinator for a project to send young survivors who were suffering from tuberculosis to Switzerland for treatment. I went there several times to negotiate for their entry into sanatoriums, always on the insistence of the Swiss that they must return to Germany after treatment. They made it quite clear that they did not want to keep them.

Of course going from Belsen to Switzerland, this jewel, was a remarkable experience. I'd never been to Switzerland. I'd never seen the mountains. And there I was in this beautiful country with lovely things – cheese and coffee, and everything very, very clean.

Belsen had a certain smell which I have never been able to forget. It smelt somehow of geraniums, that rather sweet, dank smell. Sometimes I go out on to my little patio where I have some geraniums in pots, and I smell them. I'm not quite sure why I do it. I think it's something to do with retaining a memory, not wanting to forget, saying to myself – was it really true? Was it as bad as I think it was? It was, of course, dreadful. But I have never regretted that I did it. Never. I learned so much. I grew up very, very quickly.

When I came back to England I was appointed to the Committee for the Care of Children from Concentration Camps, an organisation caring for 200 young orphan children from Auschwitz who had been brought to this country under a special scheme.

I worked and trained there for seven years. It was there that I began to understand fully the enormity of the burden carried by people who had been subjected to mass atrocity. When I first came back from Belsen I couldn't talk to those around me. I was intolerant, I couldn't understand how people could be so pre-occupied with rationing and coupons. I went to live with my husband-to-be. I could not have lived with, talked with, suffered with, or been rehabilitated with anybody else. He knew it all, he had seen what I had seen, and he understood.

I was asked by my previous unit to give talks about the former concentration camps and the plight of the displaced persons. I found people's desire not to hear, to forget, and to get on with their lives difficult to bear. I understand it better now but I was very angry at the time. I couldn't be angry in Germany because we needed to negotiate, to coax officials, to obtain supplies, to be advocates. I felt despairing and sometimes very guilty, as survivors do, for I, too, was a survivor.

One painful symptom of those who survive overwhelming traumatic events is the 'if only' syndrome. If only I had been with him, if only I had not gone out that day, if only, meaning: I might have prevented death and disaster. Survivors are constantly punishing themselves, although they know in their hearts that there is no 'if only'. For the Holocaust survivors it was terrible and inevitable. Present-day survivors we see in the Medical Foundation are equally anguished about 'if only'.

We have to face them with the imagery that people have internalised, difficult as it is. There are men who made tremendous sacrifices and suffered immeasurably in the Second World War, but who feel that their tragedy is not recognised.

There is often what I call casual brutality at the end of a war. I know of one man who was tortured by the Japanese and was at the point of death by the time of his release and at the end of hostilities. He had shown consistent courage and steadfastness. On his return he received a 'thank you' letter from the King and a bill for twelve shillings and sixpence for an unreturned pair of boots. Society found many different ways to brush aside his tragedy and that of thousands of others, to say, our men were not damaged, we were not damaged, we won the war.

I think women who were in the last war will speak of the fun they had, perhaps in the ATS or on the land. And yes, I can speak of the fun we had when I was working in Belsen. Yes, I can remember laughing and joking and dancing during the bombing of London. I can remember all of that. What I don't like to remember is the fear I had then and the fear I have now that it could all happen again. That the same intolerances exist now as existed then. Indeed, if we look at the world today, humanity it seems has learned very little.

ODETTE HALLOWES
A Different Kind of Courage

In the year that France surrendered unconditionally, French-born Odette Brailly left the air raids of London and moved to the safety and beauty of Somerset with her three beloved daughters. There she expected to spend the war.

Instead, to her surprise, she was approached by British Intelligence – 'or someone or other', as she put it. They asked if she would work for them in the part of France where she had been brought up as a child and which she still knew very well.

It was a very difficult decision to make. She was being asked to leave the children whom she lived for. But in the end she accepted – for their sake, and for that of her two countries, France and England.

After completing her training, Odette was smuggled by boat into occupied France as an undercover agent in the autumn of 1942.

Within months, she was captured by the Germans, tortured and then kept for two years in solitary confinement. Once, as extra punishment, she was left for three months and eleven days in complete darkness. The guard would open the door of her cell once a month and ask if she had anything to say. She would say, no, and the door would close.

Odette never gave in.

Where did she find the courage to face such mental and physical hardship?

I go back to my family, because my family had experienced all that. My family were always on a battlefield, in every war, so they knew all about it.

My grandmother had known three wars: the siege of Paris, the First War and the Second War. War was a way of life, if you like, and I was brought up by such women. I'll show you the kind of women they were. When my grandmother was told that my father had been killed thirty days before the Armistice, she found out on which battlefield he had been buried. Then she said to this British officer she had nursed: 'You always said if you could be of any help to me, I only had to ask. Well, could you lend me a lorry and a driver?' The poor man thought she was going to move furniture from the town house to the country, or the country to the town house. Certainly, he said.

She was given a lorry and she told the driver, 'We are going to Verdun.' He asked incredulously, 'To Verdun? But that's a battlefield, we can't go there.' She said, 'Oh yes, we are going there.'

They arrived at Verdun in the moonlight, about one in the morning. She found a wooden cross with my father's name on it, and she said, 'We are going to dig up the body of my son.' Which they did, and with her own hands she put what was left of my father's body on to the lorry in a tarpaulin, and then drove back to Amiens where we lived.

She went to the town hall where she knew the mayor, and said, 'There outside is the body of my son. The law is against me for having done what I did. What do you want me to do with it?' Well, of course, he said the obvious thing: 'You've got a family grave …' So my father was buried in that grave where he belonged.

That shows you the kind of women I was brought up with. I was born not long before the First War, and I was born practically on the battlefield, because all my family come from Picardy and Normandy and Brittany. As I said, my father went all through that war only to be killed thirty days before the Armistice, so it left me and my brother without a father. My mother always lived with Germans in her home in the First War, and she lost everything again in the Second War – my brother died shortly after it. So I was, if you like, a war-born child.

I was so young when I married and came to live in England. But it was not a happy marriage after a while, and that helped me decide to take my children from London to Somerset. I loved it there. But I kept getting bad news from my French family and other people through the Red Cross. I used to feel torn. I felt, aren't I lucky here under these lovely trees? And yet, when a lot of people I know in France are already suffering so much, and parted from their children, here I am, useless, not doing anything. So I thought, well, at least I could offer to do some translation, or adopt two or three French soldiers, or this or that.

Then I read an article in the paper asking people who had photographs of a certain part of the French coast to send them to such and such an address. Well my brother used to take endless photographs there because that's where we lived. You can imagine what photographs they were. Photographs of our youth on the beach, useless, absolutely. All the same, I thought, all right, I know that coast, so I sent my photographs. I was already regretting it, thinking I would never get them back.

To my amazement, I got a letter asking if I would go to London to be interviewed. I thought, what do you know about that, I am going to get my photographs back. So I went, and they talked to me, but nothing really was said. So I went back to Somerset a bit puzzled. They were the Ministry of Defence or something. I thought, well, if they are going to conduct the war like that!

I forgot about it until some time later I was asked to go back again. Then I got very cross, because when I arrived, the officer who was going to question me said, 'We are very pleased. We have found out all about your background in France.'

I said, 'Wait a minute, what do you think I am, a spy or what?'

He said, 'No, no, calm down and we'll tell you why.'

'I think you'd better, ' I said, 'because I take a poor view of this.'

'Anyway, what are you upset about?' he asked. 'We are satisfied about you and I'll tell you why we wanted to find out. You will not know this, but we train agents, and send them into the field – into different countries – to do this and do that. And we could do with a woman going to France.'

I said, 'I can't do that, for two reasons. First, I'm not capable of it, absolutely not. Furthermore, what about my children?' He said, 'Well, fair enough,' and I told him I was very sorry.

Back in Somerset I thought about it for three or four months. I asked myself: are you going to let other people save the future for your children, without lifting a finger? I thought, I can't go on like this, so I went back and said, 'Now look, I'm prepared to do one thing, go to the training. Then you will soon see that I am not the type to be sent to France to do what you expect me to do.' This, I thought, would put my mind at rest. I was sure that I would not be able to do what they wanted, but I'd be satisfied that I had tried.

Instead, at the end of the training they said, oh yes, they would like to send me. By that time I knew too much. And you know, it was fair what they did, but it was clever also. I had been in touch with people who had managed to escape from France, who had been going through a bad time already. They told me what it was really like. And I felt it would have been practically impossible to say, I don't care, I'll just close my eyes. By that time you couldn't let those things happen and not try to do something about it. Especially to children and be satisfied that other people would do something about your children.

My children were my entire life, I had no other life. It's not as if I had been happily married. I don't think anybody realised that I was absolutely heartbroken the day I left this country.

I couldn't go back on my word, and in a way, I was waiting to go. I had organised the children's life and everything else to the best of my abilities and I was satisfied about that. At the same time I knew it was going to be a terrible heartbreak, because I'd never left them for a single day before. And I knew the day I left that nothing that might happen to me would ever match that. And nothing ever has.

It was only my upbringing that saw me through. My brother and I were brought up with my grandfather taking the place of our father. After church every Sunday, we used to be taken out to the grave of my father, and my grand-father would tell us that in twenty, twenty-five years' time there would be another war with Germany. It will be your duty, he'd say, to do what you can, as your father did. The fact that I was a girl didn't matter. We were supposed to do our duty for our country. But I was a girl, and I forgot about all this for a little time, and got married. But it was there, the seed was there.

I got to France in 1942, but only after several attempts. Every time they put me on board an aircraft, something happened and I had to come back. We lost a wing with one plane. We nearly landed in the sea with another. After three failures they declared at the War Office that I was too costly. I wasn't lucky for an aircraft, and they would send me by submarine. The Navy refused, because they said they'd never had a woman in a submarine. Oh well, they said, we'll put you on a troop ship to Gibraltar, and from there we'll send you to France in a Spanish fishing boat. It took ten days.

From the moment I arrived in France I was a Frenchwoman who had not left France at all. I was a widow. I had a new name, new identity and everything. I did not change my appearance in any way because I went to a part of France, as an adult, where I was completely unknown.

Peter Churchill (whom I later married) was in charge of the Resistance Réseau there, and he had his own wireless. So any information went through Peter first, and then by radio to England. We were working with a vast Resistance network. England wanted to know about certain people in it, or whether we would be able to blow up this or that, or do certain things. And it might be something you could do, or something you couldn't.

We were captured because we were sold out by a man who, funnily enough, I never liked. One day, Peter said I was to go to Nancy and meet a man he would like to have working with us. He had been a prisoner in Germany and had escaped after the collapse of France. He'd got a very good record, and he could be very useful to us. So I went to meet him, and afterwards I told Peter, 'Well I'm very sorry, I don't like him for some reason. I'll never trust him.' And I've never forgotten what Peter said. 'You'd call that woman's intuition, I suppose.'

I said, 'Probably. After all, I don't know any more about him than you do.

A Different Kind of Courage 241

But my what-you-call feminine intuition tells me that I don't like him.' He's the one who sold us. Never mind. Never mind, that was that.

After I was captured I was taken on a wonderful day to a lovely house over-looking the Bois de Boulogne. The window was open and I could see the trees. When it happened, I thought, I'll just look away, look into the distance, into the sky and the trees. They burnt my back and then they did my feet. They pulled all my toenails out, one by one. And they were going to do my hands, but the German commandant in charge of the operation said, 'Stop, you'll kill her, she'll collapse. She won't talk.' So they didn't do my hands. They decided that they would not get anything out of me, so it was pointless going on. That day, any-way.

You see, I was used to suffering. As a child, I was blind in the right eye. I had always been. Then I had an accident to my good eye, the left one, and I was com-pletely blind for three years. That taught me a lot, because my grandfather took me in hand. He told me you were not to sit back and be sorry for yourself; you had to find other ways of being alive. So with his strict discipline, I managed those three years very well indeed. And, poor man, he used to get so sick of read-ing me fairy tales that he passed on to other things. He used to read to me all the books of Jules Verne, I knew everything about Jules Verne before I was ten years old.

I suffered that, and then I probably had a touch of polio at one period in my life. Of course in those days they didn't know about polio, so I was paralysed for nearly one year and had to learn to walk again.

The man who physically tortured me was French. And the Germans were clever that way, because you were nearly always tortured by a man of your own nationality. So if you were say Polish, it would be a Polish man. So you could never say you had been tortured by a German. He was a young man, the son of a well-to-do family from Elbeuf near Rouen. I saw him again when – and this shows you their demented mind – one day in November they came to fetch me at about ten o'clock at night. I was put into one of their cars, and he took me around the Arc de Triomphe twice, and said, 'Well, I thought you'd like the Arc de Triomphe with the German guards there.' I said, 'Yes, I see the Arc de Triomphe. I will come again without the German guards being there.' And with that I went back to my prison.

I think he was a pervert. I said to him, 'You obviously like what you are doing.' I thought, he may kill me, but I'll tell him before I die that I know he's having fun. I had nothing to risk by telling him.

While in prison, I could only survive from one minute to the next. I did spend two years in solitary, and that is quite a long stretch without seeing anybody. I spent more than two years never washing my hair, or having a drop of water, never washing my face, or anything, you know. Absolutely destitute, nothing whatsoever.

I came back to England in the clothes I was wearing when I went to France, and which I wore in captivity all of the time – turning my skirt an inch every day, so that it would be worn all over. I came back in it. The jacket of it is at the Imperial War Museum. That kind of thing, yes, I think I was conditioned to resist. Because, let's face it, after I was transferred in the summer of 1944 from Fresnes prison, on the outskirts of Paris, to the Ravensbruck concentration camp in Germany, I had three months and eleven days in complete darkness, without ever seeing a face. They didn't even open my door. They used to pass me my food through a little square in the door. Then I was punished altogether for ten days without any food. The complete darkness would have been a terrible ordeal for somebody who had never been blind. But because I had been blind, it didn't affect me. It did affect my eyes, but it didn't affect my mind. So I was more lucky than a normal person, if you like. What happened to me before made me accept some of the things that happened then.

I would say that the most difficult thing when you are in solitary as I was – in deep solitary with never a book to read and no one ever saying anything to you – is employing your mind. Particularly for twenty-four hours a day, because you don't sleep. There are days when I used to wonder, now, what can I think about to develop today? Days when you are weaker, and you can't find a thought. But you really have to pluck one from somewhere, for the most painful thing is to be left without anything to occupy your mind that day.

In my mind I used to make clothes for my children, which I always did anyway. I imagined what I wanted them to wear, then I would get the pattern, then the material, lay it out, cut it out and stitch it. Every single stitch I'd sew until it was all finished.

Then I would refurnish all the houses of people I'd known, starting with walls, carpets, curtains, this, that and everything. Every room of every house. In fact it used to be funny, because when I came back I would go to some of those houses and think, oh yes, I saw that room with green curtains. They thought I must be mad to have refurnished their homes. And because I had nothing to write with, I had to memorise it. But it kept my mind busy trying to remember.

The other way I was lucky, I think, in having been blind, was that my grandfather taught me quite a lot of poetry, and much of it came back to me. Then I tried to be clever and put words to pieces of music I was especially fond of. You have to try to occupy your mind, if you don't time is perfectly appalling, and every second is like an hour.

I never cried in prison, never ever. No, I couldn't let myself be that weak. A lot of things make me cry now, but in those days nothing did. I had to keep my

Odette with her medals for bravery.

strength, my reserves, and I wasn't going to be seen crying anyway. To show you how very strange one can become – knowing that I had been officially condemned to death, and they could put me to death any time they chose – I had kept the shreds of my silk stockings so that I could put them in my hair as curlers every night. I thought, well, if I face death tomorrow morning, I'll look more decent. It used to surprise the Germans when they opened my door, to see them.

I couldn't wear shoes after what they did to my feet. I used to shuffle along without shoes. But twice I had to go to see the commandant. I carried my shoes right up to his door, and I put them on before I went into his room. The man who was taking me looked absolutely surprised, but I wasn't going to go into his room with naked feet.

You ask me if after all this time I smelt? Probably. But you see, as you have no food, in the end you don't smell. You are probably clean in a way. You don't even have your period for most of the time, because, you know, you had been tortured and because you were starved. So yes, in a kind of a way, you were, I suppose, bodily, as clean as possible.

I think, for example, our normal way of life is rather tough on us, because we never have time on our own to think of certain things, to develop certain things, to even discover about ourselves. I think if everybody could do a retreat at some time or another, they would discover quite a lot of things they never knew they'd got.

I think people are so pressurised by life, that we have no time to discover possibilities completely. I know it sounds very arrogant to say it was an extraordinary experience for me. I feel a thousand years old. But it was extraordinary.

I feel I was being put to a test, and it was up to me not to crumble under it. To go along with the test, even if I were not to win at the end. I used to think well, I've survived today, maybe it will be tomorrow when I do not. But I have to battle on until tomorrow, and tomorrow is another day.

It is true about me, the more I suffer, the quieter I get. I do that in ordinary life too. I'm like an animal in that way: if I'm hurt physically I get quieter and quieter. I do not want witnesses to my suffering. I've had a lot of things done to this miserable carcass of mine, and I've always been quiet. And what has always surprised the medical people after my many different operations under the anaesthetic, I never have a nightmare. Never ever. Nor in prison.

I think it is because in my own mind I used to dismiss what went on around me. I wasn't going to be part of it. They were not going to reduce me to taking part, so not to have a nightmare was a protection.

I had TB in prison, and I remembered I had read a book written by a Belgian doctor who claimed the treatment of TB was wrong. To ease the mind you should starve the body and make it as clean as possible. So I thought, well, I'm in the best place! I decided to stay flat on my back. I didn't have a bed, just a shelf on the wall. And I lay there as much as possible, not using any of the little strength I had.

Now, if you had TB in prison, they got rid of you as quickly as possible to protect their own personnel. They had taken me to the hospital for X-rays which showed I had TB, so I thought, oh well, you are condemned to death. So I prepared myself for 'it' to come the next morning. It didn't.

The long and short of it all is that when I came back to Britain, I passed all the possible tests. The doctors said, 'You had TB, but you haven't got it now. How do you explain that?' I said, I can't explain it. But did they give you any medicine? I thought it was such a farcical question. Not even an aspirin, of course.

One evening the commandant of Ravensbruck came to my cell and said, 'You will leave this place at six o'clock tomorrow morning. Don't bring any-thing.' I thought, how stupid, I haven't got anything, just myself. Anyway, the next morning I was taken out of the place and put in the commandant's car, a wonderful car, white with red leather. Beautiful. He was wearing his smartest uniform, and following us and in front of us, there were cars full of these SS men, ready to kill. We departed and I thought, this is funny, what does he think he's going to do with me? I thought well, he's going to kill me in some woods so that nobody will ever know.

We drove all day, and at the end of it he asked me, 'Are you interested where we are going?' I said, 'No, not at all.' He said, 'Well, I am taking you to the Americans.' I said, 'Really? With these cars full of young men prepared to attack everybody? The Americans are going to fire at us; it's the first thing they'll do. They'll kill us. Is that what you are aiming at?'

After a time he told his minions to hang back a bit, and at ten o'clock one night we arrived in a little village in the snow. There were the Americans. He told them, 'I am bringing this lady who has been my prisoner.' And I said, 'This is the commandant of Ravensbruck, make him your prisoner.' They took his gun, broke it and gave it back to me, and then marched him off.

They told me they would find me a room for the night. I said no, I have not seen the sky for a very long time. It's full of stars. I want to spend the night in this car. Which I did. It was cold. There was snow, but I also knew that the com-mandant had a lot of documents in that car which I wanted to see.

I think I weighed under six stone when I came back. I had terrible stomach ulcers. I could not eat. In fact I didn't have a proper meal for four years. I had to be nursed back into ordinary life, to ordinary health. Things went wrong one after the other.

I did not have psychological help. I had no problem that way, none at all. I don't dwell on the past. I think of tomorrow permanently, and what I'm going to do tomorrow. So no, I never did suffer that. I was back and that was that. I was going to start life again, which I did.

So how was I able to take so much? As a young woman, I knew I could take quite a lot, because, as I told you, I was brought up with this idea. When you've got children you can accept a lot of things for yourself that you can't accept for them. But funnily enough, my daughters are rather like me. When things happen to them, they go quiet also. They can bear quite a lot. I can see it in some of my granddaughters, too. One especially, she accepts everything my way. She's been through a number of riding accidents, but she loves horses and has never complained. When she was a little girl about five, she fell into a bonfire, and the insides of her hands were burned. But she never complained. She is one of those.

How did I prepare myself to meet my children when I left prison? I had a feeling that it would be as it used to be, as if we had never been apart. And that is how it was. We never had to re-establish communication. We more or less took up as we had left off. We never had a problem like that. Now I live very near them: one daughter five minutes away from me, the other one not even ten minutes away, the third in Old Bosham. We are a very close family and see each other every day, one way or another.

Returning to them was something I had never expected. Obviously I would have been very stupid in prison, being condemned to death, to think this enormous joy would ever be mine. But at the same time I never gave up, and it happened, and we took off from there.

My daughters never wanted to talk to me about it, not really. I mean, they knew about it. Sometimes they asked questions, and I answered them. They also wanted to see the film *Odette*, with Anna Neagle playing me. I didn't especially want them to, but they said they would prefer to see it because everybody at school was going to talk about it. I thought that was fair enough, so it was arranged that they should see it one afternoon, quietly, with me. They all burst into tears, and I burst into tears with them. We gathered each other and I said, let's go and have some tea now. And that was the end of that.

In 1993 my daughters came to Ravensbruck with me. For fifty years I had wanted to put a plaque up there with the names of some of my colleagues who had been killed. But it was in the Russian zone, and the Russians wouldn't let anybody go there. It was only when the wall came down that we got permission to do it. My daughters wanted to come. After all they were old enough to face reality; they saw the crematorium and the whole set-up. But I've never put them into any situation that they have not wanted. And there are a lot of things I have never ever discussed with them, or with anybody else. I have seen the worst of humanity, the worst, and I'm not prepared to talk about it, because no good can come out of that.

I do accept that for some people suffering is just too much and they become demented. They behave like animals, and you have to accept and understand. It's best to be quiet about it. One should keep back such things. They can only hurt the minds of people who have not had the experience, and why do that?

The hardest thing to take was the unexpected limelight. I never thought I would have to face anything like that. I was really taken by surprise. I had rented a little cottage and I was sitting happily with my daughters, when a newspaper reporter came to my door, and said congratulations. I thought, what on earth is he talking about? Is it because I'm alive? 'Congratulations about the George Cross.'

I asked what he was taking about, what was the George Cross? He said, 'You don't know?' I said I was sorry, I'd never heard of the George Cross. 'Well, you will tomorrow morning,' he said. 'It's going to appear in the Gazette, and you'll have to learn to be more clever than you are with the press.'

'Why?' I asked. 'You'll soon know,' he said, and he was right. The next morning we had forty-three newsreel and newspaper photographers and reporters in the garden of my little cottage. I thought, what kind of monster am I? And he had been right. I had to learn fast not to make a complete fool of myself, not to be disagreeable, not to throw the lot out, not to run away. I had to learn to be gracious about it.

The government gave me a 100 per cent Disability War Pension. They said we can't give you more, we wish we could, because you haven't got long to live. I said, thank you very much, you'll be surprised. When I came back to Britain, the doctors thought that with their skill and treatment, I might perhaps survive three to six months. When I asked them why they thought that way, they said, for one thing because of your spine. They were right up to a point, my spine is bad.

They started seeing me every two months, then every three months, then so many times a year. And every time they were surprised. I used to say to them, oh no, I'll come back again on my own two feet. It took me eight years, mind. But they made a terrible mistake. Only my mother believed that perhaps they were wrong.

Here I am, fifty years on, still there. That's why I believe in women. I have seen women, and I admire their courage. I've seen women in such desperate situations, reduced in so many ways, and still proud. I can give you an instance of one. When I was in the big prison in Paris, I wasn't able to communicate with anybody, but the woman in the next cell could probably because her window was open right at the top. Her other neighbour was a woman who had already been a prisoner for three years, and one day I heard her say what a dreadful thing it was for her to be spending another birthday there. The reply was, 'Where else would I want to be?'

I thought, well, there you are, Odette. You know what's what now, don't complain. They are fantastic, women. It's only men who don't want to know. They are frightened of women. I don't like to say that to them, but they are. They know very well that in a different way women are as courageous as they are. I'm not reducing men, I'm saying they've got their own kind of courage, but it's very different from the courage of a woman.

MARY WESLEY
Hush-hush, whisper who dares…

It is sometimes difficult for the reader to draw a line between fiction and fact in Mary Wesley's The Camomile Lawn, *which covers the period of the last war.*

You might just as easily, though wrongly, mistake her account of her real life adventures in that war for extracts from another of her novels about to be made into a television film.

This is how the plot begins: Lady Swinfen has left her eight-month-old son at her aunt's in the country, along with his nanny, while she goes to London to help the war effort. She is frightened about what's going to happen, but as far as her own experience is concerned, the war proves far less alarming than she had imagined. Now read on:

One day a friend of mine said that a friend of hers – John Bolitho – was looking for girls to work for him. She gave me his telephone number, and I rang up. He asked me to send a description of myself, what my father did and, if I was married, who my husband was.

I did this and then forgot all about it, until one midnight, when I was asleep, the telephone rang and a voice said, 'Is that Mary? This is John Bolitho. Meet me outside St James's Park tube station in half an hour.' So I leapt out of bed, dressed, drove to St James's Park tube station, and sat in the car in the dark. There wasn't a soul about. I waited and waited. I had asked John B how I would know him. And he'd said, 'I'm six foot five. Find me.'

I was outside a place called Broadway, which was where some so-called top-secret offices were, though I didn't at that moment know it. Presently, I opened the window, and shouted, 'Six foot five!' and a Special Constable came up and asked what I was doing. I said I'm looking for a man. He said, 'Looks like it.' And then this individual, six foot five, hove up into the darkness, and said, 'Come along in.' He did what was strictly illegal, against all the rules – he took me up to his office, where we talked about dairy farming for an hour. Then he said 'Right, you can start on Monday.' I said, 'But what am I going to do?' And he said 'Oh, you'll find out when you start.'

I turned up on Monday, and what we were doing was decoding German, Russian, all sorts of messages. We were a very small part of what became Bletchley. This man had started it by collecting six of us in a group because he was impatient to get something going. We weren't paid, but it was very enjoyable because we were all friends – although the work itself was remarkably boring. Collecting German code signs: every tank, every platoon, every company, every regiment, every aircraft practically, had its code sign, which we had to try and unravel.

Where this John B was so clever was that he took people who had never done this sort of work in their lives before. So they used their imaginations, took incredible short-cuts, and arrived at discoveries through sheer guess work.

I remember going to him one day and saying, 'I think something's going to happen in Schleswig Holstein, John, because all the people I've been following have suddenly moved from the Maginot Line to the edge of Denmark.' He said, 'Oh rubbish darling, run along and do something else.' And next day the Germans invaded Denmark, and we became quite popular because we were the only people who knew anything about the movement of Reich troops.

Just after we invaded the Faroes, my brother rang me up at four in the morning and said, 'You've got to tell somebody we've visited the Faroes.' And I said, 'Oh for Christ's sake, shut up.' Next morning as a joke, I said as I went into the office, 'My stupid brother woke me up and said I'd got to tell somebody we'd been to the Faroes.' My boss let out a scream. He seized me by the arm and telephoned the Admiralty with the other hand to tell them one of his girls had been to the Faroes. Because in those days nobody had been there.

They quizzed me about the soundings, and the depths. I didn't know any of this. All I could say was it never stops raining and there's wonderful trout fishing. 'Where did you get your maps?' they asked. I said as far as I could remember we got them in Germany. This country had no maps of the Faroes: we had nothing.

It was all so extraordinary, and that's where the amateur came into everything in intelligence in England. There was an advertisement for holiday snaps in all the newspapers every day, month after month. And they built up the entire coastline of Europe from these. [See Odette Hallowes]

Mary Wesley as Lady Swinfen, at the start of the war.

We weren't allowed to say where our office was, or who we worked for, what we were doing. I had a husband who was a tremendous know-all, and at a dinner party I heard him tell the woman next to him how my job was being done. And I couldn't say, shut up, you fool, you're just inventing from the top of your head, because I'd not told him what I was doing. Nobody knew, and I had to sit there fuming, and roaring with laughter too, because he hadn't a clue.

Also on another occasion – this was so ridiculous – I was having lunch with a former boyfriend who said, 'I'll give you a lift back to your office.' I said I wasn't allowed to say where I worked, so he got into one taxi, I got into the other, and we met in the lift going up, because he worked on the floor above me. It was terribly funny. Everybody one met would say, 'I can't tell you where I work, it's terribly hush-hush.' Evelyn Waugh made fun of it in *Put Out More Flags*. We couldn't have given anything away because we knew so little. We were such a tiny part of the jigsaw puzzle.

I worked away at this job until I became pregnant. The doctor then said, 'You've got to get out, we can't have pregnant women in London. No doctors here.' So I collected my son and went with my friend, who was also pregnant, to her father's house in south-west Cornwall. Apart from our children and another friend's little girl, we had fifteen evacuees. It was a big estate. The eight girls lived with us in the house, and the boys were dotted about in tenants' cottages. One lived with the cowman and one with the gardener, and so on.

We eventually had three lots, one from Perivale, a posh school where they had school uniforms, another, who were really enchanting, from the East End. And a third lot, from Plymouth. None of them mixed. Perivale wouldn't talk to the East End because they were lower class, the East End wouldn't talk to Perivale because they were posh, and they all hated Plymouth, and Plymouth hated all of them. They didn't fight, they didn't talk, they just ignored. You would see them coming out of school in three lots, like different nationalities.

Only one boy was assimilated, and that was because his parents never claimed him. They vanished, and he was adopted by the couple who had him all through the war. He's still there.

Our children were tremendously happy. They used to sing and do tap-dancing round the hot-water boiler, and charge off to school together. And at night they used to gather round my four-poster bed, and I told them ghost stories. They weren't at all frightened; they fell about laughing.

Why they were really lovely, especially the East Enders, was that they were very good with pregnant women. They'd all seen their mums pregnant, and they were beautiful with babies. They latched on jolly quickly to country life. To start with they all threw stones at cows, and were frightened in the dark. And one had to say, you won't get any milk if you throw stones at cows, and you won't get any eggs if you throw stones at chickens. So they stopped.

There was one child, he stole, and my friend and I tried to deal with him. We called him into our sitting room and told him that we heard he stole wherever he went. He said, 'I've got to practise. My dad's a burglar, and I'm going to be one when I grow up.' I didn't know what to say to that, but my friend in a very grand voice said, 'We don't steal in the country.' And he said 'Oh, don't you, then I won't', and stopped. But fairly soon he asked to be taken back to London to his parents.

We used to keep in touch with the children's parents, write to them, or telephone, and every time we went to London we'd have them to tea and talk to them. When the raids stopped, which they did at intervals in the war, there was a tremendous amount of, 'I'm putting Jackie on the train.' And they'd be sent back to us to resume life as usual in the country.

Were my children put out at sharing with all these children? They didn't mind in the least, they were too small. I mean my eldest son was only a year, and the other was born while this was going on. They just quite liked all the activity and the children used to play with them like brothers and sisters. So, because I only had the experience of ours, I thought that evacuees were happy children. We only had one unhappy little girl, and she was unhappy from inverted snobbery. She said she wasn't going to stay in a house where there were servants. Didn't approve. So we found her one where there weren't any.

I saw two sides to the war. In the country and in London. To begin with we had our house in town. Then half way through the war we shut it up, and my husband moved out of London. He was working in the Ministry of Information. We were parting by then anyway.

London was very strange. You never saw a child in the streets, parks were empty of prams. No dogs – people evacuated their dogs. I did, until it pined and I brought it back. The only people around were those who were working there. I know in 1938, when we thought there was going to be a war, my next-door neighbour, a lovely woman called Lady Powell, came rushing in. I was pregnant then, and she said, 'Mary, I've taken a house in Wales, you're coming.' She was collecting a sort of house party to take to Wales. People who could, got out. My parents went to live in Somerset. A great number of old people left. London was empty of people and traffic.

The war gave me two opportunities, one was to work, which I'd never done in my life, because my father wouldn't let me, except charity work. The other thing was to escape my husband, which I did, by just drifting away and being in Cornwall, and eventually never coming back.

When I left the War Office I promised I would go back, but it simply wasn't possible with two children. What we did in Cornwall was WVS, and we worked with the Belgian fishing fleet, who all came to Newlyn with their wonderful fishing boats, and their dogs and cats and their umbrellas, and their priest, and their grandmothers. They'd piled everything onto their trawlers and come to England in 1940. The French came, too, but they didn't get on with the Belgians and moved up to Brixham.

At the house, we started taking in officers and men who had nowhere to go on leave. We had practically everybody who was fighting in the war, I should think – Australians, New Zealanders, Dutch, French, Belgians, but we didn't ever have a Pole. One way and another we always had room for visitors. The evacuee children were terrified of sleeping alone, so they shared four to a room.

It was a proper little community. And the owner of the house, a marvellous old man, really loved the children. When he went anywhere, he'd pack his car full of children and take them with him; they'd sing as they drove along. But I never allowed my children to go because he was such a bad driver.

Our friends would come and stay, too, if they were frightened of the air raids. They'd arrive for a week or two's peace, or to get some work done. And there were other friends around various air stations who would come for a bath or a meal. I took his hospitality as a matter of course, but I've since realised how wonderful he was.

There was a home farm, and I kept chickens, geese, ducks and turkeys. We also had our own pigs so there was never any shortage of food. Because there was a huge walled kitchen garden, we had an enormous amount of vegetables. And I used to make the butter in the Cornish fashion. Cream in a tub, stir it round with your hand and it becomes butter. Magical, great fun. Another thing, if you have fifteen people, you have fifteen ration books, which goes much further than if you're managing with one or two.

The war sounds like a joke but there was permanent anxiety. Practically everybody I knew, man and woman, was in danger. The first casualty I suffered was a girl friend who had gone out to Cairo to be with her husband. When she became pregnant, they decided it was safer for her to come back. She was torpedoed on the way home and spent six days in an open boat. I met the woman who was holding her when she died in her arms. A wonderfully beautiful girl, a very great friend. The first friend I lost.

And the men were being killed. Because there were so many air stations for night fighters and bombers in Cornwall, you never knew whether they'd come back. I lost quite a clutch of friends by the end of the war.

Two people who used to come and see us, just sort of wander in for meals, appeared to be doing nothing. One was French, the other English. Only five years ago I was told that they were going across the Channel in submarines or torpedo boats, putting on wet suits and diving to measure the depth of the sea for the Mulberry Harbour landings. And they were doing that week after week after week, all along the French coast. Incredibly brave. The war brought out an extraordinary amount of courage from the most unexpected people.

There was a lot of bravery, but in the last war men [like Oliver in *The Camomile Lawn*] said how frightened they were. They weren't like my father's generation, who buttoned up and didn't ever let on they were terrified. I remember somebody in bed with me bailing out in a nightmare. He'd been shot down and he was having a dream about it again. He talked about it, and was quite open which made it a bit easier, I imagine.

I heard about the end of the war as I was coming up the cliff after taking my little boy down to the sea. I got within earshot of the house, and somebody shouted the news to me. I burst into tears, and I said to my son, 'It's over, it's over, the war is over.' And he stamped his little foot and shouted, 'I want my war, it's not over, I want my war!' I had taken him to London a month or two before, and he had simply adored the raids and the doodlebugs, thought they were the greatest thing in his life. But I was thinking of the people who had been killed.

Acknowledgements

The author and publishers are grateful to all those who have kindly supplied photographs from their personal collections and given permission for them to appear alongside their interviews.

Acknowledgements are also due to the following for use of illustrations: Johnny Mans Productions Ltd, Hoddesdon, Herts, for photographs of Anne Shelton on pp. 8 and 14; Imperial War Museum, London, for illustrations on p.6 ('Ruby Loftus screwing a breech-ring' by Dame Laura Knight, IWMID2850), p.43 ('Come and help with the Victory Harvest', IWMPST0146), p.62 ('Serve in the WAAF with the Men who Fly', IWMPST3069), p.106 ('Join the ATS' by Abram Games, IWMPST2832), p128 ('Join the Wrens' IWMPST0759), p.200 ('Women of Britain ...' IWMPST5184); and the Public Records Office, London, for illustrations on p.4 ('Be like Dad keep Mum' INF 3231), p.2 ('Just a Good Afternoon's Work' INF 3/400), p.70 ('ATS at the Wheel' INF 13/42/8).

Thanks, too, to Dr Christopher Dowling and his colleagues at the Imperial War Museum for their help at the start of this book.

Index